Carry Your Candle...
Go Light Your World

USHA JESUDASAN
SULOCHANA ABRAHAM

INDIA • SINGAPORE • MALAYSIA

ISBN
Paperback 979-8-89673-304-1
Hardcase 979-8-89984-237-5

All I have needed Thy hand has provided,

Great is Thy faithfulness, Lord unto me.

(Thomas Obadiah Chisolm)

This book is dedicated to:

Our Parents

Our Children

Our Grandchildren

Go to the people.

Live with them.

Learn from them.

Love them.

Start with what they know.

Build with what they have.

But with the best leaders, when the work is done,

the task accomplished,

the people will say,

'We have done this ourselves.'

Lao Tzu

Contents

We would like to acknowledge:

Our daughter, Priya, and our son, Vinod, for encouraging us to tell our story. Thank you for this wonderful experience.

Ms. Susheela Koshi, for her meticulous editing of our book. Thank you!

Mr. Rajan Babu Thanji, our dear neighbour and friend, for his kindness in coming to our aid and rescuing us from all our computer glitches. Rajan, we also appreciate your help with digitalizing our photos and making life a little easier for us on the technical side. Thank you!

A very special thank you to Mrs. Sumithra for her patience in typing my notes. Sumithra, I could not have managed without your help.

Dr. Kuryan George and Dr. Christopher Moses for the early photos of COP. Thank you for the time spent in digging up these old photos.

Our heartfelt thanks to our nephew Rohan Mathew Daniel for taking the photos for both the front and back covers.

A very special thank you to our loving nieces and nephews who took the time to share their memories of us. We deeply appreciate this and love you all dearly.

Thank you also to our friends and colleagues who shared such lovely memories of us.

Sulochana and Usha

A Note From The Authors

When Priya Alexander invited me to write the story of her parents, Dr. Sulochana and Dr. Abraham Joseph, I was really excited. Excited because thirty-seven years ago (1987) Sulochana Abraham requested me to write the biography of her father Mr. Kuruvila Jacob, a renowned Indian educationist. I took on this project with great enthusiasm and we produced a little booklet for the family. It was my first biography and I learnt the skills of a biographer as we went along. Once a week, I would visit Mr. Jacob at his home in Kamalakshipuram and ask endless questions about his childhood, his early life as a student, the years he raised his family and then his ideas and values as an educationist and his hopes for the future. I would listen and write and then shape what I had heard into a chapter, until it became a little booklet. It was a very meaningful project as not only did I get to know Kuruvila Jacob and his charming wife Grace, but also their children Rebekah, Chakko and Sulochana. More than a decade later, I was commissioned by the Old Boys Association of the Madras Christian College High School of which Mr. Jacob was Headmaster for many years, to rewrite and enlarge the book so that his students too could be a part of the documenting process. That little booklet took on another avatar and became *Shaping Young Minds.* During this period, Sulochana and I became good friends.

I applied the same process as before – of visiting Sulo and Abraham in their Kamalakshipuram home where their parents once lived, listening to them, and writing down everything on large sheets of yellow lined paper. Abraham at first was shy about answering very personal questions about his childhood, his romance with Sulo and how their relationship blossomed. He was the perfect host – would make me a wonderful cup of coffee just the way I liked it or mix a glass of juice and then discreetly disappear on some errand leaving Sulo to answer the questions. Our chats extended to lunch and this was an informal time when I didn't write or record, but just listened. Abraham was a little more forthcoming over lunch. Sometimes I wondered, am I ever going to get this man to open up about his life?

It was a slow journey of building friendship and trust until he was comfortable enough and eager to share the stories of his life. His humility was striking. Credit for all the success was shared – everything was 'we' and not 'I'. 'We were a dedicated team,' he would say and add, 'God gave me a life partner in Sulo who really understood me and shared my vision every step of the way. He also gave me a wonderful team to work with at every stage.'

I think it is a gift if life's purpose is given to you clearly when you are young, for it enables you to move forward with dedication and discipline – and young Abraham was lucky for it was a definite 'call' given to him even before he began his career. As most 'calls' are, there was no easy way through it. He was no visionary with his head in the clouds – his farm boy's practicality was evident in everything he planned and did. There were two parts to his vision; one was his innovative and experiential method of teaching the subject Community Health to medical and allied health students. The other was his idea of every village community being responsible for its own health.

Sulo was the tireless, nurturing and supportive partner at home and at work. As her father's biographer, I recorded that one of the elements of his life was his deep sense of gratitude to God for everything he was given to do and for people to help him do it. I noticed the same in Sulo's life too. Almost every other sentence began with, ' I'm so grateful for....' A notable feature in Sulo's life is her inability to gossip. In the year that I have known her during this writing project, I have not heard her utter an ill word about anyone. She is as straight and simple as her starched cotton saris. Her compassion is legendary. From the watchman at the gate, to the ayamma in the ward and her many friends from all over the world. Everyone has a story to share about her compassion.

As I delved deeper and deeper into their lives, I got to know two amazing people – quite different from each other – yet who had glued themselves together so firmly that they could work in the same department day after day, live in peace and harmony at home as husband and wife and remain friends as well. An incredible feat indeed. What was the glue that held them together? A deep unwavering faith in God who brought them together, held them in the palm of His hand, and guided them step by step through challenging times. So too their shared values.

What sustains a marriage for so long without it turning sour or bitter or into complacent boredom? It touched me deeply when Sulo said that their day begins with prayer, with both of them surrendering their day to God and ending it this way too. Could there be a better glue than this? Apart from their deeply anchored faith and shared values, their love of music and singing, it is their unconditional devotion and love for their children first and then their grandchildren and the larger extended family that also unites them. There is nothing they wouldn't do for them. This is so evident from the way they proudly share recent photographs and bits and pieces of news from them.

It was such a privilege to be able to write down their stories as they remembered them; to listen to those who worked with them; those who were the recipients of their vision; to see them through the eyes of their children and grandchildren and nieces and nephews. The large dining table would be strewn with photographs as each picture was remembered with accuracy and often great emotion. Sulo was quite handicapped and found moving around painful and difficult. Abraham was always at her side, giving her his arm to steady herself or his hand to hold her so that she would not feel so vulnerable. Abraham found his memory failing at times and Sulo was there to remind him of things gently and lovingly. Their cheerful banter across the dining table, the appreciation of each other and the compliments they so easily gave each other was a marvellous thing to behold – Abraham's eyes would twinkle and Sulo would smile sweetly and shyly – even after fifty-five years together.

There is no doubt that Abraham and Sulo are a very uncommon couple. They both exude charm, grace, and elegance. They are warm, compassionate, gracious, and hospitable. They are easy and fun to be with as their families of children, grandchildren, nieces, and nephews tell us. But what makes them unusually special is that they, especially Abraham, saw and felt something as a young lad that touched his heart. He saw poor, hungry, sick people living on the streets of Calcutta. He could have so easily ignored what he had seen, as so many who have seen hungry, poor people on the streets do. But he allowed what he saw to seep deep into his heart and when the time was right, set about doing what he could to prevent such poverty, disease, and hunger. His vision for the health of an Indian village community brought about changes in the curriculum in medical education. He introduced innovative practices at a time when it was unheard of for medical students to go and live and work in a real village amongst villagers for three weeks. In holding fast to his vision and seeing it to fruition, he changed the lives of millions—especially children who otherwise would have succumbed to disease and death.

If Abraham was the vision catcher, Sulo was the vision keeper. Not only did she keep the vision alive by being the supportive partner, but also took it further when she took over CHAD from Abraham when he retired. Hers was the more difficult task because besides being 'Aunty Sulo' at CHAD, she was also 'amma' at home – the caring devoted mother; the dedicated and loving daughter and daughter-in-law; the sister the siblings relied on; the aunt everyone wanted to be with. Sulo played all these roles with great aplomb and joy, with no resentment even when the demands made on her time and energy were enormous. Both their rewards are a life filled with wonderful memories and love from every side.

I ended Kuruvila Jacob's biography *Shaping Young Minds* with these words. It seems apt to end this biography too with the same. *Their own special reward at the end of their careers, is to see their vision, ideas and life's work, living and progressing in other capable hands throughout our country and abroad. It is my wish that those who read this story of Sulo and Abraham Joseph will be inspired to follow their own dreams and thus make our country a place, 'Where the mind is without fear and the head is held high.'* (Rabindranath Tagore)

USHA JESUDASAN

November 2024

———•●•———

I would not call myself a writer, although I did try my hand at it at a very young age. Childhood eczema forced me to be home-bound for almost a year. My mother in her stoic, matter-of-fact manner assumed the role of teacher, health provider, friend, and mother, all at the same time. Colourful stickers from Moore Market, and her brilliant guidance was all I needed to let my imagination run wild, and in no time I was scribbling page after page of short stories in my very first 'leather-bound' diary. Then with the busy years of studying that ensued, all seeds of creative energy were forced into dormancy.

Years later with my children, nieces and nephews to entertain (mostly over plates of unfinished food), I was forced to nurture those dormant storytelling seeds once more. This 'storytelling' saved my four grandchildren on many a dull evening. They even refused to believe that I was a doctor, and labelled me 'the storyteller.'

When Priya and Vinod asked us to write down our life stories, I decided to put on the robe of a 'storyteller' formally. It has been a wonderful experience to work with Usha as she patiently and painstakingly encouraged me to recall the memories. The script of my stories was handwritten by me and handed over to her. I learnt that the craft of a writer involved writing, editing and rewriting, and editing again and again until it was transformed into a clean, perfect manuscript.

This endeavour would not have been possible without our faithful friend Sumithra, who helped me type these stories and give them a desirable shape. My very sincere thanks to her.

And last, but certainly not least, I must mention Abraham – my constant guide, companion, and friend who has spent several days, evenings, and late nights compiling and telling our story with me and without whom there would be no story to tell.

Sulochana Abraham

November 2024

———•●•———

Preface

This is the biography of my friends for many decades: Abraham Joseph and Sulochana Abraham.

Why another biography?

The answer to that question will emerge as one enters into this wonderful life story. I must say that it was a moving experience to read the manuscript of this book and through that, knowing Abraham and Sulo again at another level, deeper than ever before, understanding them much more.

Yes, it is another biography. No biography is the same as another. This is a unique one. A uniquely different one. Because it is life in flesh and blood, 'warts and all'.

There is a message in it. Here are the messengers. They, in fact, become the very message.

Let me share some thoughts about this real-life story as unfolded in this book.

Call obeyed, vocation discovered.

What was their calling?

'Building the Kingdom of God', as Aunt Ida Scudder said.

Abraham and Sulochana concurred with this goal with all their heart.

What was their vocation?

Community Health...... Both in serving and training.

A whole lifetime was spent on this. It was a passion, not only a vocation.

Fredrick Buechner says, 'Your vocation is born when the deepest hunger of the world meets with the deepest gladness of your heart.'

Leaders, yes, but they were more than leaders.

First and foremost: they were leaders. Leaders par excellence.

Each is unique in his or her own way and style, but both are different – complementing and completing each other for the common goal they joyfully share.

They *Initiated. Inspired. Innovated.*

*W*herever they worked, whether in nearby Vellore or Karigiri or faraway Nagaland.

They *initiated* many a new venture.

Inspired generations of students, graduates, and postgraduates, investing themselves in them.

Innovated many pioneering projects, because they understood and interpreted the time, and responded with creativity, wisdom, and courage.

What was unique about their leadership?

In them, I see masterhood and servanthood melded together.

Expertise and humility conjoined; such a union of diverse qualities is the true excellence they practiced.

That way of humility and simplicity is what endeared them to one and all in the CMC community.

That is how, I feel the nicknames, 'Uncle and Aunty', became their real names in actuality.

Pioneers all the way.

They were quintessential pioneers.

What is pioneering?

It is first, recognising what ought to be there but missing in any situation; then bringing that into the situation in a new way.

They were pioneers in Community Healthcare to the most unreached hinterland of villages around Vellore town. See the originality of the vision and creativity of COP (Community Orientation Program) as a live-in learning experience for medical and allied health students, a first of its kind, in the medical curriculum. Another glowing example is the conception of novel ideas resulting in the establishment of new institutions viz. CHAD, CHTC etc.

Community as the core.

Community mattered most for them. It remained at the centre of their lives. Both the inner community of CMC and the outer community of the people. And every person in the community mattered to them. They built community. The community built them.

They believed in what Jean Vanier, the community builder, wrote, 'To see the beauty in others and communicate to them that they are beautiful – this is community.'

Resource within.

The question naturally arising in your mind, I am sure is:

What is the secret source of such a robust river of life that they lived?

As in the grand vision of Prophet Ezekiel in the Bible, the tiny trickles of drops of Grace for this dear couple were from the very Presence of God. The spiritual resource was the daily 'trickle' from the Almighty. These tiny drops of mercies gently and quietly flowed into them right from the early days of their lives through the rich spiritual heritage of their parents and their families.

The tiny droplets coalesced, as Prophet Ezekiel describes, and slowly but surely, swelled up into a mighty stream through the constant nourishment of a vibrant CMC community. This river of life of this couple flowed on transforming the arid deserts and dead seas on its way. The intellectual/professional property of their life is thus deeply connected to the spiritual property, and values of their life in God.

This is what one can see clearly unfolding in the pages of this book.

Invitation.

I am inviting you as readers to an experience.

A deep experience of reflection, inspiration, and action.

To walk along this wonderful river of life of Abraham and Sulo, savouring each turn – its source, course, and resource for transformation.

Let the book read you, as you read it, provoking fresh thoughts, and evoking newer actions.

'Move with those who move…..' the wise aphorism says.

That is why I am writing these words. That is why you are reading this book so beautifully and graphically written by Usha Jesudasan.

Let us together move inwardly with this dearly loved couple- Abraham and Sulochana.

Here are people who were moved by God; people who moved others in turn; initiated movements with ever-widening ripples of change impacting generations of people.

They moved on even after retirement; never allowing moss to gather beneath their feet. Though age inevitably slows one down physically, I wish that the horizons of their minds and hearts remain ever wide, open, and renewed.

Kuruvilla Varkey

Christian Fellowship Hospital,
Oddanchatram,
November 2024

A Beautiful January Morning

It was a beautiful January morning. The sun was gentle and the cloud-less skies were a clear blue. The Abraham Joseph family had come together to celebrate the wedding of their eldest granddaughter, Elsa. The family, along with close friends was to gather for the Haldi ceremony under a large colourful tent – a shamiana. This ceremony, a pre-wedding ritual, is an ancient Indian tradition to ward off bad luck, and negativity of any kind and is a wonderful de- stresser for the couple getting married. The bride and groom are seated on the ground in informal clothes, often yellow in colour. Members of the family and close friends smear a paste made of turmeric, water, milk, and coconut oil on their faces, hands, and feet. Turmeric, in Indian culture and the Ayurveda way of medicine, is a purifying agent with medicinal properties. It is smeared to cleanse the couple's skin and keep it fresh and glowing for the wedding ceremonies that follow. It is also a deeply spiritual act that symbolises the cleansing of their minds and hearts, preparing the two souls who are to be married, to focus on an inward union as well as an outward and physical one.

The ceremony has deep significance for the family. It is a joyous time, with much laughter as the bride and groom swerve and try to avoid being smeared on the face by playful cousins. Much of the stress of the wedding planning is removed as the couple and their parents join in the fun and laughter. It is also a time when the two families come together, to celebrate the union of not only the couple, but also their families. Turmeric is a bright golden yellow – representing richness, prosperity, purity, and joy. So often, shades of yellow – a deep orangish sunflower yellow, marigold, to pale butter yellow – are worn for this ceremony by those attending it.

On this day, the Haldi ceremony was held at the Community Health and Training Centre campus in Bagayam, Vellore, under a huge shamiana which shielded the guests from the warm morning sun. The lawn was fresh and green and velvety soft, inviting one to walk on it with bare feet. The place was decorated with flowers and ribbons, and tables were laid out for lunch. At the far end of the lawn, was a platform adorned with strings of yellow and orange marigolds to signify the Haldi ceremony.

Priya Mariam, the daughter of the family recalls,' It was such a wonderful day. Everyone had come from different parts of the world and within India to celebrate the first wedding of this generation in our family. My father Abraham Joseph and mother Sulochana Abraham were hugely excited. Elsa was Vinod (my younger brother) and Priya Aley's daughter. Family was everything to my parents and they had worked tirelessly, despite busy schedules at work to keep the family unit strong and precious and bound together with strong chords. Elsa was marrying her beloved Enoch, a fine young gentleman from Chattisgarh, Northern India. To merge the customs of two different Christian traditions, we were celebrating the Haldi ceremony, which is not usually celebrated in Malayali Christian families. In our home, hurdles, boundaries, and challenges were viewed as events to be met with a positive attitude. So, the fact that we were harmoniously celebrating the union of two different communities was nothing unusual to us.

' The guests were asked to wear shades of mustard. How handsome Appa looked wearing a mustard kurta and how lovely Amma looked in a lighter mustard saree. The two shades complemented each other beautifully, just like they both had with their different personalities over the years. Priya Aley and Vinod had taken great care to make sure that Yohan, Lisa, Alex, and I had beautiful mustard outfits as well, and everyone looked perfect.

'As I looked at my parents, I felt overwhelmed with love and affection. I knew that nobody could have loved me more than my parents did. They always made me feel like a precious rose, their kindness and gentleness falling on me like soft dew drops. It was just perfect. We were not a wealthy family and our childhood was simple. We didn't own a car until my maternal grandparents moved to Vellore from Mumbai when I was around ten years old. However, my brother and I never felt like we lacked anything. I always thought I was incredibly special – like a princess, so the fact that my other friends had travelled all over the world, and owned televisions and videos at home, didn't really matter to me. I was just happy to have a beautiful and loving home and wonderful parents who loved me so much. It's interesting that my son and daughter feel the same way; they too believe that they are so special and that my parents love them just as much as they did us. I can't help but wonder how two people have a gift of showering everyone within their close network with such tender love, making everyone feel so special.'

But this was the charm of Sulochana (Sulo) and Abraham Joseph (Manu). Everyone who came their way felt this warm embrace of being made to feel special. Sulochana tucked the string of fragrant white jasmine buds into her hair. She glanced at the mirror once, to make sure that her mustard-coloured sari was draped elegantly and pleated to perfection. Then she walked out to meet her handsome grandson Yohan, who in his usual manner offered her his arm when he saw her. Yohan too was wearing a mustard kurta, just like his grandfather Abraham. Sulo gave Abraham a broad smile when she saw him. There was no need for words – the smile acknowledged how good he looked. His return smile and slightly raised eyebrows told her that she looked lovely.

Each in their own mind went back years ago to a time when everything was different. There was no haldi ceremony. No mustard clothes or stunning golden floral decorations. No huge shamiana or crowd of family and friends. No big feast. Their own wedding had been a simple quiet affair. Perhaps the only thing that was the same was the way the young couple – Elsa and Enoch, looked at each other – the way they themselves did so many years ago on that very special day – with tenderness, excitement and hope for the years to come.

1

Abraham: A Happy Childhood

My parents had been living in Ceylon (now known as Sri Lanka) since 1928. Our home was located in the charming city of Kandy, which was the capital of Ceylon before British rule. Kandy is surrounded by gently-rolling mountains which are home to tea plantations and large bio-diverse rainforests. It was a beautiful place to live. Except for my eldest sister and me, the rest of my siblings were born in Ceylon. During World War II, there was a great fear that the Japanese would bomb Ceylon. So my mother who was expecting me, travelled back to India for her delivery. I was born in my mother's family home in a small rural village in Kerala called Vadaserikara – a picturesque little village through which the river Pamba, the longest river in Kerala flowed. Vadaserikara was on the route to Sabarimala, the abode of Lord Ayyappa, a pilgrim centre that attracted millions of devotees.

My mother and I returned to Kandy when I was a few years old. Our family lived on a farm on top of a hill overlooking Kandy. From our home the view around was quite spectacular – lush green mountains, tall Buddhist temple spires and white colonial buildings. The Kandiyan way of life was slow, hospitable and full of tradition and festivals which were celebrated with great joy and colour.

Although we had helpers at home, my mother did most of the household tasks herself. Her daily routine consisted of cooking the family meals three times a day – we always had the traditional Kerala breakfasts of puttu, aapam or iddlis and dosas along with bananas, jackfruit and mango when in season. She also took care of the provisions and helped look after the cows and hens making sure they had food and water. Sometimes she even milked the cows herself. There were so many fruit trees in our garden. Guavas and mangoes of different varieties just hung there begging to be plucked and eaten on the spot. Bananas of different kinds and passion vines also thrived well and produced baskets full of fruit. The best-tasting pastries were in Ammachy's pantry in the dining room. This was a special place – delicious cake, cookies, and mouth-watering sweets of different kinds were stored there. It was one of my favourite places too.

Our home often served as a guest or rest house for friends and relatives who visited Kandy. My mother, fondly known to everyone as Maamie or Ammachy, was both an excellent cook as well as a gracious hostess. As the youngest, I loved having guests especially if there were boys around my age. A favourite was Cyril and his brother Cecil. As they were new to farm life, they enjoyed all the activities I did as a routine. Together we would take out the cows and fasten them to a tree or peg where there was ample grass for them to graze. Then we would go to the well to check if the pump was working. If it wasn't, we would have to carry buckets full of water up the many steps to the kitchen. I was used to it, but the city friends got tired easily. There was a huge family of about twenty to twenty-five rock pigeons that had to be fed. Ammachy would give us some uncooked rice grains and we would feed and play with the pigeons. Then there was the big German Shepherd dog that needed looking after as well. There were also many cats that loved to be chased. It was a good and happy childhood.

A step below the dining room was the living room overlooking scenic green paddy fields and colourful flowering orchids climbing halfway up coconut tree trunks. This is the room where we played pinball, ludo or snakes and ladders when all seven of us were together or when our friends came around. If we got bored, we would be out running around with our catapults chasing birds or whatever else there was to chase, or running up the hill to the cemetery scaring each other. Often when family or Malayalee friends visited, all of us would go on a picnic. A favourite holiday spot was in Yala where Cyril's father had a property.

The river provided us with many activities and fun. My father was excellent at throwing a wide-spreading fishing net that would drop on the water like a huge open umbrella. Ammachy was an expert in cutting, cleaning, and drying fish on hot rocks. One season, in the mid-1950s, when we were picnicking in the jungle with other families, the river nearby was unusually full of fish called 'Thuli'. The fish were big, averaging about 3 pounds each. We grabbed the bigger fish by hand and must have collected over 100 fish in sacks. Our mothers with some help from our cooks went to work, cutting, cleaning, frying, salting and drying them on the hot black rocks.

When the house helpers were absent, my brothers and I had to fetch water from the well, bathe the animals, gather the eggs, feed the chicken and milk the cows. I enjoyed all this farm work. It was also my job to distribute milk to a few households in the town. The revenue generated from the sale of milk and eggs was Ammachy's 'pocket money', which she kept safely tucked in the folds of her saree. My brothers and I also helped our father to tend the vegetable garden. The soil surrounding the house was rich and fertile and we enjoyed growing and harvesting fruits and vegetables. All these outdoor activities sowed in me the seeds of my love for Nature.

My father was a teacher and the sole breadwinner of the family. Our life was simple and followed an agricultural pattern of sowing and harvesting what was seasonal and possible. We lived well and did not want for anything. Milk, eggs and fruit from the farm supplemented our diet and the family income.

On Sunday mornings, the entire family, including my older brothers who were choir members, attended St Paul's Church. This ritual from my early days helped form my faith and involvement in church activities as I got older. We did not have many holidays as a family, but the one I do I remember well was to a cousin's house in Hatton. This cousin was the tea taster of a well-known tea factory and we enjoyed being in the ambience of a tea estate.

Christmas was always a special time for us. Ammachy would make her delicious Christmas cake, full of raisins, plums and nuts and we would all gather around the table to carefully wrap each piece in oil paper. Much of this cake would be distributed to friends and neighbours and anyone who visited us on Christmas Day. At the end of the holidays, the siblings studying in India would get ready to leave. They would pack their trunk with clothes and some snacks and goodies which Ammachy would make. Saying goodbye was a sad moment for all of us as it would be another year before we could all be together again.

Coming home again for the holidays was always a joy and sometimes it had its funny moments. My sister Ammukochamma often reminded me that when I was about four years old, when she and Kunjamma kochamma came for their summer vacation from college, I chased them around the house waving coconut leaves saying, ' go back, go back,' little realising that they were my sisters. I was the youngest and the darling of the family.

My two brothers and I received our education in Kandy, while my four sisters were sent to Tiruvalla in Kerala for their schooling. I was lucky enough to attend the prestigious Trinity College in Kandy until the tenth grade. I was good at academics – being selected as the best all-round student in the junior school – I loved and excelled in sports too. Because of my skills and speed in sports and athletics, I was chosen to represent the school in athletics and cricket.

During my high school years, I had to choose between studying Mathematics and Biology. Being interested in engineering and how things worked and were put together, I decided to focus on physics and advanced mathematics while I did my schooling at Trinity College, Kandy. My older brothers and four sisters left for India to pursue their college education. Once my older sisters, Kunjamma kochamma (Mariam) and Ammukochamma (Susan) and my eldest brother Rajuachayan (George) graduated, they returned to Ceylon as school teachers to support the education of the four younger siblings, Moniachayan (Thomas), Leelakochamma (Elizabeth), Saro (Sara) and me.

When my father retired in 1957 after 30 years of service, the plan was that we would leave Ceylon and go back to live in India permanently. Many of my father's friends from Kerala preferred to take Ceylonese citizenship and settle down in Ceylon, as life at that time was more comfortable in Ceylon than in Kerala. My parents however chose to go back to their home roots. I had to stay in Ceylon for another six months to complete high school. My oldest sister Kunjammakochamma was almost 28 years old and unmarried which was unusual for a girl from Kerala. Soon, a suitable partner from our community in Kerala was found. This was a good time to repatriate, so our family quickly packed up our home and our belongings of 30 years and sailed to Kerala, in time to organise my sister's wedding.

Throughout their married life both Appa and Ammachy kept themselves busy doing various things for the family; educating seven children in the best of schools and colleges – two as doctors, one as a senior teacher and all four daughters as graduates who could stand on their own feet with confidence. It was not an easy task at all on a teacher's salary, but it was supplemented together with Ammachy's savings from the sale of milk and eggs from her mini farm. As I look back after so many years, I realise what a happy childhood I had.

———— • ● • ————

2

Sulo: Memories Of My Childhood

My earliest memories are of the stately house in Chetpet, Madras – 'The Napier Gardens' where I spent 16 happy years of my childhood.

Coming down from Harrington Road, and through the gates of the Madras Christian College High School, what strikes you first is the majestic, imposing house with its tall, white pillars supporting the porch leading to the long steps and the ground floor of the Napier Gardens, which was once the residence of Lord Napier. As you entered, you couldn't help but notice the large hall with beautifully polished wooden floors. This room was probably the ballroom during Lord Napier's days when the British held such events. During my time as a child living there, my memory was that this room served as the main dormitory of the Hostel of Madras Christian College High School. There were smaller rooms on either side that housed resident schoolboys. There were two more rooms one on either side, one where the Hostel Doctor resided and the other where the warden resided.

As you turned the corner past the warden's residence, several long stone steps led to massive wooden doors. As one entered through it, a winding staircase with broad wooden steps took you to the landing of the Headmaster's house – our house. The rooms were large and airy and the ceilings were so high, that I remember my mother saying that there was no question of having curtains.

As you entered the gates to the school premises, to the right, a vast stretch of manicured lawns led to a large ring of antigonon creepers with clusters of pink and white flowers. As a child, I imagined this to be a garden where fairies and elves danced around on moonlit days.

My Father

Appa, my father, was the tall, stately, solemn-looking Headmaster of the Madras Christian College High School. One angry word or look from this 'gentle giant' would fill my eyes with unshed tears. I loved my father so much that I didn't dare disobey him. I have fond memories of the endearing terms by which he would call me as a child – 'Mama or Bama' and for the next couple of days, that was sufficient pampering for me.

I can remember from a very young age, that the only meal that we sat around the dining table for during the week, was at dinner in the evenings, and all meals on Sunday. Dinner time was very special. After dinner we would sit around and talk about the events of the day. Achachan, (my brother Chakko) would have many jokes to share with us. Appukochamma , (my sister Rebekah) usually sat opposite me and if I came out with anything awkward or rude, she would stretch her legs from under the table and pinch me with her toes. I didn't dare complain or cry about this, for fear that whatever naughty thing I did would come to light. Sunday afternoons were special; all of the cousins from Women's Christian College and other institutions would join us for lunch. My sister Appukochamma's friends too would join us after church service. Our dining table which could normally seat 6 of us comfortably, would be extended to seat double the number on Sundays. Amma's beautiful table linen would be laid out on Sundays, and a lovely lunch would be served. I can remember the fun and laughter during these Sunday lunches. I was a slow eater and there were several occasions when lunch was over, I would be shifted to a smaller table with the unfinished food on my plate. According to my siblings, I would still be eating lunch when everybody else came for tea, after a short snooze.

Family prayers were a regular feature of our home before dinner was served. Appa would read loudly and clearly from the large Malayalam Bible. Then we would have prayers which ended with the Lord's Prayer (also in Malayalam). Since the three of us studied Malayalam as our second language, this was not difficult at all. We were encouraged to speak in Malayalam at home, and that too in good Malayalam. Going to church both in the morning and for the evening service at St George's Cathedral was part of our Sunday routine. As a child, I thought the church belonged to us, as my father and two of my uncles were Trustees of the church and were also the ones who collected the offertory.

Appa was a strict disciplinarian, but to me he was always a soft-spoken, gentle, loveable soul. One thing Appa was so very particular about was my getting back home by the time the street lights came on. As a child I had the freedom to go and play with my friends who lived in the Nathan's Colony which bordered the Napier Gardens, as long as I followed the unwritten rule of getting back home by 6 p.m. I do not remember coming in late, although many a time I would run home panting, to be at home before the street lights came on. There was no question of avoiding Appa's eyes when I had been naughty or perhaps disobeyed him. He would correct me gently by telling me that a person who looked you in the eye while talking has nothing to hide. In the same vein, he emphasized that you can never trust a person who avoids looking at you while he talks. Some of the little lessons that I learnt from him are still fresh in my mind. Appa always stressed the fact that it was a luxury to have helpers in the house. He told us many times that they were there to help my mother, and that we were to always treat them with respect. We were forbidden to use bad words or even words like 'eda' and 'poda' or 'edi 'to our siblings. Neither could we address our helpers impolitely.

I remember only too well, the only occasion when my father raised his hands against me was when Shivan, our faithful helper kept following me around with a cup of milk. It was a daunting task getting me to drink milk and Shivan cornered me just outside Appa's room. At this point, as the only means of escape, I stamped Shivan's foot and said 'Poda' to him; (poda is a rude way of saying 'get lost'). To my surprise there stood my revered, gentle father at the doorway, with his hand raised. I knew there was no escape. I had to touch Shivan's feet and ask for forgiveness. Shivan pleaded on my behalf. 'It's okay Sir, she's only a small girl. Please don't punish her.' But my father was adamant. I slowly bent down and touched Shivan's feet and said, ' Sorry, I won't be rude to you again.'

Much later in life, I understood Appa's 'teachings' much better. I can remember complaining to my father about small fights that I had with my siblings. He would hear it out and then ask me to go to my mother. She would send me back to Appa. After running back and forth a few times, I would give up. Again when I complained to Appa about somebody being mean to me or that someone was bad, his calm reply would be, ' Everybody is good till otherwise proven'.

Appa's work table was a treasure trove for me. I was permitted to mess around only in the top right drawer and I did this till I was almost 9 years old. It had pencils of various colours and shapes, erasers both used and unused, paper clips and rulers. I do not know what was so fascinating about it, but I do remember finding something new each time I peered into it.

Although my bedroom was at the other end of the house, I can remember creeping out of my bed and climbing into bed between my parents to get a little more cuddling and a little more sleep. Appa would wake up early in the morning, kneel beside his bed, say his prayers and after a quick wash, get into his Kakhi shorts and vest and go down to the playground to take part in PT along with the resident students. Appa took a great deal of interest in sports, games and extracurricular activities. I remember him being the anchor for the tug of war between staff and students on sports day. Having been a President's Scout himself, he would be there training the scouts.

My sister Appukochamma's birthday was during our summer holidays when we would invariably travel by car to Aymanam, our home town where we spent a week or two with my father's brother, Dr. Appappa and his family. My Uncle's birthday was a day before my sister's. Her birthday was celebrated with all our cousins, uncles, and aunts. My birthday was almost always a school holiday, as it fell during the heaviest time of the monsoons. This was indeed a source of much unhappiness for me, to always have a wet birthday with no real celebration. Appa was on a tour of schools abroad when my 8th birthday came around. This added to my sadness and on one of those rare occasions when he called us, I cried to him, ' I also want a birthday party.' We had no phone at home and occasionally when there was a phone call, we had to go to my father's office on the third floor of the school building to use the phone. Appa promptly asked my mother to call a few people for a birthday party for me. No sooner had I heard about it, than I ran to Nathan's Colony and invited all the friends and relatives whom I came across. On the 21st of November, there was chaos and as friends with family and neighbours both young and old turned up for the party, I was delighted. I was not only thrilled with the numbers but more because most of them had come with a gift.

My mother did not lose her cool with all the extra uninvited guests. She managed to get some titbits and sweets to feed the 'multitude' as my brother put it. Later, he called me aside to reprimand me, ' I'm telling you, this will be your first and last party, and don't even dream of one even for your wedding.' I didn't care. I had my party and loved every moment of it!

A week or so later we, the children of 'Miss Bain's School' had assembled at The Museum Theatre for the Annual Day entertainment of our school. The School did not have an auditorium and such functions were held in the Museum Theatre. All the school children had some part to play in the entertainment. I was dressed and ready to recite a poem. As the curtains drew open, I walked onto the stage and started my recitation very confidently. I had just about managed a couple of lines when I saw my father standing at the far end of the hall carrying a large doll. I could not believe my eyes. My father was back home and he had brought me a big doll. I was so excited, that I could not continue with my poem, but just stood there staring at the doorway. The curtains had to be closed and I do not remember anything after that!

My Mother

Appa was a good 6' 2 ½ inches and my mother was barely 5 ft tall. Amma claimed to be 5' tall, but when I reached 5ft in height, Amma was a good inch or two shorter. While you could hardly hear Appa around the house, Amma was the one telling us what to do and what not to do. She would reproach me gently at first, scream at me, pinch me, and even beat me, but at the end of the day, I would snuggle up to her. All the punishments of the day were instantly forgotten as she put her arms around me and cuddled me, and what I can remember distinctly today is all the sacrifices she had made, all the loving care that she showered upon me. Amma grew up as an only child and although her father doted on her, her mother- my Ammachy – did not spare the rod with her. Amma did likewise too. She insisted that everything on the plate should be eaten, including the curry leaves. Both Appa and Amma insisted that as soon as we got out of bed in the morning, we had to first say our prayers. Then we had to fold the covering sheets and make the bed as if no one had slept on it. An unwritten rule was to change into 'decent' clothes instead of parading around in our night clothes. Amma was always neatly dressed and prim and proper. It was surprising to see her after a short nap, with her sari pleats all in place and not a single crease in her starched sari.

When I was about seven years old, I had severe eczema and needed a lot of care at home. For almost a year I couldn't go to school. According to my brother, my legs which were very scaly resembled crocodile skin. To begin with, it was just a small white patch and I remember Amma using a pin to test for pain. I recollect her asking me if it hurt. Of course, it did, but I imagined that it was abnormal to feel the pain. A vehement 'NO' as an answer must have sent shivers through my poor mother. After months of treatment, I was confined to the house and I remember Amma putting me in a tub of warm water with potassium permanganate. After soaking my feet for an hour or more, I was taken out of the tub, and dried with a towel and Amma would rub me down with ghee. Just at that moment, an elderly cousin would turn up at home and tease me saying that I smelt like a fried banana! Amma was there to pacify me and see me through those trying times.

To keep me abreast of my studies, Amma would take a bus to Moore Market, buy stickers with stories and she would sit with me for hours and make attractive books for me to write the stories. It was Amma's home schooling that helped me to improve my language skills and my handwriting. Amma would often have to help the school children with their English and Scripture lessons. I have heard that residential students who came down with diarrhoea, fever or some infectious disease would be isolated from the rest of the students and accommodated in a room at the far end of our house. I have heard from old students of MCCHS that some students would even pretend to be sick to have the Headmaster's wife pamper them with home cooked food and tender loving care.

Amma loved to have flowering plants and I can remember her giving instructions to Baliappan, the school gardener. Although I do not remember Amma cooking, I have heard of Amma's skills in advising and teaching the school cooks and insisting on cleanliness. I can remember the cooks, the helpers or the gardeners coming to Amma for ailments. Her all time remedy was a spoonful of sugar with a few drops of eucalyptus. It seemed to be the magical cure for all ailments.

Appukochamma, My Sister (Rebekah)

Appukochamma, my sister was 9 years older than me. From a very young age, I called my older sister Appusma. Later, when I changed it to Appukochamma, she told me in no uncertain terms, that she liked me calling her 'Appusma' better. To me, it didn't matter, as I loved and respected her anyway. Appukochamma was very meticulous in whatever she did. She was tough on the exterior, and as my Aunt Mariamma Kochamma would say, ' Appukka is an unpolished diamond.' That she surely was. A 'no nonsense do it all' person who would go to any length to see that I was happy, be it finding a magnifying glass or large eyed sewing needles or anything small or big that looked cute. While we were in Madras, all three of us siblings shared a large room in the Napier Garden house. My little storage space was a drawer in the ironing table where I hid all my knick – knacks. Appukochamma would stay back during the holidays with my mother when the house help and cook took leave. My sister would go on a cleaning spree and the house would be spic and span when we got back. On our return after the holidays, my first job would be to inspect the drawer, and to my utter dismay, one year, I could not spot the bracelet with the Binacca charms. I had spent quite some time getting the charms and bracelet, which came as an offer along with the Binacca toothpaste. Even though I could not stand the taste of the toothpaste, I would brush my teeth day and night to acquire as many charms as possible and the bracelet too. All hell broke loose then. My sister had nothing to say to appease me. A few days later she handed me a cute little doll that would walk if I held it under its arms. This was a gift sent by my penfriend. A customs duty of rupees thirteen had to be paid, which my sister did as a compromise for her unforgivable misdeed. She even cut up bits of attractive cloth and made dresses for my little doll. Her actions were such that I knew that she loved me in spite of my being quite a brat!

Achachan, My Brother (Chakko)

When I was about 6 or 7, I went to my brother with a question, 'Achacha, why am I dark-skinned when both Appu Kochamma and you are so fair? Why is my hair so curly and springs back even after I comb it so vigorously, although both of you have lovely straight hair?' He didn't even have to think for a second, took me by the hand to one corner of the verandah, and said, 'Now this should not be repeated to Appa and Amma. Ever. They will be very, very sad if they hear it. When Amma delivered you in Rainy Hospital, the war was going on and there were a lot of 'dark-skinned people ' who had come there for delivery as well. All of a sudden there was a bomb blast, and each mother picked up one baby and ran for shelter. Amma was a little too slow and the only baby left behind was a little dark-skinned baby with curly hair. That was you. Now, not a word from you.' That explained the difference. I was certain that my parents loved me just as much as they loved the others. So I kept the secret for a long, long time. Later on, I came across a picture of my maternal grandmother, and I noticed that I had a lot of her features. Many years later, when my brother was in the U.S. and needed a stem cell transplant, both Appu Kochamma and I offered to donate blood for his transplant. On testing, my sister and brother were a perfect match while mine didnt match at all.

When I told him that, now, I was sure I was adopted, he refused to believe that he had been so nasty to me.

Achachan would offer to straighten my hair with a hot iron or by tying a heavy stone with a string onto my hair at night. Most of the time, my mother had to get me out of his clutches. I can remember one day when my mother and aunt sat on the verandah washing my eyes with cold water because my brother had smeared chilly paste on my cheek to make them rosy. In spite of it all, I would go back to him with all my requests.

My Maternal Grandmother – My Ammachy (Anna Mathai)

Ammachy who lived with us for several years, was very fond of all of us. My sister was my maternal grandfather's favourite and Ammachy respected that, but my brother was her favourite. I had a place in her heart too as I was named Anna after her, and I did make use of that. I would run to her when I got into trouble. I can remember her from the time I was a child. She would sit on the verandah and use all her skills – embroidery, knitting, making little bags. In her early days, she would make cakes, and whatever she laid her hands on, would turn out well. At night as I lay down on the bed beside her, we would look at the stars and she would talk to me about all God's creation. She would talk to the plants and sing to the birds, 'All things bright and beautiful,' in her gentle melodious voice.

My School Days

I went to Miss Bain's School in Kilpauk at the age of four. My cousin Chikku and I went to the same school. After Chikku's mother passed away, my uncle and Chikku moved into our house. Not only were we cousins, but were the best of friends too and inseparable. I would protect him all the time, whether it was in class or outdoors.

I can remember one day when our parents were to pick us up from school at noon and drop us at 4 p.m. at the Museum Theatre. The school entertainment was held once a year in the Museum Theatre, in Egmore. Chikku and I waited for quite a while. Almost all of the students had left the school and the two of us were left alone. I picked up my bag and convinced Chikku that I knew the way home. Although he was not as daring as I was, he too picked up his bag and hand in hand, we walked on the pavement heading for the house in Chetpet. A little later a rickshaw driver who recognised us, offered to take us home. I had seen him several times, taking a neighbour home and I readily accepted the offer. When we got home, I rushed up the stairs, ran up to my mother and asked her for 4 annas. 'What do you want four annas for?' she asked. 'We were asked to bring four annas for the entertainment,' I said coolly. My mother had her doubts. But my father standing behind me said, 'I don't know about the collection, but I do know that a rickshaw driver is waiting for his 4 annas for bringing the children safely back from school'. That he knew I had fibbed was punishment enough for me. I never did it again.

From Miss Bain's School, I went on to the prestigious Vidyodaya Girls High School and Chikku went on to Madras Christian College High School to join standard 6. When we were twelve years old Chandypappa, Chikku's father married Mariamma Kochamma and they moved to Nathan's colony close by. But studies and other activities separated us now to an extent.

I loved being a student at Vidyodya. Some of my friends, Thangam and Rani and Elsie and Lalitha had joined Vidyodaya too. Thangam and Rani and I joined the dancing class and learnt Manipuri dance. I had many friends of whom, Thangam and Rani, were the closest. Ammu, Lalitha and Elsie later joined the Christian Medical College, Vellore. Seethamma (Sita) who was from one of the villages in Andhra was my classmate and good friend. In the final examination, she stood first and I second. As outgoing students, Seethamma got the medal for the best outgoing student and I was awarded the silver medal for Service and Sacrifice and the State Award for the first place in Malayalam.

I remember the handwork classes taught by Mrs. Kannamma. Thangam and I would alternatively get the first prize in handwork year after year. My schooling in Bains and in Vidyodaya gave me so much confidence.

———————•●•———————

3

Abraham: Pre – Medical Years In Calcutta

The years from 1959 to 1961 were significant for me, as they brought about many changes in my life. I did well in my high school exams, but as I struggled with languages, I failed in my second language – Tamil. This meant that I could not pursue a pre-degree course at the prestigious Madras Christian College in Tambaram, Madras, where my oldest brother had studied. I had hoped to prepare for engineering entrance examinations alongside this course. My failure in Tamil meant that I was not eligible for admission to any South Indian college for a pre-degree course. So I had to travel back to Kandy to retake my Tamil examination.

Before leaving for Kandy, I stopped in Madurai to stay with an aunt to prepare for my exam. To my surprise, I received a telegram from my father asking me to come back home to Kerala. Unknown to me, he had applied to various North Indian universities that allowed Intermediate studies without a second language. The telegram stated, ' Come home immediately. Seat offered at Scottish Church College, Calcutta.' Here I could study Advanced English instead of a second language. Furthermore, I could take Biology as an additional subject, despite focusing on

Mathematics for my engineering studies. I was thrilled at not having to retake my Tamil exams and immediately set off for Calcutta, embarking on a two-day journey alone, leaving home for the first time, and looking forward to the excitement and independence of staying in a hostel.

When I arrived in Calcutta, what a culture shock I had! Everything was new to me, from the local language-Bengali to the timings of meals and the way food was prepared. The first meal of the day was something made of wheat – either chappathi or poori with plenty of dhal served between 9 a.m. and 9.30 a.m. There was no lunch break and we returned to the hostel by 5.30 p.m. for an early dinner where rice and dhal curry was served. It was so different from what I was used to. After dinner, I sat with my books till I fell asleep. As I was determined to pursue engineering I worked hard in a disciplined manner, using books with exercises meant for engineering students and paying little attention to Biology. As a result, my university grades in Physics and Mathematics were excellent, but I just managed to pass in Biology. I enjoyed the freedom of the hostel, and the friendly hostel mates, especially those from the North East of India also known as NEFA, (North East Frontier Area)

The two years in Calcutta, a large city far from home, where I did not know a word of Bengali, helped shape me in several ways: I learnt to look after myself and live a simple frugal life. I learnt to eat food cooked in strongly flavoured mustard oil which was totally different from my mother's home food cooked in fragrant coconut oil. I learnt to eat two meals a day instead of three and not to be fussy about food. Duff Hostel where I stayed had students from other parts of the country and I enjoyed their friendship.

I was able to continue the practice of going to church every Sunday. Since there were hostel mates from different backgrounds I went to different churches including the Marthoma Church. Since my brothers and sisters were very active in the SCM and they spoke about this often when at home, I joined the Student Christian Movement in Calcutta. The SCM inspired us and nurtured values of integrity, unity, peace, justice and compassion in us. It was a decade after independence and much focus was given to serving the poor, improving our country and being Christ-like. Being a part of this movement touched me deeply. The SCM meetings and the triennial meeting in Lahore which I attended helped to make me aware of the need to be sensitive to the lives of those who were less privileged and wanting to do something about it. Walking through the crowded streets of Calcutta, seeing beggars in torn clothes, homeless hungry children, and men and women with leprosy and other diseases made me realise the needs of those who lived in poverty and sickness on the streets. This prompted me to participate in the feeding program for the street children a few days a week.

After completing my intermediate studies, I focused on preparing for admission to various engineering colleges. My father secretly hoped that I would become a doctor and urged me to apply to Christian Medical College, Vellore. Though I did not want to become a doctor, I did this out of respect for my father. Despite doing the admission tests for several engineering colleges, I was disappointed that I was not selected by any of them. However I was very surprised to receive a letter to attend the selection interview at Christian Medical College, Vellore. Dr. A.S. Fenn and Dr. George Cherian were the group observers who interviewed me. I shared with them that engineering was my first choice and what I had always wanted to do. I also told them that if I got selected to study in an engineering college, I would take that up. This surprised my group observers. 'What's wrong with this boy? Does he not want to get in?' they thought. We had two days of intense interviews. During the personal interviews, the group observers enquired about my family, my school days, my activities and especially why I wanted to be a doctor. In addition to the interviews there were outdoor and indoor tasks and group discussions on various topics.

The results were to be announced in the 'Sunken Garden,' outside the chapel in the college campus. All of us waited nervously. Soon they started calling out the numbers of the candidates who had been selected. I did not expect my number to be called out since I was in the open category and not sponsored by any church. But then I heard 'No 31' (my number) being called out loud and clear. I was quite shocked. Was my heart beating faster? For a while yes, but I was also strangely calm and happy.

After three-days of interviews, listening to the story about Dr. Ida Scudder and her willingness to obey God's call; learning about CMC's rich history of commitment to serving the poor and meeting teachers who lived a simple Christian life, I felt attracted to this way of living. With the SCM nurturing Christian values which I had come to believe in, and my experience of seeing life on the streets of Calcutta, I felt in my heart that this was where God wanted me to be at this point in my life. I knew that I would have to lead a very disciplined life and make the best of what was being offered to me.

It was an incredible moment for a young seventeen-year-old who had grown up in a semi – rural community in faraway Ceylon dreaming of becoming an engineer. The door to becoming an engineer had been firmly shut, and most unexpectedly, the door to becoming a doctor had opened out for me. I went through this door with the faith that, *'God works in a mysterious way, His wonders to perform.'*

When I thought about the events that led me to CMC, I realised that if I had not failed in Tamil, I would have done my pre degree studies at Madras Christian College, but then I would not have been able to study biology. Fortunately, I studied in a college in Calcutta where I was able to study biology as well as mathematics, which made me eligible to apply to a medical school as well. Being in Calcutta, allowed me to study Advanced English and do well in this, instead of struggling with Hindi or Bengali. Since I wanted to pursue engineering, my hard work studying mathematics and other general ability exercises helped me to do well in the entrance examination at CMC, which included speed and general ability tests. Young as I was, I marvelled at how God's guidance working through my father and a failure in Tamil, led me to the reputed Christian Medical College, Vellore.

4

Sulo: College Days In Madras

My mother and sister had done their college studies at Women's Christian College in Madras. I joined the college in 1961, when the Principal was Miss Renuka Mukherjee, a dignified and affectionate person. What I enjoyed most was the early morning worship in the beautiful Chapel where Miss Mukherjee led the short worship. With many of the students attending the Chapel, I could feel the presence of God guiding us in all our activities in College. I enjoyed the classes taken by my aunt Mariamma Kochamma, the Professor of English. Logic was taught by Miss Shanthi Manuel. I took part in sports and Miss Oommen though very fond of me, did not think that I matched up to my sister who excelled in games and was the games captain in her 4th year.

I knew for sure that I wanted to do medicine at Christian Medical College Vellore. In June 1962, I was called for the interview. I was very sure that I would be selected as my brother had done exceedingly well in CMC and had a good reputation. Besides, I imagined that I would make a good doctor. I left for Vellore by bus, and my brother met me at the bus stand. One look at me and he was horrified as my body was covered with rashes. He took me to the dermatologist at CMC Hospital who examined me and made a diagnosis of German Measles. Achachan accompanied me to the Women's Hostel where one of the senior students took me to her room. Being Chakko Kuruvila's sister, I got a lot of attention. All of the women students who came for the interview had to stay in the hostel. The next day all 50 of us met at the Sunken Garden where we were given interview numbers which were pinned in front of our chests and at the back. We looked like jail birds. The two group observers, Dr. Mrs. Mammen Cherian and Dr. Mrs. Centerwall were with us all the time, questioning us about our hobbies, studies, Bible knowledge and observing us doing the various indoor and outdoor tasks. On the third day we gathered near the Sunken Garden and Dr. K. G. Koshi, the Vice Principal called out the numbers of those selected. To my utter dismay, my name was not called out. I sobbed non-stop and my dear brother was at a loss. He called my sister the chief dietitian at CMC who was at work. I was not allowed to go to her house as I had German Measles. To my brother's query, ' What shall I do, Sulo is crying non – stop?' my sister's prompt reply was, ' tell her to stop crying.' Achachan did just that. My parents came to take me back to Madras in a car. I was inconsolable.

The next day, I went back to Women's Christian College in Madras and the first thing I did was to go to the chapel and sit in a corner with a sorrowful expression. To my relief, there was Vasanthi, a classmate who was in the same boat. Ms. Mukherjee began the chapel service with a verse from the Bible, *'The remnants have returned,'* (Isaiah 10:21), which was soothing. It certainly seemed that this was God's plan for me.

In July 1962, I joined the hostel at WCC as my parents were no longer in Madras. My father was now the first Indian Principal of the Hyderabad Public School and they lived in Hyderabad. My room in WCC was in the Garden Hostel with three others. Opposite our room was Nirmala George, the senior in-charge of the ground floor. Padmini Kurien, my friend from earlier days was also in the same hostel. During the weekdays we had to sit at the tables allotted to us for meals. During the weekends, we could sit at a table of our choice. Nirmala, my friend and guide took me to the table where her friends were. This was the first time that I was staying in a hostel and away from home. I felt loved and was pampered quite a bit.

The year went by quickly and for Christmas holidays I went to stay with my parents in Hyderabad. They lived in a beautiful stone house with large rooms, a beautiful lawn in front and fruit trees – mango, guava trees and grape fruit – surrounding the house. A stone's throw away was the Hyderabad Public School built like a Mughal Palace.

When I got back to college after the holidays, my father asked me to apply to CMC again. I was not in favour of applying, but decided that I would, just to please him.

My mother reminded me of a story about myself when I was a little girl. One day, a lady doctor had come to visit my parents. She was decked in gold jewellery and wore an expensive Kanchipuram sari with a border woven with gold thread. Apparently I overheard her mentioning to my mother that all these were gifts from her patients. After they left, I approached my mother saying, 'I want to be a doctor!' Years later, I had this great desire to be a doctor, but not for the gold and gifts. I honestly felt that I would make a good one.

After my first year in college, I applied to CMC again. I bid farewell to all my friends in class and my good senior friends telling them that ' the remnants may return!'

———————•●•———————

5

Abraham: College Days At CMC

After three days of initiation into college life and 'welcome' to the Men's Hostel, regular classes started. Three of us were selected from our interview group – the other two being Lee Hoo Teong from Malaysia and Graham Morrit. Teong and I were open candidates, but Graham was sponsored by the Church of South India, Karnataka. Teong was a Chinese Buddhist, Graham an Anglo-Indian, and I, a Malayalee who grew up in Ceylon. Though we came from three different backgrounds, we got on very well and remain friends even today.

As soon as a new batch of students joined the institution, they had an orientation programme that included the story of Aunt Ida and the 'three knocks', and her commitment to building a medical college for women. We also had to learn traditional songs that were sung both at chapel services and get-togethers, including the College Song led by Dr. John Carman, the Director of CMC, Miss Treva Marshall, the Warden of the Women's Hostel, and Dr. Poonnoose Mathew.

On the first day of the orientation, a staff member read out the names of each student so that both staff and students could get to know each other. When I registered, I entered my full name as, 'Anjilivelil Abraham Joseph.' Shortly after the last name was called, an attractive girl approached me and said, 'Is your family name Anjilivelil? My mother is also from Anjilivelil. So we must be related.' After a few minutes of conversation, she exclaimed, 'So actually you are my uncle!' She had figured out that my father and her maternal grandfather were brothers. One of my classmates, Albert Johnson on hearing this exclaimed loudly, 'Hey Machan, (a term equivalent to today's bro) you're Gita's uncle!' That nickname ' Uncle' stuck with me. Everyone started calling me Uncle – I was barely out of my teens and yet even seniors and some faculty and almost all the students began to call me 'Uncle'. Over time it seemed that my real name Abraham was forgotten.

During the first year we were not very studious, especially the three of us – Lee Hoo Teong, Graham Morrit and me. We decided to create a study group after dinner so that we could take our studies more seriously and encourage each other as well. Thus a few weeks before the first year mid-term exams we decided to sit down and do some revision. Recalls Lee Hoo Teong of this period, *'This was a good idea, but after two days we suddenly realised that one of us started to doze off and snore after we began studying. That of course was our 'uncle'. Graham and I had to wake him up by startling him. He woke up reluctantly with his most innocent infectious smile and after half an hour or so began to drop off to sleep again. This happened for about two or three nights.*

'One night Graham and I decided to play a prank on him. We allowed him to sleep soundly and decided to tie him up with a bed sheet in his bed. Then we wanted to drop him into the Men's Hostel pond.

'We managed to tie him up, but he woke up suddenly and was very startled. We made a lot of noise with our laughter. One of our seniors Chandu –Karna Dev Budden, the gold medallist of his year, came out to investigate why we were making so much noise. After we explained what we were doing, he suggested, 'Take him across the road to the Women's Hostel pond and leave him there.' That seemed like a better idea. Now with all the commotion, a few more of our block mates joined us – Pappiah Naidu, Fredrick John, and Albert Johnson. They too were very keen on carrying out this prank. But 'uncle' pleaded with us to let him go and finally, we decided to let him off.'

It was a wonderful first year for me since I had already completed the intermediate course, the science subjects that were being taught were a repetition of the ISC course I had done. I focussed more on extracurricular activities -games, dramatics, the choir, and being involved in religious activities such as the Student Christian Movement. Dr. P. Zachariah, the Professor of Physiology and Warden of the Men's Hostel was my mother's cousin. I had never met him before, though he knew who I was. It was only a few weeks after I joined college that he introduced himself to me and in time became a trusted and beloved mentor who kept a close watch over me.

I enjoyed my student days in CMC, especially the Christian atmosphere, singing hymns and choruses, and going to daily morning prayers in the hostel chapel. Although there was no compulsion to attend these, it came to me naturally because of my upbringing. I absorbed the history of the college, its work ethics, values, and ideals especially for the less privileged, until it became part of me. Daily interaction with our teachers and seeing their lives of commitment, contentment, and simplicity – not only in words but in action as well, made me want to be more like them. The retreats and Sunday worship and Bible classes led by teachers like Drs. Paul and Margaret Brand, Dr. V. Benjamin, who motivated me to do Community Health; Dr. Fritschi who later motivated me to work in Karigiri Hospital, and Dr. Ida B. Scudder (niece of Aunt Ida) all of whom influenced me greatly at a very impressionable age. I too wanted to serve the poor in their own communities and live as simple a life as possible.

The encouragement to be involved in activities other than studies like drama, sports and the choir was part of CMC life. I learnt that the good things of life which were given to us in abundance were to be enjoyed fully and joyfully. But to a certain extent, they also kept me from focusing on my studies. I was fortunate to have passed the initial exams without failure. But my luck did not last long – my first failure was in Ophthalmology, which surprised me as it was a subject that I liked. One of the lessons learnt at this time was that nothing is fully under your control; that one has to do one's best and then accept the outcome even if it is not favourable.

The days passed by quickly and although I enjoyed all the fun and boyish pranks, I also became more studious. As I came nearer to my final year, I often thought about my future. Where should I work? What speciality should I take up? What should I do with my life? CMC had many role models but one person was special to me, Dr. Benjamin, the charismatic Professor of Community Medicine, who had moved from a senior position in Clinical Medicine to start the Rural Health Centre and be part of the Community Health Department which was headed by Dr. K.G. Koshi. Dr. Benjamin was the epitome of simplicity and modelled in every way how a Christian should live. I admired him immensely. Slowly the idea of taking up a speciality where the work was among the poorer sections of the community and not necessarily in a large hospital grew within me. With Dr. Benjamin to inspire me, the idea began taking serious shape and over time I became very comfortable with it. I also realized that in order to do this, I should have a life partner who thought like me and had the same values and desires to work for the upliftment of the poor and marginalized. As the idea grew on me and once I had decided that this was what I wanted to do, I was keen on finding a like-minded partner.

6

Sulo: Student Days At CMC

I took the preliminary CMC test which was held in Hyderabad. To my delight, I was called for the interview. Although I was afraid of not being selected a second time, I was better prepared to face it this time.

Once again, we gathered in the Sunken Garden. I heard Dr. Koshi announcing the results in his loud booming voice. And yes, this time he did call out my number and I closed my eyes in relief and offered a prayer.

The Women's Hostel orientation for the Freshers was hugely entertaining. The seniors derived pleasure from watching us making mosquito pickle – no ingredients provided; repairing a large hole in a carpet with a few strands of thread and a regular needle. Jennifer Decunha, the senior, sternly said, 'Is this all you can do?' when I showed her my effort, 'I was told that you are a good seamstress.' The baby elephant walk early in the morning; covering the books in the hostel library and Indira Nair, the Library Secretary supervising all our activities was great fun for us, who were new to this. I remember too the acting General Secretary, Shanta John, and her roommate Sheela Thomas, who was my fag mistress. They were exceptionally kind-hearted.

The entire initiation process brought all of us, the seniors and the newcomers very close to each other. We moved into the renamed 'Kiddies Corner', originally the Small Bungalow, after the initiation. Twenty-five of us young girls were put in 'Kiddies Corner' as the administration decided that we should be under the close supervision of the Warden.

My roommates in college were Padmini Kurien, Maya Cherian, Shantha Joseph, and Ammu. Most of the girls slept at night in the dorm on the terrace. Maya and I had beds in the small veranda adjacent to the rooms. The veranda had 2 doors, one leading to the staircase at the back and the other to an open verandah where we could hang our washed clothes. Even though our little bedroom was airy and unique, we ' kiddies' were targeted often by the 'daredevils' of the Men's Hostel, who would throw water balloons at us or burst crackers when we were fast asleep.

Ms. Poonnen, our Professor of Biology who was also our warden, was an excellent cook and good food was provided for all our meals. In our second year, we moved to the Women's Hostel. Hostel life was enjoyable except for the monkeys which often invaded our rooms. Pranksters from the Men's Hostel Union would occasionally climb up the pipeline, all dressed in black with black masks and – parade in single file through the dorm throwing water balloons at the sleeping girls.

In the Anatomy lab, we did dissection working in pairs. Ragini Muthaiah, my partner was a joy to work with. Her attitude to life and pleasant demeanor was something which made us good friends for life. Maya, Padmini, and I were roommates for two more years. Among the seniors, Indira Nair, Mary Ponnaiah, Sheela Mathew, and Krishna Menon were good friends of mine and the friendships have continued all these years. Rachel Mira Joseph whom I knew from childhood was two years my senior and a special friend.

Since we were in the hostel, some of the senior staff who lived on the campus, kept their homes open for us. Dr. and Mrs. Fritschi and their children spoiled us with lovely food and entertainment. Drs. Sushil and Grace Chandi, and my classmate Lalitha's parents, Dr. P.I. George and Thankammachy Kochamma and twin sisters, Shanta and Sushila made life in CMC a 'home away from home.'

7

Abraham: Choosing A Life Partner

My father had very strong views on marriage and family life. My views were very different from his and I felt strongly that I should have a major say in the choice of my life partner. I was certain that he would not agree to this easily. But knowing some of the qualities that he was looking for, I thought I would choose a person who had these qualities – a Malayalee, good Christian background, not very affluent, hardworking and used to a simple lifestyle – so that he would readily agree.

In Sulochana Kuruvila, I found the qualities I was looking for. Sulochana joined CMC in 1963 while I was preparing for my preclinical examination. I noticed that she was a girl with no uppity attitudes or airs; that she was always very polite to everyone, respectful and kind especially to the lower classes of people. She spoke well and took an interest in the chapel activities and SCM. This quality of hers appealed to me a lot. She also dressed neatly, not in a showy manner to attract attention, and was attractive too.

I did not know much about her father except that he was greatly respected as the Headmaster of the Madras Christian College High School. I knew her brother Chakko well as he studied in CMC too – a soft-spoken gentleman in every sense of the word. He was popular because of his simple disciplined lifestyle. He too was extremely polite and kind, and most importantly an outstanding student and sportsman. We played in the college cricket team and travelled together for some inter-college matches. In conversation, we spoke about our families and I knew that his elder sister was the Head of the Dietary Department of CMC.

The first opportunity to actually meet Sulo arose quite unexpectedly. Sulo along with some of her classmates, chaperoned by a well-respected senior student attended an SCM meeting in Arkonam – about an hour's train ride away from Vellore. A group of college mates including me also attended the conference. On the second day, Omana, the senior student chaperoning the junior girls asked me to accompany Sulochana back to Bagayam as she had to participate in an inter-house throw ball match that evening. I had to participate in some other events too. I offered to accompany her, but Sulochana shook her head and would not hear of it. ' How can I go with a boy I don't know?' she said. The prospect of travelling alone with a boy she did not know did not appeal to her at all. Omana assured Sulochana, 'You'll be perfectly safe with him Sulo, he's an extremely nice person. I know him. ' So I accompanied a reluctant Sulo on what should have been just an hour's journey. But the train that we were on was a passenger train which took more than two hours to cover a distance of 60 kms. The train screeched to a halt at every station and stopped for a few minutes. Porters rushed up and down calling out in high-pitched voices to those who had a lot of luggage and passengers scurried up and down the platform carrying children and bags. Then the shrill piercing sound of a whistle would blow, the green flag would flutter and the train would chug slowly out of the station. It was a long ride back. The compartment we sat in was almost empty and I could see that Sulo was most uncomfortable. She kept staring outside at the sugar cane fields, lost in thought. I had nothing to do but to read a newspaper. In between reading a few paragraphs, I would look up and ask about her family, about her school, and her friends and then get back to my newspaper. She would answer as briefly as possible. As a station approached, I would ask her, 'Would you like some tea?' and she would shake her head. When we arrived at Katpadi station, I could see the relief on her face. We got down and onto a town bus which would take us to the college. I beckoned to Sulo to come and sit next to me as the bus was getting full. My classmate Kamala had also boarded the same bus and saw us both sitting together. She gave a knowing smile and added, 'Uncle, so that's why you disappeared today.'

Sulo got down at the college gate and returned to the hostel. Not knowing what to say to her at that moment, I said, 'Don't be late for the match. It begins at 4.30 p.m.' We were both in Scudder House and it was important to win the trophy. So Sulo and I parted ways at the second gate of CMC – me to Men's Hostel and Sulo to 'Kiddies Corner' where the first-year girl students who resided there were waiting for her. She seemed so nice and so well brought up, I wondered how I could meet her again. News quickly went around that Sulo and I were sitting together on the bus returning from somewhere. Of course, it was the talk of Women's Hostel for some time.

The College had a few social functions when boys and girls met each other in the sports field or during combined dinner parties which took place three times a year – the farewell for final year students by both the hostels and the Graduation Day dinner. One Sunday after chapel and after much thought, I asked Sulo, ' Would you like to accompany me and be my guest at the Final Year's Farewell Dinner?' She stood before me silently and then a few seconds later said very calmly and politely, ' I would like a few days to think about it.' I was surprised as I couldn't understand why she would need some time to think it over. Finally, after a few days, she said 'yes'. I then understood that she wanted her sister's approval before she replied.

There were many surprised glances from her classmates when they saw me walking to the Men's Hostel with Sulo beside me. We did not speak much that evening as we were surrounded by friends. We just had dinner, watched the entertainment, and then I walked her back to the Women's Hostel. After that, we did meet more often on Sundays, usually well before chapel service in the college guest room.

Another opportunity we had to be together was working for a project for Scudder House. Fortunately both Sulo and I belonged to Scudder House. A colourful cloth pandal was put up for each house and the house members were expected to decorate it. I was in charge of decorations that year and the group decision was to have a special lamp. Knowing that Sulo was good at handicrafts, I asked her for help. Of course I offered to help her with the project. This meant we had to meet often to discuss to complete this task. Not only did she do an excellent job, but it also gave us an opportunity to know each other, our interests and our family backgrounds better. Thus began a relationship that centred on friendship and respect for each other.

One Sunday evening after the college chapel service, I stopped to talk to Sulo. I looked straight at her and asked her quite abruptly,' What are your plans after graduation?' Sulo was a little taken aback. She had not thought about ' what next' as she was only in her first year and had not decided on anything. I said,' I'm committed to working in the villages where there is no medical aid for women and children. Are you willing to go to the rural areas in our country and care for the poor? This is my 'calling'. I guess I had put my ' proposal' to her quite bluntly and very unromantically.

Sulo who came from a background where service was held in high regard replied without hesitation,' I am more than happy to work and serve the poor in the villages. ' I knew that day that I had found the perfect partner for me. Now we had to face the question,' What would our families say?'

Since all my sisters had studied in Women's Christian College, Madras, they knew that her father, a well – known educationist, was a highly respected man. Two of my sisters knew her sister Rebekah, who was a few years senior to them in college. Sulo had already spoken to her parents about me. After having spoken to Chakko, Sulo's brother, and her sister regarding me, they gave their approval for the relationship, while reminding Sulo that studies should be her first priority.

The reaction from my father was as I expected – a BIG NO; not because Sulo was unsuitable in any way, but because my father strongly believed that parents knew their children better than they did themselves, and knew what was good for them. He felt that parents should make this paramount decision and not the children themselves. He felt that marriage was such an important event in a person's life involving two families, not just two people and that the decision could not be left in the hands of two youngsters who had no experience of life. Waiting for his permission was a hard time for us both. It took many months and interventions from several family members before he agreed to us getting married.

Once permission was granted, the date for our marriage was fixed in a hurry as my sister Leela was leaving for Canada and my father was very keen that the wedding be held in Kerala immediately. Sulo and her parents had little time to organise the wedding. Sulo's brother Chakko and his wife Susie, and brother-in-law Ranji were in America and could not attend the wedding, much to Sulo's disappointment. Even so, Sulo's parents agreed to have the wedding as requested. The wonderful thing about Sulo was that she did not fuss or want things her way, but just graciously accepted the difficult circumstances and married me. We were married on the 15th of September, 1969.

———•●•———

8

Sulo: Making A Commitment

A few days after the train journey, I realized that 'Uncle ' with whom I had spent almost three hours on a train journey was a very popular young man, who was much admired and sought after, by a number of girls. He was handsome, soft-spoken, and a very good sportsman excelling in sprints, cross-country races, cricket, and hockey. He sang in the college choir and was active in chapel and SCM activities.

A week before the Men's Hostel Final Year farewell dinner, 'Uncle' stopped me after the Sunday Chapel service. 'Would you like to come with me for the Men's Hostel dinner as my guest?' he asked. I was so surprised and at the same time delighted. Butterflies were flying around in my stomach from the moment he uttered those words. I wanted to accept the invitation immediately. But I waited a moment, as I didn't know what to say. So I said very calmly,' Let me check with my sister first and get her permission.'

There was a straightforwardness in Abraham that appealed to me. He did not beat around the bush or try flirting with me and I appreciated this as I would not have known how to cope, if he had. The next day I went to Appukochamma, my older sister who lived in the hospital campus, for advice. I found Appukochamma busy in the kitchen. Hiding my apprehension, I loitered around the kitchen for a few minutes, picking up this and that, and giving myself some time to casually say, 'Abraham Joseph has invited me to be his guest at the Men's Hostel dinner. Do you think I can accept his invitation and go with him?' I wanted Appukochamma to allow me to accept his invitation. I wanted her blessing.

Appukochamma knew Uncle's sisters from her college days and had heard of the family. ' Yes you may accept his invitation,' she said with a smile. But then immediately followed it up with a strict, ' Now don't let this distract you from your studies. That should always be your priority.'

The next thing on my mind was, 'What do I wear? I don't have anything suitable.' Appukochamma looked into her wardrobe and very kindly brought out one of her beautiful saris – a Kerala sari with a thin gold border and fine embroidery on the pallu. She gave it to me very graciously saying, ' Here, I think you will look good in this.' I already had a matching blouse and with her beautiful borrowed sari, I felt like a princess going to her first ball.

I kept my 'date' for the dinner a secret. ' I wonder who Sulo is going with?' a few of my classmates asked and were curious to know. I pretended not to hear them and put on an enigmatic smile on my face which made everyone even more curious. The men would pick up their guests from Kiddies Corner, and escort them to the dining area in the Men's Hostel. It was a time of excitement for those who had steady relationships, and for those like me and Uncle who were just embarking on a relationship, it was a time of anticipation, a hope of something more.

The farewell dinner for the Final Years in Men's Hostel was in February 1964. I was in my 1st year and Abraham was in his 3rd year. I waited in the common room of the Kiddies Corner. Only I knew who my host was and I was quite shy and kept everyone guessing. I wore my sister's beautiful sari and a string of fresh, fragrant white jasmine buds on my braided hair. Then I saw my host walking towards me wearing dark blue pants and a sky blue, long-sleeved shirt folded up to the elbow. Yes, I could feel the butterflies in my stomach again. He escorted me from the porch of the Kiddies Corner to the Men's Hostel. I could hear the surprised whispers and see raised eyebrows as we walked by and crossed the main road and up the path to Men's Hostel. What a beautiful sight greeted us. Instead of the usual wooden tables, the tables today were covered in a white tablecloth. Each table could seat 6 people and was arranged with long benches or wooden chairs on either side, in all three rooms. The dining room and lawn were decorated with coloured streamers, paper lanterns and lights and looked very festive and welcoming. The seating arrangement was posted on boards at the entrance. I cannot remember the menu at all. It was in all probability a rather big helping of fried chicken, pachadi made with curds, a salad of sliced tomatoes and onions, fried rice, brinjal curry and ice cream. All this in such a grand setting was a wonderful memorable experience for us.

Following the dinner, the Men's Hostel General Secretary and some outgoing final-year students gave speeches. This was followed by the entertainment and finally, some of the boys and their partners had a dance session. I wondered if Abraham was going to ask me for a dance. But no! He was not the dancing kind. Neither was I. Instead, he guided me past the lower common room for a brief walk and took me straight back to Kiddies Corner.

After that whenever some of the hostel girls asked me, 'Where are you going?' I would just smile and say, ' I'm going to see my Uncle'. There were many real uncles in CMC for many students and I could get away with this. I could go out and meet Abraham/ Uncle without anyone questioning me or gossiping about me.

When blessings from both sides were given, our wedding was fixed for the 15th of September, 1969. Most girls dream about their wedding day. *'What will I wear? Perhaps I will wear a tissue sari with gold embroidery.' 'Or maybe a white Benares with silver border.' 'Or a beautiful Kerala sari with gold kasav.'* Most girls also spend time shopping for their trousseaus. The pre-wedding period was meant to be a fun and special time. Not for me, though. I had no time to think of such things as I was busy running around doing my internship. Each posting was so busy, with so much to learn. At the end of the day when I got back to my room, I just flopped on my bed. I had no time to think of hairstyles or clothes or jewellery. I accepted what was bought for me by my mother and wore it happily and was thrilled that everything had worked out and I would shortly be married to 'Uncle' (Abraham.)

I was sorry that my brother and Susie, his wife, and my brother-in-law Ranji, had to miss our wedding as they were in America at the time.

After we were married, I began calling Abraham, 'Manu' just as his family did. It no longer seemed appropriate to call him 'Uncle' as all the others in college did.

One of the joys as well as the anxieties of being newly married was getting to know Manu's large family. They were seven brothers and sisters and Manu was the youngest. His mother Ammachy was a very loveable, saintly, and extremely caring lady, fondly called Maamie or Ammachy by all who knew her. She would wake up early every morning and start her day with morning worship. Her beautiful singing voice would waft through the morning air and I loved to listen to the old Malayalam hymns.

When Ammachy was with me, it felt as if I was the only one special to her. But I soon learnt that she was like that with everyone, giving everybody her whole attention and care. Everyone was special to her. I, as a new bride, and as the wife of her youngest son, was given just that extra attention. Apart from her cooking which was simply perfect and delicious, she was so understanding. She knew that I had a protected childhood and was aware of my inexperience in the kitchen. The women of the family would be busy cutting vegetables using the left index finger as a base and the sharp Kerala knife in their right hand. When I joined them in the kitchen and tried to do the same, she gently told me not to do this. ' You may cut your fingers Molae, (a term of endearment in malayalam) and you have to do surgery when you go back to Vellore in a few days,' she said. As a new bride, I felt bad seeing her and the others work so hard in the kitchen making delicious fish curry and ' thoran' while I just did small jobs. All day long Ammachy would be in the kitchen, cooking, making cakes and irresistable halwa and typical Kerala palaharams. The chips made from jackfruit was one of her specialties, and everyone just loved it. Ammachy, after she returned from Ceylon, hardly left Maramon as she had to care for the family; in addition she had to tend to the cows, the chicken, the dogs, besides feeding the workers as well. She did everything with a smile. It suffices to say, she was a gracious hostess as well. On our visit to Maramon, I loved trailing behind her, as she went about doing her many chores. Soon after, Ammachy would rush to the field to pick the little mushrooms to make her delicious mushroom thoran.

I cherished those moments when we were alone together, having uninterrupted heart to heart talks, getting to know one another, cementing the bond that would last a life time.

In the two weeks that we spent in Maramon soon after our wedding, I had very little interaction with Appachen (Manu's father) as did the other women in the family. As the head of the family, he was treated with respect and deference. Appachen would go to the paddy field or the river after breakfast and return with the fishing net and a couple of fish that he had caught. He would quiz me about the name of the fish as he recognised my ignorance. I remember a night when he called Manu and me to help out with their cow that had an impending breech delivery. I had only read about such things in James Herriot's books. Manu soaped his hands up to the elbow and managed to deliver the calf himself. Appachen was adept at repairing cane chairs and kept himself occupied doing odd jobs. He would sit quietly on the verandah, playing carroms and cards with his grandchildren.

I got to know the siblings and their families slowly. I enjoyed this period of family bonding with my in-laws as it was a nice break from my busy schedule at CMC as an intern.

———————•●•———————

9

Sulo: Life As A Couple

Life for us as a married couple began while I was still doing my internship at CMC (1969). There was no time for a honeymoon. Manu had to return to work at the CSI Hospital in Nagari for a year to fulfil his obligation to work in a Mission Hospital, as he had accepted a scholarship during his student days. It was a very busy time for me, going from one department to another, learning so many new procedures, seeing patients with various ailments and complications, and learning to deal with them on my own. They were very busy days and nights with hardly any time to stop and think, but still, I desperately missed Manu. We met whenever we had a few days or a weekend off and made the most of it. This was the way of life at CMC for young couples and we accepted it as did many others.

Nagari was one of the hospitals where interns were posted for six weeks during the three months of Rural Hospital posting. I was fortunate to work in Nagari for the entire three months of my posting since there was a need for a lady doctor in Nagari at that time. When I returned to Vellore, I had a home to stay in as Appukochamma had invited us to stay in their house. Ranji, her husband had gone to the U.S. for further specialization in Plastic

Surgery. This was such a great boon to us as Appukochamma was there to support us in every way during our busy days.

In June, 1970, I finished my internship and planned to join the Clinical Pathology Department as a Demonstrator for two years. We were expecting our first child. On the day I joined for work, I had premature labour pains and had to take leave for a month and be on strict bed rest. Priya was born on 10th August, 1970. She was a 'tiny little one' weighing only 1.6 kg at birth. I was so afraid of handling her as she was so fragile. Appukochamma would come during her lunch break and over a tiny wash basin, she would hold the little one in the palm of her hands, bathe and dry her, bundle her up and hand her back to me. Amma (my mother) and I had made all her little dresses assuming that she would be normal size, but Priya being so small could almost be pulled through the sleeves! Appukochamma put the baby clothes aside and found some material for handkerchiefs and made tiny little dresses for her.

I joined the Department of Clinical Pathology two months after Priya was born. Vinod was born a year later in 1971. I was not eligible for maternity leave and so had to get back to work after a month. Though working and taking care of two little ones was very demanding, it was a joy working with Drs. Bob Carman, Annie Sudarshanam, Hemalatha Krishnaswamy and the team.

Both Manu and I had committed ourselves to working in the Community Health Department. Realising that Maternal and Child Health was the priority for India, Manu decided to do Paediatrics before specialising in Community Medicine. Having enjoyed my posting in Obstetrics and Gynaecology as an intern and recognising that the care of the mother and child was the need of the hour, I was happy to do Obstetrics and Gynaecology.

Dr. V. Benjamin, the Head of Community Medicine was happy with our choice of specialization before taking up Community Medicine. He felt that the experience and knowledge in these fields would greatly benefit the community.

After completing his obligation at Nagari for a year, Manu returned to Vellore and did a Diploma in Child Health under Dr. Sheila Pereira and Dr. Malathy Jadhav – two well – known paediatricians. There were no Post Graduate MD courses in either Community Health or Obstetrics and Gynaecology in CMC at that time. So we had to look for a place to do our postgraduate studies. Since my parents were in Bombay we sought admission in Seth Gordhandas Sundardas Hospital and King Edward Memorial Hospital which offered MD courses in Community Health and Obstetrics and Gynaecology respectively. We were lucky to be accepted there as it was the best thing for us at the time. It meant that we could stay with my parents who were more than happy to help and support us as students and take care of Priya and Vinod who were just three and two years old.

10

Sulo: The Bombay Years

In June, 1972, the two of us along with Priya and Vinod moved to Bombay where my father was the Principal of Cathedral and John Connon School. To us who were used to the small rural town of Vellore, Bombay with its hustle and bustle and noise was a very different world. My parents lived at 11, Little Gibbs Road, Malabar Hill, and that became our home for the next few years.

Parel, where Seth G.S. Medical College and King Edward Memorial (KEM) Hospital were situated, was in the heart of the crowded city. Abraham and I would take a bus from the foot of the 'Hanging Garden' and it took us a good one and a half hours to reach the KEM Hospital. Travelling to work was a completely new experience for us – we were used to just walking across the road to our workplace.

Abraham joined the Department of Community Medicine under Dr. D.N. Pai and worked there for a year and a half. Apart from regular classes, the postgraduate students were posted to the Pearl Centre, a project of the hospital where outpatient clinics and minor operations were performed. These were the years when the national focus was on bringing down the birth rate as one of the answers to all the health problems of a developing nation. Sanjay Gandhi's emphasis on vasectomy drives was carried out in railway stations, municipal centres and outpatient clinics. Many of the doctors rushed to these clinics to do as many surgeries as possible. Abraham would do about 40 vasectomies per month in the Pearl Centre earning Rs 400 / month, just enough to pay for the milk for the children. Although my parents disapproved of this, we wanted to pay for the milk as our only contribution to the home expenses. Abraham's meagre stipend took care of our daily travel expenses.

Abraham's experience from working in the Child Health Department and the Rural Health Centre of CMC was recognised by Bombay University so he was able to complete the MD course in less than two years. He was also in charge of the drought relief work of KEM Hospital in the district of Poona. Apart from this, he took classes for undergraduate students in Biostatistics, Epidemiology and Communicable Diseases, so he was always very busy. I attended outpatient clinics and assisted in gynaecology operations and teaching sessions for postgraduate students. The only practical experience I had in KEM was when I worked as a locum for a month when a registrar had taken leave. There was a clamour for these posts as residential posts were hard to come by.

I thanked God for the meticulous training in the various departments and all that I had learnt during my training at CMC. Dr. D. N. Motashaw, Professor of one of the Obstetrics Departments, under whom I had registered had so much faith in me because of the excellent CMC training that she would entrust me with the patients who had to be worked up for surgery.

I had enrolled for the Diploma in OG at the College of Physicians and Surgeons. I worked for six months in the Bombay Hospital under Dr. Jahagirdar, a person of integrity and principles. At times, working in Bombay Hospital, I had serious doubts as to whether I had made the right choice in choosing my speciality. So much seemed to be going wrong. The first caesarean I had done ended in a stillbirth. The first difficult forceps delivery was on a primi gravida who had been treated for infertility by Dr. Jahagirdar. I arrived in the labour room one morning to take over the patient and the foetal heart rate of this patient that I noted was as low as 40 per minute. I alerted the paediatrician and Dr. Jahagirdar and as the foetal heart dropped further, I applied the forceps and delivered a deathly pale baby who barely took a breath. Despite every possible effort, the baby did not survive. Having sat through the night monitoring the baby, I approached Dr. Jahagirdar. With a really heavy heart I stood in front of her. 'Ma'am have I made the wrong decision to work in Obstetrics? Am I really suited to face all these challenges?' I asked her. She had already reviewed the patient's chart and carried out an enquiry. When I told her that I would like to discontinue my studies in this speciality, her immediate reaction was rather stern. ' I am going to tell your father what a soft-hearted daughter he has,' she threatened. ' You need to have inner strength and grit to face the many problems you will face in your career. You cannot just run away at the first sign of trouble. No, I don't think you have made the wrong choice of speciality. You can do this! '

I learnt much in those two and a half years – the need for honesty, meticulous record keeping, empathy, and most importantly the power of prayer before each delivery or surgery.

Priya and Vinod were admitted to Saifi School. It was a lovely play school where the children had opportunities to do what they chose to do under the caring, vigilant eyes of the dedicated teachers. Later on, Priya went to the Cathedral Primary School. Mrs. Irani, the class teacher, noticed that Priya was not doing too well in school as depicted by the 'aeroplanes' of each child taking off according to their performance. Mrs. Irani spoke to Priya kindly and asked her whether her Ammachy needed to be told about her performance. Her immediate response was, 'Mrs. Irani don't worry, my mother is busy – she has 'exschams'. I realised at once that my child knew that I did not have much time to attend to her schoolwork. I was so hurt knowing this. I did not know how to read phonetically. So I made little cards and practised phonetic pronunciation and spelling by myself so that so I could teach Priya. Priya soon improved with my tutoring and soon her little plane was soaring high along with the others!

Vinod was happy with the activities in Saifi school. My parents had an eighteen-year-old helper looking after all the chores at home. Jose was a perfect companion for Vinod and walked him to school every day. When Vinod was tired, Jose would carry him home. One day, Chaitanya, Vinod's best friend in Saifi School, went past him in a car to school. Chaitanya teased Vinod about his parents not having a car. The next day, Vinod refused to go to school. His grandfather understood the little boy's predicament. So the following day my father took a taxi to work and left the car and driver behind so that Vinod could be taken to school in my father's car. This went on for a day or two till he was gently weaned off this practice.

It was a difficult time for Priya and Vinod, but it established a strong bond between them. The Metropolitan of the Jacobite Church, a good friend of my father came to visit him. While father was busy talking to him, Priya arrived, quietly climbed onto the Metropolitan's lap and sat very still. The Metropolitan was impressed with her behaviour and gave her a tiny little silver cross. Immediately Priya slid down from his lap, vanished for a second and came back holding her little brother's hand. 'This is my brother. Give him a cross too,' she said. They both got a cross each and a blessing from the Bishop.

Every evening after my father got back from school, my parents would take Vinod and Priya to the beach. Back at home after running around in the sand, my mother would bathe them and they would settle down to do big jigsaw puzzles. When we returned from the hospital a little later, my mother would get the food ready and my father would say prayers. After dinner, we had a little time to listen to their experiences of the day, and a little story reading time before they went to bed. This was our daily routine. Within minutes I would be fast asleep as well.

It helped greatly that my brother Achachan and his wife Susie were also in Bombay at the same time. I was busy with preparations for the MD examinations. While Achachan helped me with the typing of the thesis and getting it ready, Susie managed all four kids – Bikku, Ashwin, Priya and Vinod on all weekends and holidays. Priya and Vinod loved the sleepover nights spent at Chachachi's and Susie Ammai's house. Thus a deep bond was forged between us all.

Abraham successfully finished his training and left for Vellore after having been away for nearly two years. This period was a little more stressful as the children missed their father and needless to say I missed him a lot too. The Department of Community Health was waiting eagerly to welcome him. Though I was happy for his success, I was also a little anxious at being left alone in Bombay with my studies and the children. Time went by and soon I too had finished my course and was ready to go back to Vellore to join the Rural Health Centre as Medical Officer.

—————•●•—————

A. V. Joseph Family in Ceylon

Eight-year-old Abraham in the garden in Kandy

A.V. Joseph Family. (1971)

Kuruvila Jacob Family. (Madras, 1953)

Chakko, Sulo and Rebekah (1948)

Kuruvila Jacob Family (1979)
1st Row: Bikku, Priya, Vinod | 2nd Row: Appa and Amma
3rd Row: Ashwin and Rachel
Standing: Raghu, Abraham, Sulo, Ranji, Rebekah, Susie, Chakko, Ravi

College Chapel and Sunken Garden, CMC.

Abraham and Kamala lead the graduation procession carrying the jasmine chain (1967)

Abraham and Sulochana were married on 15th September, 1969, in Tiruvalla, Kerala.

Abraham and Sulochana. (1969)

11

Abraham: The Rural Health Centre

At the turn of the century, 1900, India was almost entirely rural, her population living in small mud huts in villages with little or no health care. Poverty and famine spread their dust and dirt around every village. Diseases were rampant. Men, women and children died of malnutrition and sickness. It was in this scenario of desperate need that Dr. Ida Scudder first established a small hospital with medical, surgical, outpatient and inpatient care in Vellore. As the hospital grew she wanted to give the same care to poor people who lived in the villages around who could not come to the main hospital when they were sick.

Her idea of taking health to the villages slowly took shape and by 1906 she was able to set up mobile roadside clinics around the villages in Vellore where patients could come and be treated for simple diseases. A medical team would go from the hospital and have clinics under the large shady trees by the roadsides. At first, she and her team rode in a bullock cart into the villages. The bullock cart was later replaced by a Peugeot van, then a Ford and then a bus.

In 1948, CMC's first Community Health Programme was held in Kavanur which was primarily a leprosy centre. For the

Community Health Nursing Programme, nursing students were sent to conduct home deliveries in the centre. In 1954, the Medical Council of India stipulated that medical students should spend three months in rural areas as part of their internship and also as part of their undergraduate training. CMC was delighted by this order and was the first institution in the country to carry out this recommendation with much enthusiasm and started the Rural Health Centre in Bagayam.

The Rural Health Centre (RHC) started with an outpatient department and a 12-bed ward. It was called the 'manga thope' hospital because it was in the middle of a mango grove. There was a great need for an experienced clinician to run this centre. Dr. V. Benjamin, a reputable clinician was working in the Cardiology Department at the time. Hearing of this need at the Rural Health Centre, he offered to join and was appointed as the Medical Officer in 1958. The MBBS batch which passed out in 1957 was the first to do an internship in Community Medicine in the new centre.

By 1955, the Community Health Department was set up. Initially the plan was to identify a few villages where students could be taken for exposure to the health needs of the village community. For this purpose, five villages were chosen for medical and nursing students. Public health nurses and social workers from the department went to these villages and spoke to the villagers about preventing common diseases through immunization and better sanitation and hygiene. But their advice fell on deaf ears – the villagers were unwilling to listen. They just laughed at these very young women from the hospital who tried to advise them on how to live.

Community-Based Education

The founders of the department strongly believed that 'community health' could not be taught in a classroom but should be taught by actively exposing students to the problems of a rural village. They felt that only by involving the students in the life of the local community could they learn what was needed to solve the health needs and problems the community faced.

CMC was the first institution in the country to start the 'Family Health Advisory Services' in 1955, headed by Dr. K.G. Koshi and supported by Dr. LeRoy Allen. At the time, the teaching of Community Health was confined to one afternoon a week in the 3rd and 4th years. Students went to the community in pairs of a girl and a boy. Each pair was allotted one family with an obstetrics patient or an infant, and a second family which had a person affected with a chronic illness such as tuberculosis, leprosy, filariasis, heart disease etc. They followed the health care of this family for two years, provided health education and encouraged them to follow the advice given by the doctors. Students quickly realised that simple instructions given in the health centre by the public health nurse or doctor were not followed at all by the villagers. Why? Because the villagers' minds were rooted in cultural practices that they had followed for several generations. They were also ignorant of changing values in present-day health and economics. To change these attitudes and practices was indeed very difficult. Unlike curative services in a hospital where the recovery from the disease was tangible and easy to observe, the medical improvement of chronic conditions and change in behavioural attitudes was very slow and frustrating both for the patient and the doctor.

This resulted in a perceptibly negative attitude among students toward Community Health in general.

When I was a medical student, the community health posting consisted of going to the village once a week for 2 hours and then coming back to class. Most of us were anxious to get back – either there was an exam the next day for which we had to study or there was some interesting sports activity or some extracurricular activity that we were involved in. Moreover, the villagers were tired at the end of a day's work and after a few years of experience, knew exactly what the students would ask and so had their answers ready. Understandably very few graduates chose to specialise in Community Medicine, so there was some surprise when I chose to work in this field.

I joined the Department of Community Health in 1967 after I completed my internship. Dr. V. Benjamin, Dr. Sojibai Samson and I were the senior members of staff. There were very few interns, and the number of patients were not many either. It was an exciting moment for me as I was on the first step of the career that I had cherished in my heart – to serve and bring good healthcare to the poor and the sick in our country. The year went by quickly and I moved to a Mission Hospital in Nagari, (Andhra Pradesh). It was while working here that I realized how much more the services of the Rural Health Centre needed to improve and expand beyond the 5 villages we had chosen to work in. There was so much need in every village – children dying of malnutrition and sickness, widespread poverty, rampant unemployment, poor sanitation and overpopulation. Every village had its share of disabled, mentally ill, elderly, visually and hearing challenged and chronically sick people who needed care. Then there was the darkness brought by superstitions and centuries-old malpractice. And the women burdened by all this grieved silently for children dead at childbirth or of sickness.

In their world of darkness, who was to light a candle for them? Who was to show them a better way to live? Whose responsibility was it to care for them? My mind kept working on these questions all the time. With the questions, came the answers too. I realized that the community itself could be the best caregiver. However, we needed to show them the way. How were we going to make this happen?

Having gone through the process of learning community medicine as taught in the traditional way of one class a week, I realised that we needed to change the learning process if we were going to address the problem of the health of the community. Routine village clinics went on, but still, I felt that something was missing. We were a teaching medical college and yet we were not able to ' teach' community health in a way that students could learn and reach out to make a difference to healthcare in village communities.

At the RHC we had about 50-60 patients every day and barely 10 deliveries per month. Our main focus was to prevent disease through health education, immunization and antenatal care. We were good at what we did but whatever we said went right through the ears of the villagers. Nobody paid any attention to us or cared enough to listen to us as they thought they knew better; after all, this was how they had lived and practised health for centuries. They were unwilling to follow our advice regarding immunization, antenatal care, better nutrition or use of toilets. Our health workers had a hard time during every visit and were most dejected. So was I.

This rejection of what we were trying to achieve bothered me a lot and I took my concerns to Dr. Benjamin. It had been troubling him too. The idea of raising the level of health in the villages by using the village community to be responsible for their own health was the obvious answer – we both agreed on this. But how were we going to achieve this , given the difficulties we faced?

Dr. Benjamin now had a like-minded comrade in me and together we talked late into the night and worked out schemes that we thought might work.

Community Orientation Programme

Soon after I returned from my postgraduate studies in Bombay, I was invited by the Principal Dr. Fenn, to demonstrate a better model for teaching Community Health. ' Show me something different and new,' he challenged me. This was what I was waiting for.

Though there was much respect from the administrators and those working in the main hospital for The Rural Hospital, it was seen as a poor relative. Nobody wanted to work there – no exciting operations, no demanding life-and-death situations where the adrenalin flowed and you helped save a life. For students too, it was a most uninteresting posting during their internship.

'How do we make it more interesting and inspiring for them?' ' Why isn't it challenging for the students? Why do they not want to make a difference to healthcare in Indian villages?' I wondered.

There was something very wrong with how we taught this subject. Students would go for the village clinic, come back and have a lecture to attend. Lectures and classes alone were not going to serve the purpose of teaching community health. I realized 'the classroom' needed to be the village itself, allowing students to see and experience the problems the villagers faced concerning their health. They had to know first-hand about the villagers' way of life and traditions. Only with this personally experienced knowledge, could they come up with solutions and changes.

This was my vision and great desire – to take the students to the villages so that they could interact with the villagers, understand their needs, identify their problems, and then work towards finding solutions. It was a process of learning. I spent most of my time talking about this idea to anyone who would listen.

We made provisions to take the teaching of Community Health into the villages; a very new and exciting idea. The idea was that the students would live in the villages for a period of time to experience what the villagers went through. Farmers – both men and women – would get up by 4.30 in the morning to work in the fields before the heat of the day set in. Sowing, reaping, and harvesting were all done during particular seasons. Water had to be carried from wells often far from the village. They faced drought when there was insufficient rains which meant that there was not enough food for the family to eat. Even cattle and goats suffered during the drought or summer as there was neither food nor water for them. I felt that our students had to see this and experience it to understand what the ordinary villagers in our country went through every day.

Dr. V. Benjamin and Dr. Christine Mathews, a Public Health specialist from the UK, approved of it wholeheartedly. The

Principal, Dr. Fenn also agreed to it. Then came the hard part; getting the teaching faculty to agree to this idea. We had to bargain with the faculty for more time than was allotted for Community Health so that this experience could be meaningful to the students. We needed at least four weeks so that the students would have enough time to do proper research projects. The basic science faculty was very much against granting students three weeks off for community health as they felt that they had insufficient time for their own subjects. It was not an easy period at all — facing opposition, running the normal village health programmes, doing duties in the Rural Health Centre, writing protocols, and seeking permission from the administration. Nevertheless, I persisted and kept presenting our ideas to various pre-clinical faculty, meeting with them separately and in groups. In preparation, nurses, health workers and social workers visited one village after another for several weeks to identify a suitable village, large enough to accommodate 80 students and staff for two weeks. Meetings were held with the village leaders and elders to seek their approval. Armed with this success, a detailed hour-by-hour plan was drawn up as to what exactly the students would be doing. With Prof. P. Zachariah, the Head of Physiology interceding on our behalf, permission from the Principal was finally granted. The first three weeks of December after the students' examination were to be set apart for the Community Orientation Programme (COP). Finally, with all the permissions granted, we had the green signal we had been waiting for. What a day of rejoicing that was!

This was the opportunity for me to try out some of my own ideas and I was really excited. Having read about some innovative health programs of organisations from other countries, I realized that we needed to make radical changes in the teaching of Community Health in our own centre and that this was the right time and place to implement these changes.

On a personal level, this had been a particularly difficult period for me. Sulo and the children were away in Bombay and almost every day I was beset with so many problems over the beginning of the COP. I missed Sulo's sunny nature and her positive outlook and advice and the children's laughter and hugs. One particularly bad evening Sulo called – Priya had very high fever and she was very worried and I could sense that she wanted me to come and be with her and the children. I was completely torn apart – the husband and father in me wanted to fly to Bombay immediately, and hold them all in my arms and assure them that everything would be alright. But the professional side of me that had been battling for permission for the COP, just could not think of taking even a few days off. I found myself saying, 'Sulo, just this once can you manage on your own?' From the deep sigh at the other end, I knew that Sulo understood and I was so grateful for her support. Even though I was absent, Sulo's parents and her brother Chakko stood by her throughout this trying time.

---·●·---

12

The First Community Orientation Programme

Our first Community Health Programme was held in December 1975. The plan was for the medical students – both boys and girls to visit the village along with senior staff. The boys would stay in the village, while the girls would return to the college hostel every evening. For two weeks the students visited the villagers in their homes, ate food cooked in the camp and learnt of the villagers' problems first-hand, under the supervision and guidance of senior doctors and social workers from the department.

Recalls Dr. Vedantam Rajshekhar, one of the first batch of students to go on the COP. *'It must have been either November or December of 1975, when the Community Health Department informed our batch that they were introducing a new program called the Community Orientation Program (COP) for first-year medical students. It was to be a full-time program which involved living in a nearby village for two weeks. Some of us thought it was a great idea – a little holiday from nagging teachers, classes and tests; others were appalled at the idea of living away from little luxuries and others thought of it as a great unique experience that we were lucky to get.*

'For many of us, including me, it was our first exposure to village life. We had passed by little villages on the bus or on the train, and thought them to be quaint, but did not spend any time thinking about what life was like for those who lived in those villages. We quickly learnt how hard daily life was. Our first excitement quickly gave way to nervousness and a little uncomfortableness.'

'Everything was so different from what we had imagined. There was no running water – water had to be collected from a well. Open gutters ran through the village. There were flies and mosquitoes and dogs running around. There was no electricity. We had to get used to the dark nights lit only by kerosene lamps. We were not used to the scary sounds of the night either or sleeping on mats on the cow dung smeared floor. There were no proper toilets or bathrooms as we were used to. Uncle (Abraham Joseph) and other faculty and staff of the Community Health Department introduced us to village life gently. They guided us in our interactions with the villagers and through their example we learnt how to speak to them, humour them and relate to them. They patiently introduced us to the strange food we were given to eat – 'kali and koolu' – a kind of pasty gruel made with ragi and other millets and grains. They guided us through their customs and rituals which were unfamiliar to most of us. I remember Uncle telling us, 'They share their meagre food with you generously. Don't refuse what you are given to eat, that will insult and hurt them.' He also led by example, graciously accepting and eating the food offered by the villagers and showed us that this was one way of building trust.'

Recalls Dr. K.S. Joseph, 'The Community Orientation Program in the first year of medical school, and in subsequent years had a *significant impact on me, and I chose to specialise in Community Medicine.'*

During the COP students learnt sociology – village customs, practices, rituals and traditions by interacting and talking to the villagers; they learnt statistics by collecting data in the village and analysing it. Some aspects like the age distribution, sex discrimination favouring boys, nutritional deficiencies etc. came alive and made more sense when the students did the study while in the community itself rather than from an abstract paper. Clinicians from the hospital came to the village to discuss common medical problems like tuberculosis, leprosy, scabies, diarrhoea, respiratory infections – all of which had social and economic implications. The objective was that what they learnt was to be experiential, community-based and problem-oriented and not based on didactic academic lectures alone.

The first program was such a grand success – most of the students enjoyed it immensely. The boys and girls went into the homes and sat with the families on a mat on the floor. The families liked it because here were smart students from the city who were willing to sit and talk with them in their homes and identify with their poverty. They would offer the students something to eat, maybe some peanuts or corn or tender coconut. It warmed their hearts to see the students accept their sparse offerings and eat them with relish. The families were also happy as the students learnt their names and related to them individually. The community was happy because we were taking care of their immediate medical needs like coughs and colds and fevers and aches, pains, and bruises. If the family had a health problem, the students would bring them to a faculty-run clinic in the evening. The fact that the students accompanied the families showing them that they cared for them played a huge part in developing trust between them. This also gave us an opportunity to teach the first-year students how to look at and treat minor health problems.

Right from the beginning, we suggested that the students should do something for the community to thank them for their hospitality. In Tamil, we call it *'shramadan,'* which means working along with the community to do something good. Before going to a village we met with the leaders and asked, 'Tell us what you need. How can we help you? What do you want us to do in your village?' Some said, 'When it rains our roads are waterlogged. Can you do something about that?' The students then helped with making a soakage pit. Some batches of students cleaned drains, and relaid roads. The students learnt the value of the dignity of labour and manual work. Doing things for the community created a bond between them and the students. We also told the leaders, 'You, the entire community are our teachers. The students will be learning from you; from observing what you do and listening to what you say, so please help us.' On the last day, the students put up an entertainment of music, dance, and some aspects of health education that they felt the village needed, and the villagers loved this.

About a month of groundwork had to be done before we took students to a community. Usually one senior and one junior faculty would supervise a group of 12–15 students. In the first year, we provided fairly intensive, close supervision. Later on in the students' curriculum, there were two other block postings when the supervision was less intense because by then, the students had learnt the art of interviewing and how to get the cooperation of the villagers.

There were of course some students who were not too happy initially about spending two weeks in a village, working under constrained circumstances. One of the girl students recalls, '*We weren't particularly thrilled, but we adjusted quickly to the village way of life and happily allowed the village women to place strings of bright marigold flowers or purple December blossoms or orange kanakambarams in our hair. This show of affection to us was their way of accepting us, and although the flowers were garish and most of us were not used to wearing braids and flowers in our hair, enjoying what was given to us and wearing them was our way of accepting the village women and building a kind of trust despite our differences. In retrospect, I realise what an adventure this period was and how much I learnt even though I didn't expect to at the beginning.*'

Dr. Dayalan Clarke, *(batch of 1977)* remembers the COP as a great learning experience. '*The village that was chosen was Senji, a small village in North Arcot District. We set off on the college bus and moved into our residence in Senji for the next 2 weeks. A classroom in the village school was converted into a dormitory and was to be our bedroom for 2 weeks. All the male students along with the staff, slept on mats on the floor in one large classroom. The toilets were built specially for us on the school grounds adjacent to the classroom and were just holes in the ground, but built in keeping with the sanitation guidelines of the Preventive and Social Medicine textbook by Park. This took some getting used to. Food was cooked in a make-do kitchen and the meals that were served introduced us to nutritious but inexpensive meals made from lentils and cereal like millets and ragi.*

'*The existence was basic. But the students and the staff who stayed with us in the village had a great time. We lived in the school and went out into the village, meeting the members of the village and promoting public health amongst them. We were all paired in twos and each group of two covered a geographical area of the village, where we visited each house in the allotted area and collected information of each household – a sort of census that covered the whole village between us. We discussed various issues with each family to include clean sanitation, healthy lifestyle measures, immunization programmes for the children, health checks for the elderly, and advice on general well-being. The thrill of learning to give intra-muscular injections as part of the immunization programme is something I will always remember.'*

The Community Orientation Programme had taken off and was now part of the curriculum. Most students looked forward to it after hearing about it from the previous batches. Every year little adjustments were made to make the COP a better experience.

A decade after it was begun, Dr. M. J. Paul, (1987) recalls *'My interaction with Dr. Abraham Joseph and Dr. Sulochana Abraham whom we affectionately called Uncle and Aunty, began in the winter of 1987 when we as first-year students, went to the Community Orientation posting, an unusual experience for most of us city and town-bred teenagers who had never experienced village life in India. The COP was a beautifully designed part of the curriculum where we were given an immersive experience of the realities of rural life. 'Uncle and Aunty', together with other staff had designed a two-week stay in the village for budding doctors to orient our minds to the dynamics of social and economic factors at play in the health of the majority of our country's people. This included interviews with the villagers in various zones of the village to find out the social and economic determinants of health and to see for ourselves how caste dynamics operated in village life. We also dealt with water supply, drainage, building our own dry toilets, slept in a village hut – a practical exposure to community health that would otherwise have been meaningless if only read from a book. There would be evening discussions on various topics to engage our minds and enhance learning to make this one of the most impactful experiences in the medical curriculum and motivate some of us to make it a lifetime involvement. Even those who took up other clinical specialities would have an interest in making their specialty rurally oriented thus creating a far-reaching impact.'*

Says Dr. Padma Paul, (1987) *'What I imbibed from all our postings in CHAD including internship was the backdrop on which the rest of my career was to form. I had been educated in Bihar and had once visited a local village as a child. The experience that was the Community Orientation Program was so immersive and deeply inspiring as it made us connect with people and their lives really and not only as read in textbooks.*

'When I finished my training in Ophthalmology, this deep connection made me feel that we should provide eye care as well as all the other primary health care for healthy well-being. This spurred me on to do a Masters in Public Health, joining the first batch of MPH students in CMC in 2009. As part of my dissertation when I went back to talking and relating to the villagers, I got a deeper understanding of the excellent work done by the CHAD team in identifying, training, investing in, and nurturing the 'health aides' who are the foot soldiers of the programme.'

Over the years more and more students were trained, and the effect the COP had on them was the same. After this experience, some students took up the challenge of doing Community Health in places where no healthcare was available. Some who were sponsored by the church went on to work in Mission Hospitals where doctors were much needed.

After successfully running the Community Orientation Programmes for several years, we did a study to assess how our fresh graduates were performing at Mission Hospitals. After their training at CMC, which was a tertiary hospital with all the latest diagnostic facilities, we wanted to know how they were able to work with fewer facilities and a minimal number of staff.

Our graduates were also asked to provide feedback on their experiences at the Mission Hospitals where they had worked as part of their sponsorship obligation. This was so that we would be aware of some of the problems they faced from their perspective.

The feedback from the Mission Hospitals revealed that, while the young graduates were highly dedicated to their work, they were not familiar or proficient in the way the Mission Hospitals functioned. Based on this study and with the approval of the Principal and Director, a two-week program called the 'Peripheral Hospital Posting' was introduced in 1990, when I served as Vice Principal. The objective of this programme was to acquaint the students who were going to serve in such hospitals, in the way the Mission Hospitals functioned, their limitations and problems and how to face them. The program was a success, leading to the addition of another two-week 'Mission Hospital Rotation' in the second clinical year. In 2002, Dr. Anand Zachariah, Professor of Medicine, further modified the program, renaming it the 'Secondary Hospital Posting,' which continues to this day.

13

Sulo: The American Study Years

When I joined the Rural Health Centre after completing my post-graduation in Bombay, both Abraham and I were young and idealistic, deeply influenced by the SCM and the values we had learnt during our time as students at CMC. We were sure that we could make a difference. Dr. Benjamin, the Head of Community Medicine knew this and felt that I needed to have a Masters in Public Health so that I could be recognised as a teacher in the Department of Public Health. Abraham had done his Diploma in Child Health in Vellore and followed it up with an MD in Community Medicine in Bombay. Having a pediatrician and an obstetrician was a vital need for the Rural Health Centre as Maternal and Child Health was the priority of the time, considering the national birth rate of 30/1000 and an infant mortality of 80 /1000. He now felt the need for a Public Health specialist too. He was very keen that I go to New York to specialise in this. We had a difficult time deciding how to do this – for me to go to the U.S. at this point was not easy – as Abraham was so busy with his work in the department. I could not leave the children alone in Vellore with him although we had excellent house help. While we were pondering what to do, Appukochamma, my sister, and my brother-in-law Ranji, who lived in Kansas, stepped in and offered to take care of the children for a year. We were so touched by their kind and gracious offer and accepted it gratefully. This meant that there would not be a big separation between us. Appukochamma, gave up her full-time job as a dietitian and opted to work part-time so that she could be there for the children. Priya was 8 years old and Vinod, 7, and I am certain that it was no easy task to take care of them and to look after her own family as well.

Priya, Vinod and I travelled to the U.S. in September 1978. I left them in Kansas with my sister and proceeded by myself to New York to Columbia Presbyterian University to enroll for the Masters in Public Health, focussing on Maternal and Child Health. Life in New York was not what I expected at all. I had a real culture shock. I found it difficult adjusting to living alone in the Nurses' Hostel after having lived in a home of my own. Having my supper by 5 p.m. was also not easy as I was used to having a late one. I had to return to the hostel as early as possible as 164th to 168th Street, the 'Mexican Harlem' which I had to cross, was a dangerous area to be in after 5 p.m. not only for women but for everyone. Besides, I was away from the children and Abraham and it seemed like a never-ending year.

My first acquaintance was Dr. John D. Frame, the Head of the Church which sponsored me. As soon as he saw me, he said, 'I know you have left your home and country and have come here to do your MPH, and I am certainly happy for you, but would you not be happier if your husband joined you here to do the MS in Epidemiology?' I was stunned by this, as this was my heart's desire – for both of us to be further qualified from American Universities. The next three months went by quickly. There were several people who helped make me feel less lonely – Dr. Ida B. Scudder, (niece of the founder of CMC,

Dr. Ida S. Scudder) who was working in CMC when I joined as a medical student, Dr. D.V. Scudder, the widow of Dr. John Scudder of Ranipet, Mrs. Sue Swanson, a grand niece of Dr. Ida S. Scudder, all of whom took me to their homes, were very kind to me and treated me like family. Mrs. Mary Chacko (sister of Dr. V. Benjamin) and her husband not only took me to their home almost every weekend but also packed delicious Indian food to last me till the next weekend. Miss Gertrude Nyce, the acting Director of the Vellore Board, looked into all the small details to see that my stay was a happy one. In the University, the heads of MCH and Health Education were particularly kind and helpful. Dr. Frame, a fatherly figure stood by me and gave me opportunities to present our work in Vellore to a very large audience of Public Health Foundations in Washington.

A little miracle happened during this time. Dr. Indira Radhakrishnan, Abraham's classmate and a good friend of ours from our student days came looking for me. Indira, her husband Radhakrishnan (RK), and their seven-year-old son, Nana, lived in an apartment in North Bergen, New Jersey on the bank of the Hudson River. Indira had kept in touch with my mother and learnt that I was in New York. Since RK had to be away the whole week working in Chicago, and Indira was in the midst of her anesthesia residency, she asked me to come and stay with them in New Jersey and commute to New York during the week. This was wonderful for me as it meant that I did not have to stay in the hostel. Abraham arrived in December and we spent Christmas with my sister and her family and our two little children. How wonderful it was to see the first snowfall and experience an American Christmas. New Year was spent in Vancouver with Abraham's sisters, Leelakochamma and Ammukochamma. This too was a time of family bonding which we all enjoyed. After a splendid break, we went back to New Jersey and to our studies in New York. Abraham spent a month at Johns Hopkins doing his Masters in Epidemiology. We also spent time with Mrs. Naomi Carman, wife of the former Director of CMC, Dr. John Carman.

Having completed our courses with honours, we were now ready to return to our home and work in Vellore. With the support of Indira, RK, Nana, and my sister's family, we truly felt that when one door closed, several others opened to help us complete the task that we had set out to do.

On 15th July, 1979, we boarded an Air India flight back to Madras. Early in the morning of 16th July, the Air India air hostesses brought out a beautifully decorated cake with eight candles. It was Vinod's 8th birthday and what a special celebration that was on the aeroplane with passengers and crew singing happy birthday to him and wishing him.

14

Abraham And Sulo At Work

On returning to Vellore and the Rural Health Centre (RHC), we were both excited. We missed Vellore, our colleagues, and the RHC. We were even more committed to working, armed with new knowledge, skills, and a shared vision – to make health care in the village communities accessible, affordable, and acceptable.

At the time when we began our work in the RHC, the birth rate, and maternal and infant mortality were high. Eighty percent of the women chose to deliver in their homes; antenatal coverage was less than 40 %; most women had more than three children; complications of pregnancy and delivery were many; stillbirths and early neonatal deaths were sizable. Deliveries in the homes were mostly conducted by the Traditional Birth Attendants (TBA) or the Dai and only a few of them were trained. The wives of the village barbers were traditionally the TBA and the practice was subsequently handed down to the daughter-in-law, who watched and learnt. The deliveries were conducted on the floor of the house (usually a mud floor washed with cow dung); the umbilical cord was cut with an unsterile knife or a sickle.

Salamma, our oldest TBA, and later on a part-time community health worker, (PTCHW) demonstrated how she would sit on the floor of the house between the folded legs of the mother, and use the sole of her feet to support the perineum, as the head of the baby was crowning. Salamma agreed to be trained by us after a newborn child died of tetanus. The reason for the death? She had used a farm sickle to cut the cord. 'Why did you use a sickle?' we asked her. Her spontaneous answer was, ' What else should I use? That is what we have always used.' We taught her a sterile way of cutting the umbilical cord and provided her with a sterile blade and cord tie.

The RHC where we worked was not a favoured place to be for most of the doctors. There were only 3 or 4 interns posted at any time. In the mornings, in the OPD, I, (Sulo) would see general patients and occasionally an antenatal patient who needed a check-up. Tubectomy operations were done in the afternoon whenever a postnatal mother would opt for a tubectomy – a rare occurrence at that time.

Maternal and child health clinics were held in the OPD mid-afternoon on the first Wednesday of the month. The junior doctor's role was to send for the routine lab investigations, take the patient's history, and do a physical examination. The nurse would do the antenatal examination. My role was to see that all was well after going through the notes and then to prescribe the medicines and the tetanus toxoid. Gradually when the patient numbers increased, we had to bring about some changes so that we could cope with the increasing numbers. There were some objections from the nursing staff because until then they had fewer numbers to contend with, but soon everyone settled down as they realised that the changes were necessary, considering the ever-increasing number of patients. The afternoon MCH clinic had to be increased from once a month to twice a month and subsequently to every week.

The RHC (base hospital) had twelve beds for obstetrics patients. The labour room was small with one labour cot and a large drum to store water. There were 8 – 12 deliveries conducted in a month and occasionally a forceps delivery. In the early 70's, one or two caesareans sections were done. Most of the complicated deliveries were either referred to the Government Hospital or the CMC Hospital.

In the early days, Abraham and I alternatively attended the mother and child health clinic in the village two or three days a week. The van would set off at 3 p.m. with a public health nurse, one or two nursing students and a medical intern. The first visit that I made was to Pennathur village. The nursing student brought the patient in and after the routine tests were done, the intern had to collect blood and transfer it into a tiny sterile bottle. Haemoglobin levels were determined using the Sahli's haemoglobinometer. If the blood clotted, the patient was asked to get her blood tested again at the next visit. Blood was also collected for VDRL, blood group and Rh. The doctor took the history and did the physical examination and the nurse, the antenatal examination.

On my first visit to the Maternal and Child Health village clinic, I played the part of an efficient 'highly trained' professional. I asked the only patient who had turned up, to pay Rs 40/- for the blood test that had to be sent to the hospital. Just as we were about to leave, another patient strolled in. At the next visit the following week, there were no patients at all. Nurses who visited the area later were told that the women who had come to the clinic the previous week complained as, 'the Missie' doctor who wore a long white coat and glasses made us pay Rs 40/- and took one bottle of blood for testing.' There was resistance to the money that was charged, the blood being collected, and the unfamiliar look of the new doctor. The complaint taught me many lessons. The first was to look at everything from the women's perspective. To the village women, all this was new and frightening – even how I looked was strange to them – my long white coat, the glasses, the severe pulled-back hair. I had come to them with my newly acquired knowledge and training to tell them in a crisp, no-nonsense voice what to do to take care of their and their children's health. I quickly learnt that it was more important to get to know them, become a friend, and understand their problems as village women first, before giving them my treatment plan. I had to come down to their level of understanding and get to know their way of life. They needed to trust me as a woman before they could trust me as a doctor and entrust me with their lives. And the road to gaining trust was through conversations.

Dr. Vinohar Balraj recollects, 'As an intern in 1977-78, I remember going to one of the villages about ten kilometres away from the RHC on a scouting expedition, since Dr. Abraham wanted to know whether mothers and babies had come to the clinic. He said, 'Try to convince them to attend the clinic.' The clinic was empty. I walked around the village trying to convince the mothers and grandmothers, but nobody turned up. I remember the first immunization session in the community – the women just did not trust us. We had to overcome the mistrust and suspicion before any immunization could take place.'

Very soon we understood some of the reasons for the poor attendance at the MCH clinics. The older generation felt that they had gone through pregnancy and delivery without attending any clinic, so why was there a need for all this fuss? The young antenatal mother saw a new intern at each visit and was rather confused. It was easier to approach the TBA who knew them and understood their problems. The women dreaded the routine practice of blood being drawn for the investigations. We had to find a way of putting them at ease and telling them what these blood tests were for before we could do anything. Some of the women who had attended the MCH clinic felt insecure when we had to refer the complicated cases to RHC. There was a reluctance to come to RHC because the women felt more secure with the dais they knew from the village, to being with unknown people in the hospital. Traditionally, births took place in their homes in familiar surroundings under the supervision of the TBAs. The pregnant mother had support at home, where she could also continue to oversee the household needs. The women needed a lot of convincing and persuasion and were often brought to the hospital in the late stages. Another important factor was the lack of transport from the homes to the hospital. There was an instance of a woman in obstructed labour who had to be carried on a cot across a stream which was flooded. On another occasion, I had to go to the patient's home on the back seat of her husband's bicycle to remove a retained placenta. Some of the women were anaemic and it was a nightmare getting the husband or close relative to donate blood. Deliveries were even conducted in bullock carts or transport buses. All the passengers were asked to get off the bus till the delivery was over and the bus cleaned up!

In 1981, we realised that we needed to expand our work to more than just the five villages. We extended into the whole of Kaniyambadi block with a population of 80, 000, in phases.

We put our heads together and realised that we needed a person in each village who would be accepted by the community. We discussed the problems with the village elders and leaders. The dais (most of them trained by now) were the obvious choice. The selected dais were then trained as the PTCHW. The training of three months began with what they were familiar with already – the care of the mother and child; conducting deliveries in a sterile manner, postnatal care, the need for immunization of the mother and the child; how to treat diarrhoea, the need to boil water; how to treat cuts and bruises and when to refer a person. We introduced a home based ANC card with symbols that an illiterate person could recognise. This card helped the PTCHW to recognise the 'high risk' factor and refer the woman on time. The PTCHWs were expected to work for two hours and also to motivate the mothers and children to attend the mobile clinic. They were paid accordingly. The fact that they were part of the CHAD team gave them a special status in the community. The grateful villagers paid them in kind – rice, ragi, lentils, vegetables and occasionally a sari for the help rendered.

We then divided the entire block into smaller units of 3 to 4 villages making up a population of 5,000. The PTCHWs who were illiterate could not document births, deaths and other vital events and turned to their children for help. It was evident that they needed supervision. Auxiliary Nurse Midwifes (ANM) who were trained in good Mission Hospitals were appointed to stay in the villages; one ANM covering three villages. Though the ANMs were sincere, there were problems which we hadn't anticipated which made their work difficult. There was always the issue of what caste they belonged to. If they were of a lower caste, they were not allowed to live along with the higher caste within the same village or use the same well. There was the lack of security for them if they lived outside. To add to all of this, the villagers were always suspicious of someone new, especially if they were unmarried women. The government also faced the same problems of ANMs not staying in their allotted villages.

Abraham soon realised that there should be a cadre of workers similar to the government ANMs, but one who resided in the village; one who had studied up to the tenth standard and could maintain records; who had children herself so that she could motivate the village mothers regarding diet, milestones, and growth of the child. Importantly, these Health Aides would reside in their own villages and would be easily available to anyone when the need arose. All the village leaders were informed and more than sixty women applied for the first training programme, went through an interview, and seventeen of them were selected. The training began in 1982 – six months in the CHAD Hospital, (formerly known as Rural Health Centre) six months in the labour room, community visits and clinics. In 1984, seventeen Health Aides were appointed by CMC to work in CHAD.

Nirmala, one of our first Health Aides recalls, *'I was just twenty years old. I came for an antenatal check-up and spoke to the 'big doctor' there – Dr. Sulo. I desperately wanted a job. But the baby was due soon, so they couldn't consider me. I waited for six weeks after the delivery, and when I went for immunization with the baby, I searched for Dr. Sulo. She listened to me patiently and compassionately and when she understood how desperate and eager I was, she asked me to join the training class. Just like that – no interview. Seventeen of us who were selected were trained for a year. We could not give injections but could give prescribed medicines and see that the patients took them. We gave the women health education, advice about good nutrition, good hygiene and encouraged them to attend the clinics for their health problems. Dr. Sulo was 'Aunty' and of course Dr. Abraham was 'Uncle' to us. Our stipend was Rs 75/per month for the first six months and then it was raised to Rs 150/per month. We were so happy with it as it was the first time any of us had money in our hands. We were all 'raw' young girls from the village. Dr. Sulo showed us how to wear a saree neatly and pin it to our blouse, how to comb our hair and tie it into a 'kondai' so that we looked well–groomed and professional always. This way, people would take what we said seriously. With my first salary, I opened a bank account. Because of family problems I could not stay with my in-laws; so I looked for a place where I could stay with my child. Dr. Sulo gave me a small cross to wear as a 'thali' as otherwise a single woman with a child living in a village would not be respected. In time, Dr. Sulo helped me to get admission for my child in Vidyalayam. My daughter joined the Compassion program run by the school and did very well.'*

As the department made new inroads into the community in different ways, it was the women who benefitted the most. Says Manimegalai who trained as a Health Aide in 1982, *'I met Dr. Sulo at a Madhar Sangam meeting and asked for a job. She asked me to apply for the training. I was smart and was selected and given a lot of responsibilities. In time, I learnt to help with conducting deliveries, death reports, follow up of patients with chronic diseases, checking baby weights, counselling and a little bit of detective work on why patients did not come to the clinic or take their treatment seriously. I loved my job.*

In the early years we were like a big family. We all looked up to Dr. Sulo and Uncle. I cannot tell how good our relationship was; not only between them and me, everyone felt the same too. We were never scolded in front of others and when we made mistakes, both of them would take us aside and talk to us privately. They made us feel that we had a serious job to do.

'Once Uncle took a few of the health aides, social workers and doctors to Salem on an evaluation project for DANIDA. We were given chappatis for lunch. Uncle saw that we were not eating the chappatis. He knew that as village women we were used to eating only rice. Later he went to a far off place and brought us rice to eat. Nobody ever cared about us this way before. I used to live in a house with an open gutter nearby before I became a health aide. I realised that before I could teach others, they have to see the changes in my own way of life. So I cleaned up the gutter and built a proper little house with a bathroom. When the other women saw this, they also wanted a house like mine and worked to achieve this. What a difference CHAD has made to my life and theirs.'

Recalls another Health Aide, 'A *few years before I started working, because of a family feud, I tried to commit suicide. I was brought to Dr. Sulo and she saved me. I came to her door with nothing in my hand – just my unhappiness. She took me in, counselled me and told me I had everything to live for. She found a small house for me to stay, gave me clothes, groceries, pots and pans and everything I needed to start life again. And I did. At every step she was my guide and mentor. Now I am doing well, I still have her spoons and use them. I wear the clothes she gave me and feel that she is close to me. The compassion she showed me, taught me to be compassionate to the women who had drunkard husbands or whose mothers-in-law used to harass them. I became a kind of counsellor using Dr. Sulo's words.'*

It was not just the women workers in the village who recalled the kindness and friendship at work. Vijayapandian joined the community health team as an attender in the hospital when he was twenty years old. His job was to clean the theatre, the OPD and to transfer patients from the trolley to the operation theatre and later wheel them back to the ward. Recalls Pandian, *'I worked for forty years in the CHAD Hospital and since I had worked as a plumber with my father, I was also asked to do any work connected to plumbing in CHAD. I have made many mistakes, but never once was I scolded or shouted at. One day I locked the operation theatre after cleaning up, put the key in my pocket, forgot about it and went home. The next day, as I was getting ready for work, I noticed the keys in my pocket. My heart almost stopped. I was sure I would lose my job. When I went to Dr. Abraham's room to apologise, he just looked at me and said, 'Don't ever do it again, we might urgently need the operation theatre.' Of course I never repeated that mistake again.'*

Many changes were introduced to strengthen the base hospital and the existing programs. With a steadily increasing number of patients, we realised that it was not possible to provide the needed attention to the antenatal women with 'risk' factors in the regular MCH clinics either in the village or the base hospital (CHAD). In the mid-eighties, we introduced the concept of 'high-risk' approach. A high-risk clinic was organised once a week in the morning. I sat through this clinic which sometimes went on and on. On one such day, I was so relieved when one of the postgraduate students, Dr. K. S. Joseph offered to help me. Seeing that it was a good learning experience, posting postgraduates at this clinic was made part of the routine. The number of patients referred from the mobile clinic to the CHAD Hospital increased steadily, and another high-risk (HR) clinic was started in the morning to fulfil the needs. After initiating the HR clinics, over the years we did see a steady decline in the perinatal mortality rate.

It was a great relief to have Dr. Daisy Singh, an experienced obstetrician who had worked in a Mission Hospital in North India, join the department in the early nineties. Dr. Daisy took on the responsibility of screening high-risk antenatal patients. Dr. Daisy and Dr. Jasmine, a postgraduate, alternatively took the women who came for antenatal check-up to the Rehabilitation Institute for the ultrasound screening twice a week as CHAD did not have an ultrasound machine till the late nineties.

The visible increase of antenatal coverage from 20 % in the mid-seventies to well over 95% in the late nineties was not only because of the inclusion of the PTCHW, the health aides, the nurses, the doctors and the mobile clinic but also due to the improvement of the quality of care in CHAD Hospital; from a single bed labour room to four beds in the eighties and to 10 beds in early 2000. The operation theatre was also upgraded to a higher standard.

It was a slow process and it took several years to change the existing practices, but it materialised with education and motivational talks done by the entire team. With safer deliveries, and even complicated deliveries being conducted in the CHAD Hospital, the number of home deliveries decreased dramatically.

Interestingly, women would come to MCH clinics more often than required. This was not only due to more confidence in the team, but also because it was an opportunity to get out of their houses and have social interaction with other women.

———•●•———

15

Empowering Women

The more we became involved with the local communities, the more we became aware of the social status of the women. A woman's life revolved around work in the fields – sowing, planting, harvesting. Their lives also revolved around looking after the children and elders in the family, cooking, cleaning, washing the family's clothes and putting up with abusive, drunken husbands, difficult mothers-in-law and facing all the vagaries of family life on their own. They had very little income and no rights. We realised that this was our starting point. If we had to make an inroad road into the health of the community, we had to begin with the women. A meeting with the local Madhar Sangam, (women's group) showed us the impossibility of keeping a family healthy if the women had no land to grow their food, no income of their own to buy food or clothes, no real work to sustain them other than seasonal agricultural work. They had to be dependent on their husbands who themselves had only seasonal agricultural or building work. We saw that there was no value for a woman's or a girl's life. Girls dropped out of school as early as standard 4 or 5 and were a burden on their families – both financially and concerning their safety – until they got married and went on to their husband's families.

We realised that we needed to empower the women to be economically independent before we could discuss their health issues. Our next thought was how could we do this? A village woman had few skills. We would have to teach them new ones. So we began a series of simple, easy-to-do, income-generating activities. CODES (Community Development Society) was set up to train women in small local crafts like basket making, making sisal products like table mats, weaving colourful cloth, tailoring shoulder bags, embroidering saris, making macramé plant holders and other crafts. Says Abraham, ' We were so lucky that Sulo was a wonderful seamstress and a real master with the needle and thread. She taught the women how to embroider on terry voile saris and these sold so well.' Recalls Sulo, 'I would rush to the sewing room across from CHAD during lunch break and teach the women a new stitch having started from the basics like hemming and tacking. It was wonderful to see the talented ones take to it and enjoy their work.'

The craft products were sold through various outlets and became very popular and soon the women were making enough money to look after their families and to even save a bit for things they needed. Women who were trained in tailoring and embroidery were able to earn Rs. 2500/- to Rs. 3000/- per month for the beautiful work they did. With this new economic independence came self confidence and the feeling that anything the men could do, we could also do. The women now wanted to be in control of the family finances. Men masons were often absent from work due to heavy drinking the night before. The women said, ' Why not train us? We don't drink. We need the money for our families.' So we started training women as masons and bricklayers. We were delighted when the women masons of CODES constructed a two-storey building to house the created products. As the women became more independent and vocal about their health and rights, the men wondered why they were left out and wanted us to train them, so that they too would be employable. So we began training some of them in automobile repairs.

Recalls Uncle, 'While organizing all these activities, we came across a most unexpected problem: that of caste in the villages. Some villagers felt that weaving was not a suitable job for a high caste woman. These women did not want to work with the Dalit women. They wanted separate workrooms. We could not agree to this. To us, social and economic development also meant integration and living in harmony. So we said, ' No work, no income, unless all of you work together.' In time, economic independence won and the women of both castes began working together. This was truly a big success for us. Working together happily, in harmony with each other was what we had dreamt of and to our great delight and pride, it was happening.

We also got banks to give loans to poor villagers to earn a livelihood. We started what was called the 'passing the gift' scheme. The bank loan was used to purchase 10 sheep or a calf which was given to disabled persons. Once the calf grew to be a cow and delivered a female calf; it was given back to CHAD and was then passed on to some other deserving individual. PTCHW's were also given a calf to help supplement their income.

Women with small children found it difficult to work. They were used to taking their children along to the fields or to collect firewood. But now with specific workplaces like the weaving sheds and tailoring rooms, they could not bring them to work. Many of them could not leave small children behind with a mother or mother-in-law either. What could we do to help them? We began balwadis (nursery schools) where they could send their children both for safety and for some learning activities. This was a great help to them as it meant that they could come to work knowing that their children were safe and looked after. When the women realized that we really cared about them, they also began trusting us with their health and that of their children. They were open to our immunization campaigns and programmes and learnt to take their own health seriously. They realized that if they fell sick, they could not work. And if they could not work, their families could not eat.

Most of the women were illiterate and were very keen to learn to read and write. So we began literacy programmes. As the women began to read and write and sign their names, their self-confidence soared and they were ready to take care of their own, their families' and the community's health.

Health Education became an important part of CHAD's outreach activities. The village meetings where everyone gathered in the evenings and Madhar Sangams were the right place to introduce and discuss these ideas and ways to care for their family's health. The women who could barely afford rice and dhal for their families were sorely tempted to buy expensive baby food, tinned milk and cereals which were advertised on TV showing plump, happy babies. The ' breast is best ' campaign was a very necessary one. Our health workers taught the women about the good nutritious values of locally grown peanuts, grains like ragi and millet, and taught them how to make dishes with rice and home grown vegetables. Mothers were educated when to change a baby's diaper, how to keep the baby safe and clean and how to look after and feed a baby with diarrhoea. A nutritional rehabilitation centre was set up for severely malnourished children. Here mothers could bring their sick children, admit them, stay with them and learn how to cook for them and look after them until they were better and ready to go home.

The women began trusting us and realized that our concerns for the health of their children were for their good. The vaccine and immunization programmes took off, keeping children safe from communicable diseases. Says Abraham, 'As we progressed from trying to solve one need, we found that another one cropped up that had to be solved too and so it went on.' So with the mother and child's programmes taken care of, we turned to caring for adolescent girls and boys who needed a different kind of health education – sex education. Our health workers gave classes on how to prevent teenage pregnancies, STD and AIDS. We began youth clubs where the boys played games and were encouraged to take up different hobbies instead of wasting their time. Then we realised that with all these different sections of the family taken care of, there was one group who needed care too – the elderly. So we set up daycare centres initiated by our son Dr. Vinod so that the elderly could gather there during the day and occupy themselves doing small activities.

————————•●•————————

16

Abraham: Entering The Tribal Areas

As part of the Outreach Evangelical Group of our church, St John's, in Vellore, I realized that healthcare in the hills surrounding our villages – the Jawadhi hills – was non-existent. Groups of tribal people up there lived a very primitive lifestyle and disease and poverty were rampant. When faced with disease or illness, the tribals had to walk miles down the hills where there were no roads to reach the plains and then take a bus to get to the hospital. So most of them didn't bother to go or when they did, many of them did not make it on time. In extreme cases, they carried their children and elderly down, but often it was too late. Their lives were ruled by superstitions and unhealthy rituals performed by local 'shamans' or the 'mantaravadi'. Another problem was that they did not trust the people from the plains. The tribals felt that the people from the plains manipulated them and cheated them – and of course they were right about that. For example, the tribals who practised a barter system for the things they needed were forced to exchange a kilo of tamarind which was expensive, for a kilo of brinjals which was cheap. Often they would be denied entry in a bus because they looked different and wore different clothes. Life was not easy for them once they left their hills.

Says Sulo, 'Once Abraham saw their plight, he could not get them out of his mind. His vision now extended to the people in the hills. *'How can we just leave them there like that? Do we not have a responsibility towards them too? Now that we have a good programme in our village communities, why not take it up to the hills?' So that is what we did under the initiative of Dr. K.R. John.'*

Similar to the earlier community health programmes, the first step was to build trust and good relationships between the healthcare team and the tribals. We couldn't just walk into their villages and lecture them on their health and lifestyle habits. First, we learnt to understand their lifestyle, their habits and listened to their needs during regular visits. Slowly they understood that their children did not have to die of diarrhoea or fevers; that they could be better nourished; and that they could earn a living to sustain them with things from the forest that were available to them, like herbs and honey. Along with basic healthcare, we also introduced development projects that they could be involved in easily. Part of development was education, so setting up local schools became a necessary part of our programme. So too was developing income generating projects for women.

Underlying everything, all the innovative health, social, and development programmes was the message of the Gospel – *'Lord when did we see you hungry or sick or in prison? And Jesus replied, 'I tell you, whatever you did not do for one of the least of these, you did not do for me.' (Matthew 25: 40)*

———————— • • • ————————

Dr. L.B.M. Joseph, and Dr. Benjamin sharing the activities of the Community Health Department with visitors.

WHO Award

Dr.Palitha Abeykoon, Deputy Regional Director, WHO, SEARO
presenting WHO's 50th year award for the best institution providing
Primary Health Care in India

COP – getting to know each family

COP – participating in village lifestyle.

COP – Students show the villagers how to make a soakage pit

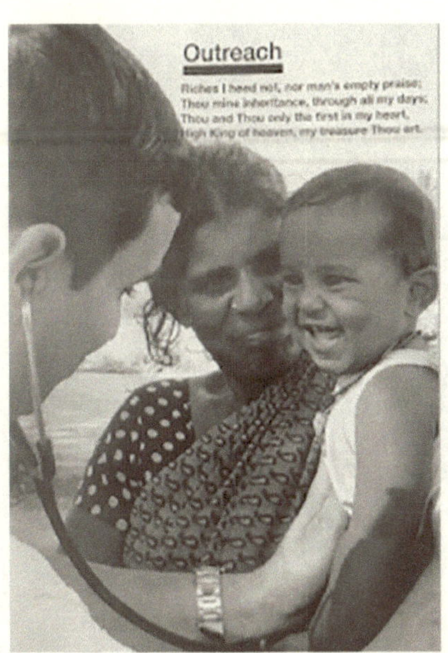

Dr. Vinod making friends before immunizing a child

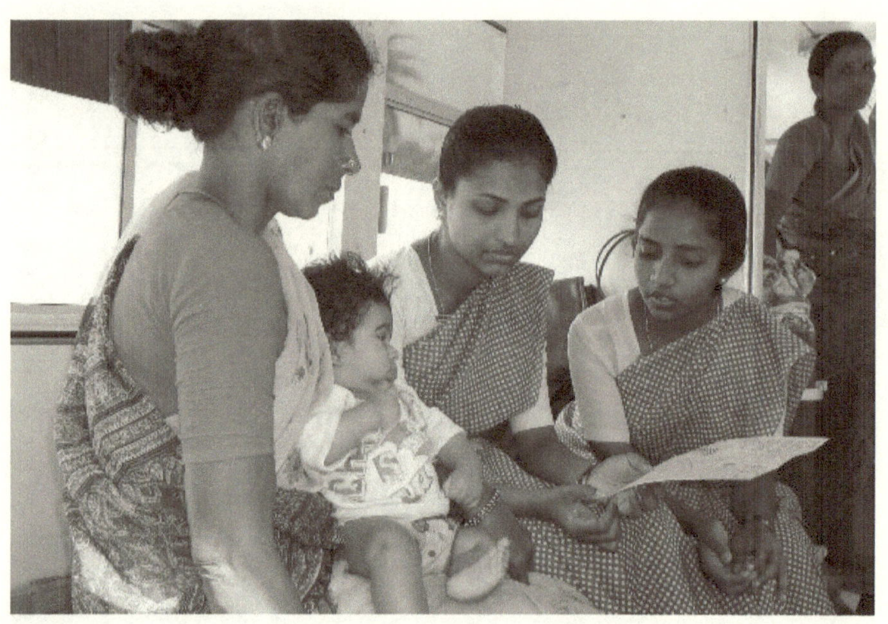

Student nurses educating a mother

*Geriatric Care: motivating elderly women to keep
fit at the Day Care centre*

Teaching Balwadi teachers to make the jasmine chain for graduation

Tailoring and Embroidery Unit

Motivating women to be masons and not just helpers

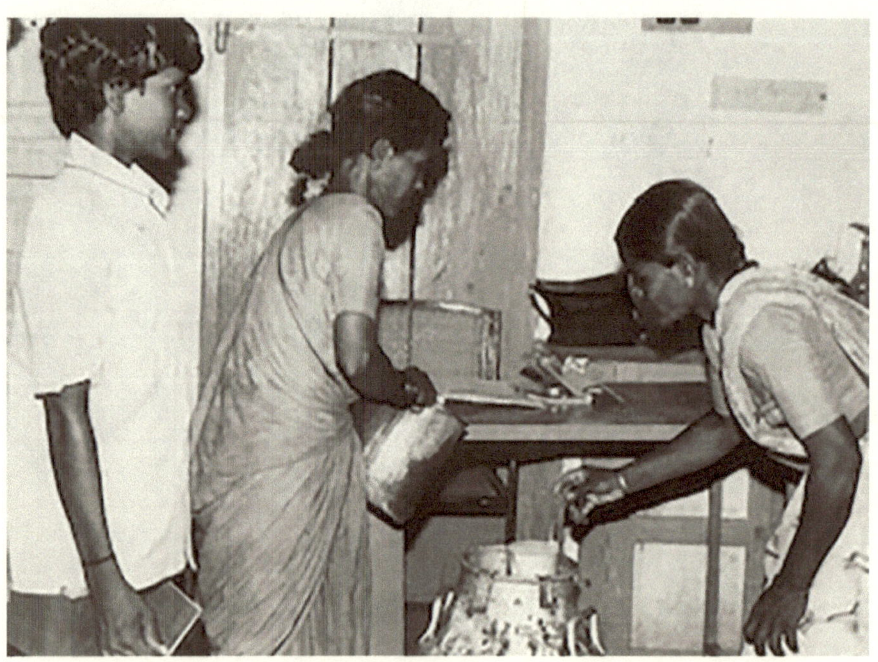

Members of the women's milk co-operative society

Women making hollow cement bricks for construction

Training men in automobile repair

Pioneering into the tribal area in Jawadhi hills

Getting familiar with tribal lifestyle.

17

The Teachers, The Trainers

Several changes were introduced on our return from America, in CHAD. The first caesarean section that I (Sulo) did in 1982, was for a woman who had come with ruptured membranes during the 7th month of her third pregnancy. On examining the patient, I could see that the umbilical cord had prolapsed and the head could still be felt in the abdomen. We rushed her from the labour room on a stretcher over the rubbled pathway to the theatre, all the while pushing up the prolapsed cord with the gloved hand and gently pushing the head up higher through the vagina. The cord should not be compressed. The hospital did not have a generator to assure a continuous supply of electricity. Nevertheless, we did the operation using a bright torch light. The mother was given oxygen through a nasal catheter till the baby was delivered. The rest of the surgery was done using a petromax lamp. Abraham was the anaesthetist and Dr. Daisy Dharmaraj, the Registrar who had a lot of experience, assisted me with the surgery. Sister Rosaline, the senior nurse also assisted very ably. At the end of the day, we were exhausted with tension, yet, we all rejoiced at what was a little miracle for us.

Training the interns and post-graduates in such emergencies became a routine activity. Recalls Dr. Madhavaram, *'On a cold December morning, I was on second call in the labour room at the unearthly hour of 3 a.m. Dr. Sulo was on third call and came to my aid for a challenging assisted labour. She remained present throughout the procedure, including the completion of an episiotomy. By the end, the labour table was in a bloody mess and disarray. Auntie Sulo told me, 'Madhu, please call Pappamma' (the attender) I stepped into the corridor and repeatedly called out Pappama's name, yet she didn't respond. Then Auntie said, 'Madhu, give me the broom and the bucket.' I didn't know what she was going to do with these. She just took them from my hand and meticulously swept, cleaned and washed the room until it was spotless. I was astounded. Here I was a trainee student just standing there, while one of the foremost social obstetricians in the country was sweeping and cleaning the dirty labour room floor. I learnt a lot that day – both in complicated obstetrics and the values of humility and the fact that no task was beneath my dignity or position.'*

Dr. Johnny Oomen too remembers his training. *'Dr. Sulo called me and said, 'I will teach you how to do Caesarean Sections, but in my way.' And it was brilliant.*

'For the first lower segment caesarean section (LSCS) I had to follow and learn the job of the attender. I learnt who all had to be called for a surgery and how. I learnt that the mop was left hanging to dry on a bush outside the theatre, and it was critical to get the theatre mopped and cleaned between surgeries. And so on.

'For the second LSCS, I had to learn the job of the Floor Nurse; where the drugs and instruments are kept. How do you keep the

supplies going while the surgery progressed, calling out the BP at each stage.

'For the third, I learnt the role of the scrub nurse. I learnt to slap the instruments in the hands of the operating surgeon just so. And then the role of the assisting surgeon.

'Finally, she taught me how to do an LSCS in about 25 minutes skin to skin. This step by step learning taught me to appreciate the roles of the many members of the health team, and the critical importance of even the meanest of tasks and the people who do them.'

Most students who first come to CHAD either as interns or as PG's think, ' What does it matter if I'm 10 minutes late? '

Recalls Dr. Vinohar, *'One of the things we learnt from Uncle as students was the value of punctuality. An early riser, Uncle would be strolling around CHAD Hospital at 7 a.m. and at exactly 7.30 a.m. he would be just outside the hospital watching staff come to work. He'd go tsk, tsk, tsk and look at his watch when someone was late for work.'*

Another of his colleagues recalls, ' None of us wanted to be later than him, not because we were afraid of him, but because we respected him so much. Even a disappointed look from him because I was late would spoil my day.'

Dr. Madhavaram *also recalls this virtue that he learnt from Uncle. 'One enduring memory that continues to resonate with me is Uncle's emphasis on 'keeping time.' Every morning at 7.30 a.m. he would stand at the entrance, greeting us with a cheerful 'good morning' for the CHAD prayers. I learnt this art of being punctual and setting an example from him, and carried this tradition forward to the PSG Rural Community Health Centre in Vedapatti, where I implemented a similar routine at*

8 a.m. including lighting the lamp and performing the Aarthi, followed by a 10-minute planning session assigned to each staff member.'

Apart from these basic values, the students were there to learn how to practice good medicine in a village setting. Recalls. Dr. Gift Norman, *'Uncle taught us the art of deductive diagnosis; to depend more on the patient's history and physical examination rather than ordering a whole battery of tests to arrive at a diagnosis. Through this approach of minimal investigations, he urged us to be conscious of the social and economic realities of the people we serve. We were also encouraged to follow up on each patient to check on how they were doing.*

'I served my bond in Karur in a village health centre for two years that also had a leprosy control program. My days were filled with field visits, interacting with patients and hearing their problems. I tried my best to apply Uncle's methodology of deductive clinical diagnosis. This phase was also a turning point in my life. I now understood that rural India urgently needed doctors and decided to specialise in Community Health and turned my back on my desire to pursue surgery.

'With Dr. Abraham at the helm of the Community Health Department, I couldn't have asked for a better mentor and guide. He was not only a powerhouse of knowledge but possessed an intuitive understanding of what ails public health in India; insights that tomes in a library can't hold. I was fortunate to hone my skills under his tutelage and closely observed how he would speak to patients and administer to them. Compassion was the biggest learning here that I try to carry forward to this day. You could say it was, 'caught rather than taught'.

Recalls Dr. Gift again, *'Work does not end at 5 p.m.'* was Uncle's work mantra. Visits into the community at 7 p.m. were quite common since that was the time people were back from their work and Uncle kept up his discussions with the local leaders and the public at these forums. We as post-grad students as part of our training had to participate and we learnt that these informal visits were a crucial part of our community health training.

'Uncle was hard-working and expected no less from all of us. On one occasion, I thought I was justified in requesting exemption from the 'Madhar Sangam', a meeting from 7 p.m. to 9 p.m. where I was to address the women of the village under a banyan tree on anything from anaemia, cancer, tuberculosis prevention, ante-natal care, vaccinations etc. It was not something I looked forward to. 'Sir, I have a night shift coming up. Can I skip this?' I asked. Uncle thought for a moment and then said, ' You have so many friends, Gift. Ask one of them to cover for you, finish MCH clinic, then Madhar Sangam, and get back in time for night duty,' as if it were the most natural thing in the world. It was a quiet lesson in prioritizing what was important. These were lessons that could not be 'taught ' in any other way.'

Recalls Dr. Varghese Philip, *'Dr. Sulo started medical audits in CHAD Hospital. This was such a terrific move. These audits were meant to improve quality of care in CHAD and included ante natal and pediatric cases as well as medical cases. Given that CHAD was a part of the Community Health teaching department, this was a great lesson for us trainees. Soon, 'ethics in clinical care' was added to the curriculum and anonymized case reports were presented by trainees to their peers and teachers. Participation from other departments was encouraged and welcomed. This was a major upscaling of relevance in the teaching of the department. Needless to say, some of the audits were painful for the caregivers but, the lessons learnt were many. Dr. Sulo demonstrated the humility to accept criticisms when they were backed by evidence. By her example, we learnt too that humility was a part of the 'mission.'*

'One of Dr. Sulo's successes was her brilliant idea of storing records. When it was time to develop an information system to support community-based antenatal care and deliveries at a low-resourced facility, Dr. Sulo designed and implemented the CHAD Antenatal Card for recording, storing, and transmitting information between patients, community health workers, nurses, and doctors. The specific items of information chosen; their location on the card and the sequence of their flow perfectly capture the mental models that treating physicians and nurses use and need to be guided in to make decisions from the time a pregnancy is registered to the delivery and the period after the delivery. When I visited government urban health centres in Vellore town during my post – graduation, they had copied the card and were using it. It manages to be concise and comprehensive and intuitive all at the same time. That card is the most intuitive health record I've come across.'

Recalls a colleague, 'Uncle towards the last few years before 'retirement' decided that all decisions needed to be taken collectively and started faculty meetings for collective decision making minuted and had it distributed. He asked for edits on this document before it's final acceptance. Uncle put this system in place and this was the only department in the institution with such a system. So everyone felt they were a part of the decision making process. Sulo continued this practice after Uncle retired.'

Abraham loved his students. Every one of them will tell you this. Wherever he went, they went with him. Teaching and training was a skill that came naturally to him. He didn't go to a school or college to learn how to do this. And his students loved him for it.

Dr. Arvind Kasturi, now Chief of Medical Services and Professor of Community Health, St John's Medical College, Bangalore, recalls. *'I joined the department as a junior Clinical Assistant' (Non-PG Registrar) in 1989. As a wide-eyed youngster, I remember being deeply impressed by Uncle's quick thinking and deep commitment to the cause of Community Health. His energy was boundless, reflected in his seemingly unending ability to work, and this left a deep imprint on our young minds.*

'He allowed us the freedom to laugh and joke together, which was again a reflection of the love he had for all of us and the pride he took in his band of post-graduate students. We had the freedom to disagree, and this was a wonderful gesture by a teacher, allowing his student to express a dissenting opinion while keeping the focus on the big picture.

'He gave a bit of himself to all of us, and this is the greatest thing a teacher can give his students. I took away some of these values in my own development as a teacher and member of my Department at St John's Medical College.'

Abraham was passionate about everything resonating with the teaching of community health. His students saw and felt the passion and were mesmerized by it. One of them, Dr. Nihal Thomas, said to himself, *' That is how I want to be. How do I learn to be like this? I realised that there were no books or classes that teach you how to become like Abraham Joseph. So I decided to watch him closely; to think like him; react like him; speak encouragingly like him; to do what he did; and not do what he didn't do. In time, I hoped that I was becoming a little more like Uncle.'*

Dr. Manoj Kurian, who is at present the Director of the Commission of the Churches on Health and Healing, World Council of Churches in Switzerland, recalls, *'These two teachers, Uncle and Aunty, were always very real and are appropriately placed on the pedestal of my mind. They are two sides of the same coin, working and living for the welfare of the community and the foundational values of the institution they led.*

'They led and trained us by example. Both of them reflected the best values that over time has helped shape my life and professional career. I remember an incident in the first year of my MD training which illustrates how they navigated the complex relationship with us students, dealing with us in a dignified manner, and catalyzing our development and growth. During a monthly meeting which brought together all the staff at CHAD – including all the outreach staff, Uncle announced the closure of a number of 'balwadis' (child care centres) in our villages due to a drop in funding and budget cuts. As a young doctor who was looking after some of these centres, I was both devastated and furiously angry. 'How can he just close these down?' I fumed, as I felt that the villages that I was responsible for were being disproportionately impacted. After the meeting, I went to his room and raised my concerns very bluntly and angrily. I questioned the basis of the decision and how the centres were prioritised in the process of closing them down.

Uncle patiently listened to my concerns and my angry tirade. 'O.K. You develop a criteria to prioritise the usefulness of the centres in light of the services available for children in all the villages, so that we can recommend the centres to be closed based on evidence-based prioritization,' he said. That was a neat and clever move. So we students went through a thorough and transparent process of prioritization and the management accepted our recommendations. This was something I learnt from him – don't make all the decisions yourself – get your team involved in the decision-making process to solve problems for themselves. That is how they will learn.

'Uncle connected us with the village community that was poor and had so many health and social needs. He taught us to be humble and to listen carefully to what the community were saying; to be aware of their needs as they saw them; and to work with them to find solutions together. In connecting with the villagers the way Uncle did, in a seemingly easy, and one-to-one basis, we too learnt to bond with them at a deep and personal level. They were not just 'villagers' or ' patients' but people and families whom we came to love and care for deeply.

'Now years later I am in a place of leadership. I try to follow the values I so admire in them. It's not easy, and yet, because they made it seem so easy, the desire to walk in their shoes has become a goal for me. Both of them were disciplined and compassionate; setting and living by the highest yet simplest standards; always very accessible and approachable. They were willing to accompany and mentor younger professionals and students, shaping them and inspiring them to go out and make a difference in whichever part of the country they chose to work in. Their ability in caring for the individual, without loosing sight of the context of the whole community was specially admirable.

'I now realize that they helped reveal a holistic, participatory and appreciative practice of public health. They nurtured and sustained, with the help of the very cooperative team they led, an institutional framework that inspired me and numerous other health professionals to mobilise our God given ability to dedicate our lives to the welfare of people, both at the individual and the societal level.'

———•●•———

Drs. Madhavaram, Manoj Kurian, Arvind Kasthuri,
Sara Bhattacharji, Vinohar Balraj,
J.P. Muliyil, Kuryan George & K.R. John
Abraham and Sulochana

18

Sulo: Building A Centre Of Excellence

As more and more women, their husbands, children and elderly parents began coming to the CHAD Hospital, it was soon obvious that we needed new buildings. Abraham had taken up the responsibility of being the Head of Community Medicine in 1981, and all his waking hours were spent seeing the department and faculty grow to their fullest potential. It was very obvious that a new building for the OPD and wards was desperately needed as patients spilled out of the old one in large numbers and there was just not enough space for anyone – neither staff nor patients. Since CMC was supporting the outreach activities and staff salary, Abraham felt that the department should raise its own funds for capital expenses especially for new buildings.

Realizing that we desperately needed a new building, he worked tirelessly writing for grants, searching out and connecting with organisations that could help us expand the base hospital. In 1980, Christian Aid funded the initial expansion and later in the mid 90s DANIDA, the Danish agency funded the new building. Everyone looked forward to a new building with well-planned wards, an operation theatre and a spacious labour room.

The whole building project took up almost all of Abraham's time as he supervised and saw to every aspect of it. There was great excitement as the new buildings started taking shape. The CHAD logo, standing tall at the front of the building has the symbol of the mother and child and Gandhiji's spinning wheel. This too was carefully thought out and designed by him.

The centre of excellence was not the building. It was the work that was done by the people in the building. The Community Oriented Program (COP) the first of its kind in Asia was initiated by Abraham in 1975 soon after he joined the department after specialising in Community Medicine. In the early nineties, the WHO recognised the department as a centre for Community Based Education and conducted workshops for other colleges in the South East Asian region. The success of the COP spread and our programme became the model for other medical colleges too.

When the Dr. M.G.R. Medical University was formed in July 1988, the Vice Chancellor Dr. Mrs. Lalitha Kameswaran was very keen that all the colleges in Tamil Nadu conduct a similar program. A three-day workshop was conducted by CMC which was attended by all the Deans and a few senior faculty from every medical college in Tamil Nadu. This was truly one of the ' firsts'. To make it feasible for government colleges, a similar program with some modifications was planned and later approved by the University. The WHO, SEARO conducted several workshops to develop a similar program which was then recommended to all the countries of the SEARO region. Abraham was invited by Dharan University, Nepal, and the Vietnamese Government to establish community-oriented teaching programs in their country for medical students as well as the primary health centre staff. The CHAD model was well received all over the world and international students started coming to CHAD to learn from us and to be trained in a similar manner.

Nurses were an important part of the Community Health Team. Thus training them became a priority for us as well. Student nurses spent about 15- 20 weeks during their training period at CHAD experiencing a practical learning environment that integrates primary and secondary care along with the developmental programmes that CHAD provides.

Recognising that Community Health has several important components, Abraham identified individuals from CHAD for each sub speciality and raised funds to send them for further training to centres where they received excellent training. Several international organisations such as WHO, UNICEF, Ford Foundation, Damien Foundation, SIDA and DANIDA helped to support the training programs.

With all these training programmes in place, a training centre was much needed. DANIDA kindly funded the Community Health Training Centre (CHTC) which stands in the former New Life Centre campus. The old site was outgrown with thorny plants and shrubs. Finding funds to do any kind of improvement work was always our problem. The staff of the Community Health Department were amazing – they offered to do all the clearing of the ground themselves to get the site ready. Tools were provided and both men and women happily worked together every Monday evening after work for an hour. This continued for a few weeks until the ground was cleared. A glass of juice and water were provided for the hard work that was put in. The staff were used to doing this kind of work as we often had shramadhan to clean the campus.

The CHTC, which included the lecture theatre, guest house and the dining hall was part of Abraham's dreams. There were some concerns from some of the administrators. ' Will there be enough programmes for it to be used?' ' Would it be a white elephant for the institution?' and so on. But in reality, it turned out to be a boon for the institution for housing students not only from other parts of India, but also from various countries during the training programmes.

I (Sulo) agreed to look after the guest house and the canteen. Right from making trips to choose furnishings and utensils and crockery, I was happy to do whatever I could to make the training centre the best. One batch of alumni decided to have their meals in the CHTC Canteen just as we were beginning the canteen. We had just employed Das, the cook. The meals started with poori and potatoes. While Das mixed the dough, I helped him roll out dozens of pooris which he fried one by one. Then I quickly cut up the potatoes, tomatoes and onions to make the potato masala. That was only the beginning. After that Mrs. Anna Zachariah helped train Mrs. Leela Ranjit who later became the Manager. Later, Mrs. Susheela George took over the canteen and did a wonderful job training the cooks, the helpers and more importantly providing good, clean, tasty food.

Research had always been emphasized at CHAD right from the beginning. Medical students learnt the art of doing research from their COP days and research became an integral part of the Community Health Programme. Recognising the importance of epidemiology, Abraham started the Epidemiology Resource Centre which was funded by the Ford Foundation. Several faculty received training in epidemiology overseas.

Dr. Jayaprakash Muliyil, who did his doctorate at Johns Hopkins took over the leadership in Epidemiology training programs from Abraham. Dr.K.R. John took a keen interest in Economics and started the Health Economics course. WHO, recognising the effective MCH program conducted by the department under Sulo's leadership, deputed senior Obstetricians from the South East Asian region for training. The Uppsala and Lund University in Sweden, Ben Gurion University, Israel, and the Panum University- Copenhagen, under Professor Ib Bygbjerg linked with the department and started internationally recognised courses.

I (Sulo) was invited as a Consultant by the Uppsala University, Sweden, from 1999 to 2003, for a one-month training course on Sexual and Reproductive Health and Rights held in Uppsala for African and Asian countries. WHO, SEARO, deputed me to Bhutan to plan their MCH program for a ten-year period and to evaluate the Diploma in MCH training program of Bangladesh. I was also invited as a Consultant by the World Bank to evaluate the Child Survival and Safe Motherhood programs (CSSM) in the country. Each consultation abroad, each conference, each exchange with other academics thinking along the same lines or with different perspectives gave me the confidence to comeback to CHAD and try out new ideas and methods of training. How to improve what we were already doing was always on both our minds.

Abraham during his tenure as Professor of the Community Health Department was deputed as a Consultant to USAID, African Development Bank, and Consultant and Senior Advisor for Primary Health Care to the Government of Vietnam. International organisations such as WHO, SIDA, World Bank and ODA invited him to evaluate Primary Health Care programs.

Further, Abraham served as a Visiting Professor in the Department of International Health, University of Copenhagen, on the Scientific Advisory Committee at the Institute of Nutrition, Hyderabad, and as an Adjunct Professor, at Ben Gurion University, Negev, Israel.

The Community Nutrition program initiated by Dr. Sheila Pereira was expanded to a community-based programme by Abraham and handed over to Dr. Sara Bhattacharji.

The Community Health Department with the 80-bed CHAD Hospital doing over 200 deliveries per month and over 80 inpatients was an ideal place to start the Diploma in Family Health. This course was recognised by the NABH in the 1990s. A few years later, a separate Department of Family Health was established in CMC.

CHAD was also in the forefront of developing a computerised Health Information System (HIS) for the community development block of over 100,000 people. Every pregnancy and birth and death was documented, which meant that all the vital events were reported. This Health Information System helped review the work at the community level by the PTCHW's, the health aides, nurses, and doctors, during their monthly meetings and helped improve the quality of the work. *Dr. Vinohar Balraj* further improved this by including spatial details of each residence in the database. This helped improve the HIS, especially for specific interventions. *Dr. Kuryan George* went to Maastrict University in Holland for further training in the Health Information System. *Dr. Jasmine Prasad* took over women's health after Dr. Sulochana retired. With the joint-family structure breaking down, care of the elderly became a priority. *Dr. Vinod Abraham* who had done his MPH from Johns

Hopkins University and a Diploma in Palliative Care developed a Community Based Geriatric and Palliative Care program which extended to the tribal community.

It was in recognition of all these pioneering community-based programmes that WHO as part of its Golden Jubilee Celebration in 1998, selected the Community Health Department of CMC as the best institution in India practising 'Health For All.'

19

The CHAD Family

Besides building a team, a lot of time was spent training the many community workers and students, both national and international, in various ways. This too was Abraham's passion. It wasn't just teaching the academic subject so that his students passed their exams that was important to him, but getting them to think about ways in which they could serve our country with its enormous needs; to have meaning and purpose for their lives which would perhaps in the long run of their career, give them greater satisfaction than all the things that money could buy. He was also passionate about passing on the vision that he had caught and was so committed to, so that his young team and students could take this vision across India and to other parts of the world where it was sorely needed. For almost every problem that he faced, he was an ' out of the box' thinker. He encouraged his students and his team to do the same and to brainstorm ideas with him so that they came up with the best solution. This could only be done with constant interaction and discussions with them whether it was in the tea shop, the clinic van or in the class room. He was a man of great energy whose day was filled with different activities from morning to night – teaching, training, planning, writing a paper, looking at research proposals, attending meetings, listening to complaints and so much more. In spite of all this, he took time to mentor his students. Trust in each other and the building of trust within a community was most essential in community medicine. This is something he taught tirelessly by example.

Recalls a former student, ' *If Uncle said he would do you a favour, no matter how busy he was, he would do it. I learnt this from him time and time again.* ' His mantra was, ' *Without trust, we cannot help each other, and trust is built by communication and being there for each other.'*

Recalls Dr. Vinohar Balraj, ' *In the early years CHAD was like a close knit family. There was care and concern for everyone. It didn't matter whether you were a doctor or a health aide or an intern. Everyone mattered. It was an exciting time for us doing things for the first time, seeing if our ideas would work, planning, talking to the villagers and the leaders. The hours were long as often Uncle would go to the villages after duty hours at the base hospital and we would tag along after him. Work in the day blended into work at night in the villages. Uncle believed that work and duty does not end at 5 p.m. He would come with us to visit the community at 7 p.m. This was quite common since that was the time people were back from their work and sitting around and talking to each other and were available and amenable for discussions. We would see Uncle talking to the local leaders and the public, listening to them keenly and with respect. He led by example and we followed.*

'Uncle's influence on my life was profound. He taught me how to be in two or three places at the same time. 'Simple enough, delegate someone to go to places 1 & 2, be briefed,

keep in touch with them and you go to place 3. The informality of the department and camaraderie was its success.'

Remembers Dr. Gift. Norman, *'Uncle would wake up at 5 a.m. eat with us, share a cup of chai, and mentor us at the same time. He walked the talk, didn't tolerate any excuses and expected the entire senior faculty and students to be present at all times. He created an unforgettable atmosphere of 'we are in this together.'*

'He had graduated from a cycle to a Vespa scooter by then and never lost his dogged determination nor his readiness to roll up his sleeves and do the work with us. I fondly remember our times in the Sethu kadai tea shop. He carried no airs about his seniority or achievements and would be happy to join in for a few laughs and good-natured leg-pulling. At work he looked for opportunities to promote you and push you up the ladder. Many of us confided our personal problems to him and he was a rock of support to us; never judgemental, always ready to offer fatherly advice when we needed it. But he was also a tough, no-nonsense boss.

'As the boss, he always gave people second chances. During the peripheral posting of my PG training, I had started off in Paediatrics and had a rough time. With no experience in dealing with even minor ailments, I desperately devoured every textbook I could find but still came up short. The Head of Paediatrics at the time fired off an angry letter to Uncle lambasting the poor quality of his PGs with a particular reference to me. I only heard of this many years later because Uncle never brought it up while I worked with him. I learnt integrity and how to treat someone with respect from him.

'Whenever we messed up occasionally, Uncle would always be there. Hands-on, practical, and staunchly behind us. I remember him particularly concerned about cases involving children (he had specialised in paediatrics). As a post-graduate registrar, I've often woken him up at 3 a.m. and he would gladly come from home in a few minutes, ready to guide and advice. I've never heard a whisper of a complaint from him and am quite sure no one else has. A mistake was never met with abuse or scorn, but was a teaching opportunity. Whenever we braced for a stern reprimand, all we heard was, 'What can we learn from this?' Our graver errors elicited a, 'What is this?' delivered in an almost pleading, only slightly disapproving tone that you would reserve for naughty children who scribble on walls.'

As we began to grow as a department, new cadres of staff joined us. Not only medical staff but also secretarial, attenders and others who helped keep the department functioning. One of them was Mrs. Arokia Mary.

Mary, a graduate in English, who had good typing and shorthand skills joined the department in 1986. An extremely willing and uncomplaining lady, she translated all my notes into neatly typed files. She also worked on the curriculum side for medical students and other courses conducted by the department.

Mary recalls that working in CHAD was like being in the midst of a caring family.

' I was very comfortable and happy working with Uncle. He recognised each person's skills and strong points and allotted work accordingly. Whatever work was given I did it to my best. I worked with both Uncle and Dr. Sulo. By the time Dr. Sulo took

over as Head, I was married and had two children. Often I could not reach the department by 8 a.m. Dr. Sulo understood this and adjusted my schedule so that I could come in a little late, but I had to stay and finish my assignments before going home. This little compassionate gesture made such a difference to me. I did not come to work as a harassed mother, but committed to doing my best that day because of her thoughtfulness.'

As we got involved with an increasing number of research projects there was the need for more secretarial staff. Sumithra, a pleasant young girl joined us in 1996. She took on an array of different tasks uncomplainingly and was always willing to learn new things.

Sumithra recalls, *'I joined as a Clerk Typist on a project when Dr. Abraham Joseph was the Head and Dr. Sulo was the Obstetrician & Gynaecologist and the Chief Medical Officer. I was very young and this was my first job and of course I was nervous and made some mistakes. But neither of them ever scolded me or made me feel bad. Instead, they would correct me and teach me how to do it without making mistakes. I worked under their supervision until I gained confidence in what I was doing. As the work in the department was increasing, Uncle requested the administration to create a post of Clerk Typist in the Community Health department and I was appointed against this vacancy. (I am still working in the Department.)*

'Both of them were great sources of strength when my father was ill and passed away. Finding myself alone and single was very distressing. They understood my fears and found a safe house for me to stay as a paying guest until I got married. When I had a child, Dr. Sulo gave me the nursery rhymes and Ladybird books which belonged to her children and grandchildren. What a

treasure chest full of goodies this was. All of us in the department were treated as their family.'

Sr. Rosaline Jayakaran was a Community Health Nurse who chose to work among the rural poor. Recalls Rosaline, *' When I was at school studying 8th std, a lesson on the life of Florence Nightingale touched my heart and inspired me. Ever since then, I wanted to become a nurse. In 1973, I joined the BSc Nursing course at CMC Vellore and completed my Midwifery in 1978. I asked for a rural posting during my internship as I was keen on serving the poor in our villages. I was posted as the village nurse in Veppampattu where Uncle was the consultant doctor. Working with Uncle gave me opportunities to learn how to work as part of a team. From day one, I was part of a team along with social workers, junior doctors, medical and nursing students. We had to organize leaders' meetings, conduct mass health education and action programmes such as immunization, mass scabies treatment and TB. Every health problem was overcome with health education and action.*

'During the day I worked in the village community, and at night did call duty in the base hospital. The night call duties gave me opportunities and confidence in conducting normal deliveries. Dr. Sulochana would teach and encourage us to use our knowledge and skills in maternity care. When I did my Masters in Community Nursing, Dr. Sulo was my medical guide. She was very supportive and meticulously guided me to complete my thesis. After I had qualified, I rejoined CHAD as Nursing Supervisor.

'All of us worked together very closely at the Rural Health Centre, and later on at CHAD as the department grew. That feeling that we are all one and that we work for the same cause

that Uncle instilled in us by his example, remained with us even after he retired.'

Apart from office staff, we had others who worked in the field who also became part of the CHAD family. Mr. Maruthamuthu was a Health Educator who came from a remote village in Tamil Nadu. After having completed his MA in Economics, he was jobless. He had the opportunity to train as a Health Educator in Gandhigram. His first job was in a mobile medical unit travelling 48 -60 miles twice a week. He had to discontinue this after his father died as he had to take care of his land and had to repay the loans incurred by his father. When he heard that there was a vacancy in the Community Health Department for a Health Educator, he applied. This was in 1974. He was the oldest who joined the department and served faithfully till he retired in 2003.

In the early days, his wife Nagaratnam, a trained teacher who had a beautiful voice accompanied him to the Health Education programs and the village street plays. The health education songs that he wrote appealed to the villagers as they conveyed the message using popular film songs with catchy tunes. Mr. Maruthamuthu along with Susila, the social worker and other field workers were always associated with the Community Orientation Program. The college students, along with the village youth would sing lively songs such as ' Muthu Muthu' for measles, 'Keerai Keerai' for nutrition, and many other catchy tunes to educate the community. He was a very popular member of the team.

Recalls Mr. Maruthamuthu, *'After I joined the department, to start with I had a bitter experience with Uncle who had entrusted me with getting some seeds for the department on my return from a program I attended in Ooty. Unfortunately in the hurry of boarding the train, the parcel was left behind. Uncle's reaction was that I had shirked my responsibilities. At that moment I could not accept that statement and even considered giving up my job. However, in the course of a few days all was forgotten. Soon after this Uncle entrusted me with health education programmes – 'kathakalashepam',drama, street plays, mass education covering several health problems. He gave me all the help I needed for all these programs. My relationship with Uncle was always cordial. He did not for a moment consider all that he did for the department as for his own glory and was always thinking of newer programs for the welfare of the community. For him 'work was worship.'*

'We often had camp fires in front of Uncle's house. These were the most enjoyable times when my wife and I were always invited and we participated happily along with other staff.

'CHAD is a place I cannot ever forget. When I retired, at my farewell, Uncle called Shivashanmugam and said, 'Now Maruthamuthu Anna has retired. Shivashanmugam have you seen Maruthamuthu at work? You need to observe him carefully, follow in his footsteps and do all that he did.' Doctor and Doctor Amma cared for all of us like we were their own family.'

Another loyal worker who was part of the team was Poonguzhali. When we first met, Poonguzhali's husband was dying of cirrhosis of the liver. It was such a difficult time for the young wife, with two small children as she waited for the inevitable end. She shared her fears for the future with me, weeping, 'What am I going to do Amma? How am

I going to raise my family?' How could I not help her? She weighed heavily on my mind all that week. Then her husband died. Now I had to help her in some way. She had studied up to the 10th standard and was bright and willing to learn. She was selected as a hospital auxiliary and worked in the Mental Health Centre on a project. When the project was completed, she came to us at CHAD as there was a vacancy. She was a very efficient, cheerful and diligent worker. Her job was to see to the cleanliness of the ward, make up beds, and assist the nurse in every way. There was nothing that Poonguzhali would not do, and we relied on her integrity to keep our wards spic and span.

The small Rural Hospital grew over the years into a large centre, with sub-sections for electrical and plumbing work, transport, accounts, and public relations. We really needed a good person in the office to manage all of this. Could one person do all this, I (Abraham) wondered. I came across Samuel Chandraraj in the registrar's office in 1982 during the time of student selection. In my interactions with him, I recognised his integrity and the honesty and enthusiasm with which he did everything and thought that he was just the kind of person we needed at CHAD. So when there was a vacancy in CHAD, I asked for Sam to be posted as secretary in CHAD. Sam was transferred to the Community Health Department and he took over as secretary looking after the transport section which contains about 8 four-wheelers & 20 two-wheelers, preparing the statement of accounts and organising the reports for the many national and international projects that Abraham had started in the department. Sam helped prepare the budget for the various funding agencies, the training programs, the accommodation of the participants and finally the schedule for the drivers and their many trips. He also looked after the overall maintenance of the CHAD Hospital including equipment, oxygen supply & other minor theatre equipment. There was nothing in CHAD that Sam did not know of or look after.

Recalls Sam, ' While I *was working in the Registrar's office, the first person I met was Dr. Abraham Joseph, Head of the Community Health Department. From that first meeting, I learnt that to him everybody was equal – whether it be a doctor, nurse, the office secretary, the driver or any of the 80-90 of the various levels of staff working in CHAD. I learnt a lot of management skills from Dr. Abraham who supervised my work. He trusted me and worked along with me. At times when I made mistakes or spoke abruptly to anyone, he would take me aside and correct me in his own gentle way. He was an extremely good boss, whom everybody respected. As Head of the Department he brought in various projects, many training programs and taught me how to look after visiting faculty and students from abroad and India. Seeing how he worked, the drivers and attenders were happy to work over – time without asking for any compensatory time off. He brought out that kind of loyalty from us all. The staff from CHAD and the Community Health Department have worked like one family under his leadership. Sometimes we worked long hours during the nights to complete the financial and other reports required for submission to funding agencies. Punctuality was his hallmark. He was always at least two minutes early and we all followed his example.*

'Dr. Sulo took over as Head from Dr. Abraham after being the Medical Officer of CHAD for nearly 20 years. She was always

friendly, strict as far as work was concerned and was very considerate and compassionate.

'During my time of more than 20 years I remember that both of them considered all the workers at CHAD as their own family. When my father died, I was away in Nagercoil. By the time I got the message, Dr. Sulo had already gone to my house, comforted my aged mother and took care of every detail in the house. This was the same care she showed when any of the CHAD family needed her help.

'People used to say that if Uncle and Dr. Sulo were away for a few days we could cope. But if Sam took a day off, there would be chaos. That was such a compliment to me.'

Recalls Dr. Vinohar Balraj, 'Uncle and Sulo lived on-site at the Rural Hospital/CHAD campus, just a stone's throw from the labour room. It was quite easy to walk over to their house to discuss a case in labour with Sulo. Most of the time she'd walk over to handle difficult cases herself.

'One weekend on-call, I remember dropping in to discuss a case. It was Sunday and the children (Priya and Vinod) were just back from Sunday School. To encourage them Sulo said, 'Children sing the song you learnt today for Vinohar uncle and sing it with actions'. There was a bit of a tussle, Priya said, 'I will sing it and Vinod will do the actions'; but Vinod said, 'I will sing and you do the actions'. Sulo settled it saying, 'Priya is older so do what she says'. Priya sang, 'Father Abraham had many sons ......' and Vinod was swinging his right hand, left hand and his legs and looking miserable, while Priya was grinning from ear to ear. The Abraham Joseph family made us all feel that we were part of their family, as well as the CHAD family.

The role of a Medico Social Worker became important as work in the community progressed. Susila Suriya joined the department as a Medico Social Worker in 1975. She was also trained in psychiatric social work. Starting with an evaluation project, house-to-house surveys and mingling with ordinary villagers she established a very good rapport with the community. Teaching mothers with malnourished children, Susila says 'further moulded her life.' Despite several challenges in her own life, she was an asset to the department, working in several areas, understanding the problems in Kaniyambadi block and tribal areas; conducting Madhar Sangham meetings, developing skills in adolescent girls and so much more. She worked with us from the age of 23 until she retired. A remarkable lady who still continues to work unofficially educating young people and motivating them to donate blood.

Recalls Mrs. Susila, *'Over the years, I got to know that Uncle was passionate in getting to know the villagers, meeting with village leaders and finding out the problems that the villagers faced, seeking to find a way to help them. Working late in the evenings he understood what a young co-worker faced and would arrange to have her to be taken back home in the CHAD van. He was strict about timings and punctuality and conveyed it very diplomatically. I learnt the art of maintaining a diary, completing the work on time and recording it. Uncle was always thinking about new projects and his advice to me was, 'never say 'No,' as soon as you are asked to try something new. Begin with an open, willing mind and then having done it for a while, address your difficulties and drawbacks.'*

'Uncle gave me many opportunities to learn and improve my skills – like attending a course in Canada for social development; to Myanmar on how to deal with violence against women, and many other programmes within the country as well. All these were learning experiences for me both personally and professionally.

'I worked with Dr. Sulo more closely especially when the tailoring and embroidery units were started. These helped the women to earn enough money to support their families. She went through each stitch, each step meticulously till their work was perfect. One year when there was a problem with the making of the jasmine chain for the graduation ceremony, Dr. Sulo took it on and worked with the balwadi teachers and flower sellers. She sat with them on the floor and worked with them till the chain was ready. This was a regular feature for several years till she was sure that the work would carry on in her absence by delegating it to the right people. It still goes on year after year exactly as if she was still here.

'One admirable quality of Dr. Sulo was that she was very happy to transfer the knowledge and skills that she had imbibed through workshops – the Participatory Rural Appraisal (PRA) and Social Mapping and many more training programs to encourage young people.'

Towards the end of my time (Abraham) at CHAD, our team consisted of 80-90 staff from all categories. Besides the doctors and nurses there were technicians, health educators, social workers, drivers, attenders and an efficient office team. Growing up in a large family, I, understood the value of relationships from a very young age. I had seen my mother delegate responsibilities to get things done and treat everyone like family whether they were the helpers or friends or family and I guess I just absorbed this value from her. So keeping a 'family atmosphere' at work came naturally to me. But Sulo took it one step further and added her unique brand of compassion to every relationship. Those to whom she had been particularly compassionate would sometimes ask me, ' What makes Sulo Ma'am so compassionate? '

Perhaps this quality stems from her childhood. *Sulo's mother told me that when she was four years old, her cousin Chikku's mother died and so Chikku came to live with Sulo's family. Little Chikku was inconsolable. To comfort him, some well- meaning people had told him that his mother would come back one day. So every day Chikku would lean on the parapet wall and wait for his mother to return. One day, the two four-year-olds were watching a black hearse on Nathan Street, carrying old Mrs. Nathan's body, followed by a lot of cars and people. Little Sulo pointed to the hearse and told Chikku, ' Look at that black van Chikku. Inside it is old Mrs. Nathan who died. Her body is being taken to the cemetery to be buried. She has gone to heaven to be with Jesus. Your Amma also died and has gone to be with Jesus in heaven, so she will not come back here anymore. Chikku digested what Sulo said. Then he ran to 'Sulukutty Amma',(Sulo's mother) with this revelationary news that he had just heard. Perhaps this was the starting point of Sulo's compassionate nature. She saw her little cousin in so much sorrow and intervened to comfort him in the way she knew best and told him the truth. After this, Chikku didn't go and look out over the parapet and wait for his mother to return any more. Sulo, little as she was had helped him accept the grim finality of loss in a very kind way.'*

As I look back, I see that my time in CHAD was satisfying and glorious. All the success of the programmes we set in place would not have come to fruition without the wonderfully cooperative team that we worked with. It was surely the grace of God that we were provided a team that could work together and help each other and for this *'To Him be the glory'*.

————•●•————

20

Abraham: Farewell To CHAD

At Abraham's farewell by the Community Health Department where he had worked from 1968 – 2002, Dr. Kuryan George remarked, 'Dr. Abraham's interest in Primary Health Care planning and management, with emphasis on Community Based Education and Health Systems Research, has won him National and International recognition. The extension of secondary care services from the first 10-bed Rural Health Centre to the current 80-bed Community Health and Development (CHAD) Hospital and the outreach work from the 5 villages in the early 1970s to the entire 68 villages of Kaniyambadi block was largely due to his initiative and vision.

'As a founder member and President of the Community Health and Development Society (CODES), Bagayam, he was instrumental in the promotion of social and economic development, along with primary health care. The healthcare activities of the department have received ample recognition as one of the best in the country. Under his leadership, the department developed training programs in primary health care, which have been recognised and applauded by the World Health Organisation. In recognition of this, the department was awarded the status of a 'Collaborating Center for Community Based Health Professions Education,' in 2002.

'The various International programs conducted by the department are due to the collaboration that he established with the University of Copenhagen, Denmark, the Uppsala and Lund University, Sweden, College of Social Work, Ohio, USA, Concordia College and Gustavus Adolphus University, USA and the Ben Gurion University of the Negev, Israel.

'He is also recognised as one of the leaders in the country in Health Systems Research. Above all, Dr. Abraham will be remembered especially for his immense contribution towards changing the image of Community Health among the faculty as well as the students. At Dr. Abraham's farewell, Dr. V. Benjamin, the previous Head of the Department said, ' Never did I imagine that this little man, Abraham Joseph, who joined the department in the 1970s, would put the Department of Community Health firmly on the world map.

'Perhaps, Dr. Abraham's biggest legacy was to introduce community exposure to medical students from their very first year of training. He was a pioneer in moving this concept from rhetoric to practice. He believed that primary healthcare cannot be taught in a *'vacuum'*. He wanted to get future medical professionals out of a plush echo chamber and into the real world. *'With no idea of who your patient is, where they come from, what they work as, what their superstitions/dreams are, how will you treat them?'* was his perspective.

'His views were challenged by several senior colleagues and members of academia who felt that a student's precious time was being wasted in taking them to villages and could be better spent in the lecture and dissection halls. However, he stoically carried on. He envisioned something that no one else saw and never let go of his vision. Years later, he was recognised internationally for it.

'His vision for postgraduate training followed a similar philosophy. Dr. Abraham believed that a public health specialist should have a good grounding in providing primary medical care. Apart from theoretical inputs, our entire three-year training was experiential and field-based. The outcome of this unique model was a better, more well-rounded understanding of public health.'

Says Sulo, 'I could see that Abraham was very touched by these accolades and a little embarrassed too, but I was happy to have his many achievements recognised and applauded. I was so proud of him. We stepped into the Rural Hospital so many years ago as two idealistic young people determined to change the world around us, armed only with our faith in God and the values we were brought up with. What a marvellous and unexpected adventure it has been for both of us.'

Abraham recalls, 'I was deeply touched and grateful for these words of recognition and praise and I acknowledge humbly that none of this could have been achieved on my own. All along I had the support of a great team. It was the end of a chapter for me and as I looked around from the podium where I sat, I saw many colleagues and friends from the early days who had come to wish me well. It was a very moving moment. When I first joined The Rural Health Centre in 1968, soon after my internship, I was a young man who wanted to make a difference to the health of people in the villages around us, but didn't know how to. I just knew that I was following a calling and that God would lead me step by step. All I had to do was follow with trust. And that is exactly what I did for over three decades.

'At the beginning, I expected the village communities to follow my agenda and my ideas because I was the specialist, the one with the 'know how' and it made sense to me. But slowly I came to realize that my ideas would only work if I humbled myself and listened to those who needed our help, saw their problems and needs through their eyes, and not mine alone. It was a learning experience which brought me closer to the community and I learnt to respect their ways, their culture and some of their healing methods. It was a slow process for both me and the community and a difficult task aligning what the community expected of us and what we wanted for them. But with time and patience it was achieved.

'Looking back, I'm amazed at how health in these villages has changed since I first visited them as a young intern. I remembered sadly an incident just behind the Pennathur sub-centre where two families refused vaccination for their small children. A few months later, one child developed diphtheria and in the other family, the child developed whooping cough. Both were really sick for a long time and sadly the child with diphtheria died. It didn't have to be this way. The immunization was available free of cost in the village clinic, it was available in the evening when they returned home after a day's work, but they still refused it because of ignorance of preventive measures. Today, 30 years later parents know the value of immunizations and safer health practices have become the norm. Children no longer die of these diseases. Immunization coverage in the community is well over 95%.

'At the farewell ceremony, as I looked around at the wonderful team who worked tirelessly with me to help achieve my vision, I had a great sense of fulfilment and gratitude knowing that God had led me every step of the way.

'Many people asked me, if I felt sad to leave and if I wanted to stay on for a few more years. I could honestly say, ' No.' I had done my best to make the teaching of Community Health wholesome, interesting and inspiring – to such an extent that many students had gone on to work in Mission Hospitals in India where there was no health care and begun programmes of their own. Others went on to regional, national and international organisations where their commitment and experience made a big difference to policies. Dr. Manoj Kurian went on to work in Geneva with the World Council of Churches; in Bangalore, Dr. Glory Alexander set up an HIV/ AIDS programme for women and children; Dr. Arvind Kasthuri went on to Head the Department in St John's Medical College and started innovative programs; Dr. Reuben Samuel went on to UNDP; Dr. Ravi D'Souza worked with the Government of Orissa; Dr. A.V. Ramani with UNICEF; Dr. Johnny Oomen to Bissam Cuttack in Orissa; Dr. Madhavaram as Medical Officer, Global Vaccine Safety in WHO. It is particularly heartwarming that Vinod our son had also chosen to specialise in Community Health and took a keen interest in developing a community-based palliative care and geriatric programme.

'Many others, though they did not specifically work in the field of community health, were hugely inspired by what they had experienced as students and allowed these experiences to influence the different specialities they had chosen. Drs. Roopa and Deva, established a program for the tribal community in Gudalur; Drs. Suranjeen and Madhulika work for the UNICEF in the less developed states in North East India; Dr. Renu John though working in Australia, comes to Madhipura Mission Hospital for a few months every year; Dr. Prabir Chatterjee focuses on the needy areas of Chattisgarh; Dr. Daisy Darmaraj established projects in Chennai and Andhra Pradesh; Drs. K.S. Joseph and Madhukar Pai, outstanding students are Professors in Public Health in Canadian Universities. Several alumni became Professors and Heads of the Community Medicine Departments of medical colleges in India. I felt enormous pride as I remembered some of them and felt deep gratitude to be a part of an institution that gave birth to all these amazing people.

'As I stood on the beautiful lawn outside the CHTC where the farewell function was held, many colleagues and friends greeted me with much warmth and affection. Several cameras flashed, blinding me. Out of the corner of my eye, I saw Sulo, concern written over her face, wondering how I was coping with so much attention. In a flash, the worry was gone and I saw her smile – a smile of reassurance. It was such a good moment and I held on to it.

'As I looked at her, I was so proud of my Sulo, my partner in life as well as at work. As a young girl, Sulo accepted my proposal of marriage which was clubbed with a rather challenging clause – to work in the rural areas where we were needed the most. It meant a life of great personal sacrifice for her, as in the early years, I was so busy initiating new programmes, visiting the villages, and holding meetings late in the evenings as it was the only time that we could get all the villagers together. Sulo was such an important part of how my vision progressed step by step. She was my first sounding board, and what she thought about an idea, her intuitions always encouraged me and gave me the confidence to take it to the team. She had the extra responsibility of being there for the children as they were growing up; never letting them feel neglected, always making special treats for them on a very limited budget and giving them a fun childhood to remember. At the end of some very difficult days, I would return home to laughter, music, wonderful meals and the joy of playing board games with my family. She also looked after our parents and siblings with the same dedication, whenever the need arose. The happy atmosphere she brought to work, the way in which she made everyone feel special, and her willingness to go the extra mile for anyone who needed it, were also something I am so proud of. Yes, she did far more than I expected at the time when I proposed to her, and that too with never a word of complaint.

'Our children, Priya and Vinod too played a vital role in helping us realise our dreams. From the time they were very small, there were many occasions when both of us had to rush to the hospital in response to an emergency call, at times half-way through our dinner. Young as they were they realised that this was part of Amma and Appa's life. They also graciously accepted that their parents had a lifestyle which included many others in ' the family' and learnt that family meant aunts and uncles, cousins, helpers in the home, students, staff and colleagues from the department.

'I knew that I was moving on to another phase of my life and to a place that needed my experience. I also knew that I was leaving the department in the best of hands – Sulo's hands – and that our vision would move even further under her nurturing.'

———•●•———

The New CHAD Hospital

Community Health Training Centre Lecture Hall

Abraham addressing the first batch of BSc nursing students at their graduation in CIHSR, Dimapur.

The first College of Nursing in Nagaland at Dimapur

Abraham Joseph Centre for Learning, Dimapur

21

Sulo: The Torch Of Leadership Passes On

After Abraham retired, the torch of leadership was handed to me. In some ways I was overwhelmed, but I knew that God would lead me every step of the way, just as he had led Abraham. The work would continue.

I had a growing concern. Even prior to the expansion of the new OPD, the existing antenatal and postnatal wards had room for only 12 patients. The others slept on the floor along with their attendants. Often due to a lack of space, the women were forced to occupy the small cubicle intended for their belongings. With the additional expansion of the spacious new out-patient facilities and larger labour room, the number of patients expanded exponentially, including large numbers from beyond Kaniyambadi block, our project area. In an effort to curtail the unmanageable crowds in the antenatal clinic, we imposed strict restrictions on these 'out of area' patients; mandated early registration by 24 weeks of gestation, and then due to persistent crowds we further limited registration to under 16 weeks. None of these strategies curbed the rising antenatal registrations. It was obvious that we desperately needed a new maternal and children's ward. We had the space, but not the funds.

Up to this point, all of CHAD's buildings were financed by various donors and funding agencies. Since CMC funded our recurring expenses (salaries, outreach work, and student education programs), Abraham's policy was for the department to raise its own funds for capital expenditure. I prayed about this project a lot as it was my dream to have a spacious centre for maternal and child care.

Ms Eta Forshamn, one of the founding members of the 'Friends of Vellore, Sweden,' was a well-wisher who had already supported CHAD through smaller donations. On one of her visits to CHAD, she enquired about the needs of the department. ' I took her to the antenatal ward where she saw for herself the alarming state of the crowded ward with women sleeping on the beds and under the beds on cement floors. She was deeply moved and concerned by what she saw. 'How much would you need for a new ward?' she asked. ' Sixty lakhs,' I told her, as we had already worked out a detailed budget. 'Write me a proposal. There is the possibility of securing funds for you through the Church of Sweden Mission in India,' she said, before she left. I immediately wrote up the proposal for the new ward that I had been envisioning for some time and sent it to her. Shortly after, I left for the U.S. to spend some time with Priya and her family. There was no news at all from Eta or the funding agency and I was disappointed in some ways, yet if it was part of God's plan for CHAD, I knew that it would happen, perhaps not in my time. A few weeks later while still in the U.S. I received an urgent call from Sam, the department secretary, requesting me to return urgently to Vellore as representatives of the Church of Sweden were scheduled to arrive for a site visit in a week's time. Reluctant to cut short a visit with my precious grandchildren, Yohan and Lisa, I hesitated. Priya, our daughter, convinced me to leave immediately for this important visit. With hopes, dreams and much excitement, I was back in Vellore on Friday, the night before their scheduled arrival. To my utter dismay, I learnt that there was no further intimation of their visit. Hugely disappointed I continued with the usual routine on Saturday. At 9 a.m. I received a call from the railway station saying that the Swedish team had arrived and were headed towards our department. It felt like my heart skipped a beat or two. Would they really see the need and fund us? I took them on a tour of the hospital and the women's ward. One look at the ward, with the many women on the floor, convinced them of the emergent need for a new facility. 'What is your budget?' they asked. 'Sixty lakhs', I replied. 'Make a new budget with additional facilities that you will need' they said. I did so almost immediately.

Once again there was a long period of waiting. Weeks and months passed by and there was not a word from them. Meanwhile, the need for the new building to be constructed had escalated.

Convinced that God would provide for us, I approached Dr. George M. Chandy, Director of the institution, to set a date for the turning of the sod. 'Have you got the funds for it Dr. Sulo?' he asked. 'No', I said, 'but it will come.' He was surprised at my confidence. In faith, we set the date to begin on the 12th July 2005. There was still no sign of any funds, but I had the faith that God will hear my prayer. On the eve of the event, as I was leaving office for the day, Sam arrived excitedly with a registered letter. I tore it open and there it was – a cheque for 80 lakhs from the Swedish Mission. Once more, God had provided, in his own time and with much more than I had asked for. At the ceremony the next day, Dr. George mentioned that 'Dr. Sulo's faith that this building was to be built according to God's will was amazing.' At this point, I walked over to him and handed over the generous donation. 'A miracle indeed', he declared. A verse from the Bible came to my mind: *And whatever you ask in My name, that I will do, that the Father may be glorified in the Son. If you ask anything in My name, I will do it. (John 14:13-14)* My prayer had been answered and my dream of a building especially for mothers and children was coming true.

The rhythm of work, programmes and teaching went on as usual. Recalls. Dr. Arvind Kasthuri, *'Dr. Sulochana Abraham was the Head of the Department of Community Health when I joined in 1989. She interviewed me for the post when I joined, and I remember thinking to myself that things can't turn out all that bad, especially with the friendly, motherly presence of Dr. Sulo at the helm. And I was proved right.*

'Things turned out very well indeed, with Madam remaining approachable, friendly and taking all of us under her wing over the next three years. We tended to be a bit wild at times in our talk and behaviour, and I will always remember her gentle admonition of, 'What's the good word?' whenever I uttered a word or phrase out of turn. With her, we could always say, 'Sorry madam, I didn't complete what I should have,' with the knowledge that she would be firm, even tough, but kind at the end of it all. Humility, friendliness, commitment and a people-centric approach – these were qualities Dr. Sulo imparted, not formally, but through her gentle and pleasant way.

For me, it (Sulo) was an honour to be asked to be a short term consultant to various international agencies such as SIDA, WORLD BANK, WHO and Ministry of Health and Family Welfare. I was always happy and proud to share my experience of women's and children's health and the pioneering work we had done at CHAD. It always elicited such interesting responses. Training for us at CHAD was a big part of our work. So when I was asked to be a resource person for various training programmes in MCH and RCH at Uppsala and Lund University in Sweden and other Universities abroad, I willingly agreed. I enjoyed travelling and meeting other people, sharing stories, and making new friends. I had learnt a lot from working with Abraham and I had the confidence to continue God's work. The years sped by and soon it was time for me to retire as well. It seemed like only yesterday that I had stepped into the old Rural Hospital ready to take up the challenge that God had placed before me.

During the farewell at my retirement, Dr. Kuryan George said, *'Our Director, Dr. George M. Chandy, during the handing over of the Headship, put it aptly, 'The retirement of Sulo marks the end of an era where Uncle and Sulo provided dynamic leadership to Community Health in CMC for well over 2 decades.' From the small Rural Health Centre to the magnificent CHAD and CHTC.*

'One cannot but pay rich tributes to the leadership which was given by Uncle. However, all of this would not have been possible without Dr. Sulo who worked quietly behind the scenes. It was Sulo Aunty who often translated Uncle's dreams and ideas into concrete plans and actions. If Uncle was the architect, Dr. Sulo was the master builder. Most people cannot even perceive the quantum of work that has been put in by Sulo Aunty to make CHAD what it is today. Where do I begin to outline her contributions? And where do I end? I will just allude to a few of them. She was the Consultant who taught her registrars obstetrics appropriate to a secondary care centre; the innovative obstetrician who got

the Bird's Ventouse for CHAD, long before CMC had got one; the person who designed, developed and brought to practice, the legendary CHAD home based pink antenatal card; the pioneer who introduced and developed the high risk antenatal clinic in CHAD; the health care manager who developed and put into practice regular audits of LSCS, maternal, and perinatal deaths as well as the OP card; the economist who costed health services even before the beginnings of Health Economics in CMC; the Teacher of Teachers who trained her junior faculty and registrars in teaching methods; the person who started and sustained the ethical reviews; the person who read every PG thesis irrespective of who the guide was; the person who taught us the chicken dance.

'I would like to think of the person beyond all her achievements and remember her as the one person all of us would run to when we needed advice or when we were in trouble; she would scold us when necessary, but always stood behind us like a rock in times of trouble. For Dr. Sulo there is no grey, only black and white. She is passionate about all the important issues. She cannot be lukewarm about anything.

'Her love for the beautiful and the aesthetic is legendary. The beautiful creations of the tailoring and embroidery unit, the well-planned gardens of CHTC and CHAD and the lawns of the Dr. V. Benjamin out patient block are all expressions of her understated and elegant taste. Dr. Sulo's meticulous care and organisation for every function are unparalleled. The elegant and beautiful function which was conducted when the new OPD block was inaugurated by our then Finance Minister, Mr. P Chidambaram is but an outstanding example. She was a gracious hostess and opened up her home for numerous dinners and parties.

Her ability to produce simple, elegant, and appropriate prose for the various reports, speeches and news items are note worthy. Working with her has enabled me to imbibe her love for simple and elegant prose.

'Above all she was a deeply compassionate human being who cared for all who came in touch with her – high and low, rich and poor – all were equally important to her.

'They, Drs. Abraham and Sulo, leave behind a department which is one of the best Public Health Departments in any medical college in India, if not the whole of South Asia. We hope that we will be able to continue the work at the same level and of the same quality which they brought to their work.'

I was deeply touched by Kuryan's speech. My mind went back to the little curly – haired girl who wanted to be a doctor; to the first rejection at CMC which broke my heart; and to all the difficulties we went through to achieve our vision little by little. 'God has been so good to me,' I thought. So many of the staff and well wishers and friends came to wish me and I was pleased to see every one of them. The happiest moment for me was when everyone had almost gone. There was just one person left and we both just looked at each other. ' *Do you remember me Doctor amma?'* she asked. I embarrassedly shook my head. *'I am the lady on whom you performed the first caesarean operation at RHC. We had no electricity that day remember? You delivered my son by the light of a torch light.'* I grasped her hand firmly with both my hands. Yes of course I remembered that day very well. How could I forget it? I was young and terrified, yet held my fear under control. I said a prayer in my heart and just did what I had to do . The lady turned and beckoned to a young man standing a little away from her. *'This is that baby, amma',* she said proudly. ' *He is my son.*' In front of me stood a tall, handsome young man who smiled at me and went down on his knees to ask for my blessings. He had just finished his Master's degree. This was surely a sign for me from God – that my many years in CHAD had indeed made a difference.

Sulo, Chakko and Rebekah

Sulo and brother-in-law, Ranji.

Two happy couples. Abraham's brother, Moni Achayan and sister-in-law Rajamma, and Abraham and Sulo.

Abraham and Sulo

Abraham relaxing playing Sudoku

Sulo doing Quilling

22

Abraham: Time At Karigiri

When my time at CHAD was almost ending, well-wishers wanted to know what I was going to do next. Quite honestly, I did not know. I just knew that God would lead me. One day in 2002, Dr. Benjamin Pulimood, former Director of CMC, and Dr. Cornelius Walter, the Chairman of the Board of Schiefflin Leprosy Research and Training Centre, Karigiri, approached me to ask if I would consider taking over as the next Director of Karigiri. I politely declined the invitation. A few weeks later, Dr. Paul Brand, one of the founders of SLRTC, and former Principal of CMC and Chairman of the Board of SLRTC, met me.' Do you have any definitive plans after your retirement?' he asked. When I shook my head, he said, ' I was hoping that you would provide leadership to SLRTC and develop it the way you have developed CMC's Community Health Department. I feel that you are the right person to lead this institution at this point.'

Sulo and I thought about this offer seriously. Dr. Brand was someone we both respected and admired enormously. He was the Principal when I was a student. If he thought that I was best suited to bring SLRTC into a new era, I felt I should surely think about it and pray about it. Once again I felt God's hand leading me. After much thought and prayer, I accepted Dr. Brand's proposal.

Sulo took over as Head of the Community Health Department and I accepted the invitation to work at Karigiri.

I joined Karigiri at a time when the Leprosy Eradication Program in India was going through a radical change. The prevalence had come down dramatically and WHO had declared that leprosy was eliminated from India, which meant that the prevalence was less than 1/10000 per year. Many people working in the field of leprosy were sceptical with this declaration of elimination and felt that it was premature. A sequelae of the declaration, made by both the Government of India and WHO, resulted in a rapid decline in funding for leprosy work. All the international organisations which were committed to eliminating leprosy and working to rehabilitate leprosy patients were financially impacted. This was true for SLRTC as well. The contributions from the Leprosy Mission Organisations were on the decline and leprosy hospitals were told to either close down or try and raise as much funds as possible locally. Many leprosy hospitals were situated in places where general health services were not available and were therefore providing basic general health care based on the specialists they employed. Most leprosy hospitals had departments of dermatology, medicine, orthopaedics, ophthalmology and clinical laboratory. The main problem was that these hospitals were situated in the periphery of the towns where access to them was poor. SLRTC was no exception.

When leprosy was endemic in Tamil Nadu in the 1950s, Dr. Paul Brand, the leprologist and reconstructive surgeon at CMC wanted to admit leprosy patients to the main CMC Hospital.

There was so much stigma and fear around leprosy at the time and no one wanted to admit them into the main hospital. It was only after much persuasion that the administration finally agreed. Subsequently, some leprosy patients were admitted into the general ward alongside non-leprosy patients. The next morning, Dr. Brand was surprised to hear that all the other patients had got themselves discharged, since they did not want to stay in the same ward alongside leprosy patients and be treated by the same doctors and nurses. By the time I came to Karigiri , the ugliness of the stigma around leprosy (in the 1950s) had given way to a more general acceptance of the disease.

When I joined Karigiri as its Director in 2002, I was impressed by the number of general patients attending the outpatient clinic for medical care and also by the number of general patients admitted in the wards. The stigma of leprosy was still present but considerably less than a decade earlier. However since the hospital was located in an isolated place, access was difficult; bus service was poor; patients either still walked the long stony road or came in autos they could not really afford. It was very distressing to see 6-8 patients crowded into an auto rickshaw travelling between the highway and the hospital. There was always the fear that the vehicle would topple over on the stony road resulting in injuries to the travellers. My experiences at CHAD told me that many more patients would use SLRTC's health services, if the outpatient service could be located close to Katpadi town, so that patients could avail of the local bus service. More patients would generate more income for a hospital in dire need of financial resources. The funds raised by improving general health care would compensate for the decreased contribution from the Leprosy Missions, allowing SLRTC to continue providing free services to those affected by leprosy. There was some opposition to this idea. Many felt that the land and funding was specifically donated for leprosy work and therefore should not be deployed for other medical needs. Some felt that leprosy, like tuberculosis may make a comeback after some years, and if it did, there should be leprosy hospitals to care for them. After much debate we decided to integrate leprosy into general healthcare. This meant revamping the entire system.

A new centre called the Paul Brand Integrated Health Centre (PBIHC) was opened in 2005 nearer the town with easy access by local transport. Different departments had clinics in the new centre. Patients with general medical problems came and sat alongside patients with leprosy. The outreach program conducted from the main hospital also integrated leprosy work with mother and child health, tuberculosis and community based rehabilitation, thanks to the committed community health team led by my former student Dr. Gift Norman.

It was not an easy task bringing everyone, especially those opposed to this idea under one umbrella. For me, it was a unique privilege and challenge attempting to integrate leprosy with other diseases. Already many aspects of community healthcare such as health education, leprosy and skin clinics were in place. We needed to add general health care to this. It was pioneering work and challenging, but slow. For years things had been done in a certain way at Karigiri, and suddenly here was this new Director bringing in sweeping changes. Of course, there was some resentment, but with time we worked through all the negativity; after all, we were a Mission Hospital on a healing mission.

Recalls Dr. Margery, ' *I joined Karigiri a few months after Dr. Abraham Joseph took over as Director. I had heard that 'Uncle', as he was universally known, had the reputation of being a strict administrator. I did not know what to expect. I had many apprehensions. But on the day we moved to our new home on the campus, he surprised us pleasantly. He visited us with a flask of steaming hot tea and welcomed us very warmly. I soon learnt that there was a very personal touch in all of Dr. Abraham's relationships with his colleagues. It didn't matter whether it was an attender or the head of a department- his courtesy and concern extended to everyone. By the time he left Karigiri, I knew that he was the best boss that I had ever worked with.'*

As Director, one of the things I liked best about being in Karigiri, was my trips to Shanthigramam. Shanthigramam is a residential centre for destitute and elderly leprosy patients. It was started by Dr. Ernest Fritschi and his wife Mano in 1980, to look after elderly, badly deformed leprosy patients who were neglected and abandoned by their families. A cluster of small houses in a village type of environment with chickens and goats and cows wandering around amidst mango, coconut and lime trees is home to those who live here. Its residents are looked after by clinicians from the hospital. When I first visited it, I was shocked by the decline in the state of the buildings and the general running of the place. One of my priorities was to revamp it. With my passion for gardening, I encouraged everyone to get to work so that more vegetables and fruits were grown. The neglected houses and buildings were rebuilt and painted. A garden with colourful flowers and shrubs was planted and maintained. Slowly Shanthigramam regained its lost charm. The elderly patients who had absolutely nothing earlier, now had colourful flowers, fruit trees to admire, farm animals and dogs to pet and love. We used the vegetables, fruits, milk and eggs for the patients. Sponsors and visitors were encouraged to come and visit the patients and talk to them.

Another area that needed inspection and change was the central kitchen. Food was being cooked in a smoky kitchen with outdated utensils. I began by visiting the kitchen regularly and seeing what could be improved. It was important that the kitchen was kept clean and hygienic and this was my constant advice to the cooks and helpers. I found that cooking was still done with firewood and coal, and with very little ventilation, the whole room was dark and smoky. The first step was to convert the cooking system from coal to kerosene, with an automatic pumping steam generator which helped cook foods more easily and quickly and also kept the cooking area neat and clean. We applied for gas cylinders which meant that kitchens were even cleaner now. The crowded dining area with long queues also bothered me, hence we extended the dining hall and added windows to make the space larger and more airy. We also built an air-conditioned room for the storage of perishables. As we were relatively far from markets and grocery shops, this new room helped to preserve freshness and prevent waste. The next area to tackle was the menu and the food.

The campus – once a beautiful place with colourful trees like the red flame of the forest and spectacular yellow chinese lanterns and fragrant ones like Queen of the Night had been felled and replaced by new buildings. These trees had not been replaced and the once scenic green forest-like place looked dry and bare. The drooping flowering bougainvillea needed pruning. The park and the lagoon in the park were also in a very sorry state. Everything needed trimming, replanting and cleaning up. The morale of the staff too was very low. It was a huge challenge to bring everyone together to work for the common good. Team spirit needed to be encouraged. So we began with the lagoon. The idea was that we would clean it up ourselves. Could we do this? I put the idea to some of the staff who seemed quite enthusiastic. Soon others also joined in the project. Around forty staff would gather after work on a hot Saturday afternoon, get inside the murky lagoon, and dig out the mud and sediment so that it could be used as manure for the gardens. The lagoon was deepened, cleaned and filled with fresh water. This brought the birds back. Then we set about to beautifying the campus by planting tree saplings and bushes. These 'shramdans' encouraged the staff to work together for the benefit of 'their' hospital. They enjoyed working together and there was good camaraderie between everyone. Although we may not see the 'greening' effect immediately, I was certain that in about 10 years time another generation would enjoy the benefits. As this exercise in team building proved to be a success, we organized more events that brought us together.

The Training Unit with its many training programmes was one of Karigiri's successes. New courses were started; Community Geriatric Health Care and a PG diploma in Podiatry care for physiotherapists. New units – Obstetrics and Gynaecology with a new labour room and Paediatrics were added to encourage women from the surrounding villages to come to Karigiri for their delivery.

My particular interest lay in the training of nurses, especially Community Health nurses. Recalls Mr. Christopher, PA to the Director, *'Dr. Abraham gave the needed support to make it a top-level school of nursing by providing the much-required facilities and making sure that a good competent Principal was employed. Mrs. Emily Amma did an exceptional job.*

Dr. Abraham's concern for student's welfare was clearly seen in the efforts that he took to ensure nutritious food and comfortable accommodation. He also made sure that poor students received scholarships and funds from other sources.'

The old rubber mill set up to make MCR footwear for leprosy patients to protect their feet from injury, was fully renovated with new equipment and an orthotic workshop. We are grateful to Madras Rubber Factory (MRF) which had set up the Microcellular Rubber factory in Karigiri at the request of Dr. Paul Brand in the 1950s. In 2004, with the help and expertise of Dr. Ranjit Matthan, we began concentrating on the diabetic foot and MCR footwear for the care of those with diabetic feet. In collaboration with Dr. Nihal Thomas of the Endocrinology Department in CMC, Karigiri was recognised as a centre of excellence for diabetic foot care by the World Diabetes Foundation.

Recalls Dr. Nihal Thomas of this period, *'As a medical student I was just another young man to Uncle. But when we began to work together on projects, a deep and special relationship was formed. I understood, admired and tried to emulate his philosophy of a team. Working together for the same cause, giving up something for the sake of a bigger picture that didn't always include you, and finding meaning in every small task helped me to work and live life on a different level. He taught me to find meaning in everything I did. Everyone who has worked with him will tell you the same thing – that he inspires you to be a better person.'*

Dr. Margery, recalling Abraham's days in Karigiri says, *'Much more than courses and new departments were set up during his time. Lives were touched and changed forever too. One young man whom he 'set up' is Muthu. Muthu was from a very poor family, who earned his paltry living in a make shift road-side shack, where he cleaned dining tables and made parathas. Dr. Abraham knew Muthu's brother, who was working in the CHTC Mess. He saw Muthu's skill in making parathas and brought him to Karigiri and employed him as a cook at his home. He then sent him for training at the CHTC Mess where he learnt to make several new dishes like cutlets, stews and ice cream. Muthu blossomed under his tutelage. Through the years I have seen his skills grow with so many culinary delights added to his repertoire. Several times in Muthu's life he needed help and every time Dr. Abraham stepped in. This is just one example of many such people whom he helped in Karigiri.'*

My time in Karigiri quickly sped by liaising with the various donor agencies and fundraising so that Karigiri could function both as a general and a leprosy hospital. The many changes I was able to initiate were made possible only because of the cooperation I received from all the staff. Soon, it was time to 'retire' again and move on.

23

Abraham: Gratifying Years In Nagaland

When I completed my term at Karigiri, I was invited to take on an even more challenging task. Drs. Verghese Philip and Lionel Gnanaraj, two of my former students were actively involved in re-establishing the referral hospital – Christian Institute of Health Sciences and Research (CIHSR) in Nagaland as a Public Private Partnership. Nagaland, in the north-eastern part of India, is renowned for its vibrant culture, diverse tribal communities, and lush mountainous landscapes. It is also one of India's strife-torn, poorest and neediest states. The Central Government had given a generous grant to the State Government to establish this hospital. However the well-equipped hospital did not function for over 5 years till CIHSR was formed. I was invited to lead this hospital and set up the Community Health Department, to serve its people, most of who lived in a mountainous terrain which for the most part could only be travelled on foot.

It was an exciting but daunting task. Several factors were on my mind – Dimapur, Nagaland was so far from Vellore. It took a car journey of around three hours to get to the airport in Chennai, then a two-and-a-half hour flight to Kolkata and finally another 1 ½ hour journey to Dimapur. It meant a whole day of uncomfortable travel and waiting at airports for flights which were often cancelled. I took the decision of going to Dimapur seriously only after visiting CIHSR with Sulo, as it was going to be even more challenging for her to be away from our children and grandchildren and the community at CMC. We prayerfully looked at the pros and cons, challenges and opportunities very seriously and after a short period, when we prayed for guidance, we felt that God was leading us once again. After our visit, Sulo especially felt that this was a very poor and neglected place which needed my skills and experience and that we should not shirk this difficult challenge for the sake of a more comfortable retirement.

It was agreed that I would join as Associate Director with Dr. P. K. John, as Director till his term was over. This would give me time to understand the land, the existing healthcare system and the needs of the local communities. It would also give me time to coordinate and work closely with the government in a tripartite system.

Dr. Sedevi, a senior Naga doctor, welcomed me warmly and introduced me saying, *'Developing an institution requires clarity of vision, excellent in-depth and onsite understanding of issues, wisdom, exquisite sensitivity to people and cultures, incisive decisions, deep compassion for people, networking skills and connection with issues and people. Dr. Abraham has the rare combination of all these qualities apart from his internationally acclaimed academic credentials.'* Everyone rejoiced when I accepted this challenge.

When I took over, there was a shortage of qualified competent healthcare professionals. Doctors, nurses, and other medical personnel often preferred to work in more urbanized areas, leaving the rural regions underserved. The first major challenge I faced was recruiting well- qualified, committed staff to head various divisions such as the clinical specialities, nursing service and nursing college, allied health sciences and the administration. Dr. Sedevi, a Gastroenterologist and one of the founders of this hospital carried out the duties of the Medical Superintendent and headed the Clinical Departments. I persuaded Mrs. Bharathy Jacob, former Dean of College of Nursing, CMC, Vellore to come to Dimapur as Dean of the first College of Nursing in Nagaland. This was a good decision as in a few years, with all her experience we were able to begin the first BSc Nursing course in the Northeast. Mrs. Christy Simpson took over from Mrs. Bharathy and continued doing the good work that she had inherited. Several senior nurses from the northeast had done their Master's degree in Vellore and so were able to set high standards which others followed.

Dr. Ravindran, the former Vice Principal for Allied Health Sciences at CMC and a Radiotherapist, joined CIHSR and established a Radiotherapy Unit, with a large donation from the TATA's. Dr. Mammen Chandy, the Medical Director of TATA Medical Centre, Kolkata was instrumental in promoting the project. The Allied Health Sciences courses were also supported by CMC, Vellore, and in a few years, CIHSR became the first institution to conduct graduate courses under the Nagaland University. The Dialysis Unit and the Radiotherapy Unit are two major contributions to the Northeast – all headed by former CMC faculty.

We encouraged committed specialists from CMC and elsewhere to visit CIHSR to provide specialist care. They also used their visits to provide Continuous Medical Education in their specialities to doctors from the region.

Husband and wife teams too contributed much to the work of CIHSR – Dr. Sedevi was ably supported by his wife Dr. Leishiwon, an outstanding dermatologist. Dr. Jacob Chacko, a paediatric surgeon was a much-needed addition to the hospital. Mrs. Christy Simpson brought her husband, Dr. Simpson who had specialised in developmental paediatrics and he set up an excellent unit for children with disabilities and has trained several therapists. Dr. Sushil Mathew Daniel, an ophthalmologist from Kochi, gave up his private practice for four years to establish the Ophthalmology Unit. Dr. Keith Ingty, an alumnus of CMC, Vellore, after a lifetime of service in Mission Hospitals in Assam, joined CIHSR to start the Orthopaedics Unit. Major road accidents are common in Nagaland and this unit provided a much-needed facility for trauma care. Handing over the baton to the local specialists was one of the objectives with which I came to Nagaland and I was happy that I was able to achieve this goal.

Maternal and child health were major concerns too. Limited access to antenatal care, skilled birth attendants and post-natal support contributed to high maternal and infant mortality rates. Infectious diseases such as malaria, tuberculosis, and waterborne illnesses also posed significant health risks to the community. Access to clean drinking water and proper sanitation was a challenge in many areas. Rural communities in isolated areas struggled to get access to even a tiny, well-stocked pharmacy. Many villagers from remote regions of Eastern Nagaland were forced to travel great distances to access the closest medical centre. These were some of the problems that needed to be addressed urgently and we had a team who were eager to do their best.

From the early days of CIHSR, community outreach services were given high priority. With poor transport services within the state and many living in small isolated villages in mountainous terrain, the great need was to provide primary care as close to their homes as possible. We initiated a mobile unit for very needy urban areas and rural clinics for those in some of the remote villages. Dr. Atsung Aier, an alumni of CMC gave valuable leadership to these initiatives and so did Dr. Viu Meru and Dr. Rohan Ramesh, an alumni of Community Medicine from CMC Vellore.

Community Health is a department which is unique to CIHSR and even Nagaland. While most other departments focus on the treatment of disease conditions, this department emphasizes on general health and staying healthy and preventing diseases. Therefore all activities of the department revolve around the preventive and social well-being of not just one patient but of the community as a whole. Slowly our presence and care for the isolated communities was being felt and poor patients were comfortable coming to our clinics for treatment.

I had certain goals when I took over as Director; to develop a centre of excellence in healthcare in Nagaland that the people could be proud of; to develop undergraduate, postgraduate and innovative medical teaching programs to empower healthcare personnel in Northeast India; to encourage and help form a vibrant community that would care for and support each other; to provide a focal point for a network of hospitals and like-minded organisations in the Northeast so as to make an impact on health in the whole of the region. They were specific goals which could only be achieved by the support of others who also had this vision for CIHSR.

Dr. Sushil Daniel recalling his early years at CIHSR says, *'The problems facing the institute when Dr. Abraham took over the hospital were many. The doctors of CIHSR were dedicated, enthusiastic, capable and young. What was required was experienced leadership in both administration and the speciality departments to channel the energy and the enthusiasm of the staff to build up departments of excellence. The backbone of any good hospital is the nursing cadre. Qualified and efficient nursing personnel were at a premium, more so since Nagaland lacked any nursing colleges. Therefore setting up a nursing institute was an important spoke in the wheel of development. And this, Dr. Abraham, did.'*

Once we had set up the Community Health Department and the Nursing College, building infrastructure was the next big challenge. Space was not an issue, since the institute was situated on a campus of 100 acres. The main challenge was raising the finances required and apportioning the work to architects and builders with integrity and good work ethics.

The Central Government had a scheme for financing the institute through the Ministry of Development of the Northeast Region. This brought in grants for the Nursing College and the NERMPI (Northeast Region Multidisciplinary Paramedical Institute) channelled through the Northeast Council, Shillong. The funds enabled CIHSR to create a good infrastructure through which the current academic programmes in nursing, Allied health sciences and DNB programmes were able to operate.

Recalls Dr. Sedevi, *'Dr. Abraham's networks with the Tata Trust resulted in the Trust providing funds to obtain the radiotherapy equipment for the cancer centre. This centre currently treats the largest number of cancer patients in Nagaland, most of whom receive free treatment under the PMJAY scheme. Scores of people now can avail of cancer treatment at CIHSR without having to travel to distant places in the mainland.'*

Once certain departments started to function well, I turned my attention to research in the institution. Research in the Community Health Department has always been important to me. Recalls Dr. Sedevi, *'Dr. Abraham helped the staff start the journey of acquiring research skills by organizing research methodology workshops and collaborative research work with CMC. Community field research started with work in primary healthcare, outlining disability and surveys of common disease conditions in the block of Dhansiripar, studies in paragonimiasis and oral cancer screening, training needs, assessment studies of medical staff in Nagaland and a host of others.'*

Whenever I remember this period at CIHSR, my heart is filled with gratitude. They were very challenging times, and I feel that I received much more than I gave. The support provided by the administrative staff cannot be expressed in words. They helped me understand the local culture and practices which are so different from the Southern states. I am so grateful to all of them for the wonderful time I had in Nagaland.

As always I had the support of Sulo. Sulo was invited to help in the obstetrics unit which she could do only in a small way because of her disabilities following knee replacement surgery. However, Sulo was soon busy training nursing students and other members of the community in 'quilling', a unique paper art that she learnt and mastered on her own. The local girls were delighted to learn an art which they could do to sell and earn extra money to support their families. Through the sales of their beautiful quilling the nursing students who came from very poor backgrounds were able to make enough money to supplement their travel expenses to Vellore for an educational meeting. Sulo also taught quilling to the women of a School for the Hearing Impaired as well as HIV affected women. During these sessions she also counselled young women who were very depressed because of family situations. She passed on her strong belief that when one door closes, God opens another, to many young people who felt that their future had so much uncertainty. Her faith too was inspirational for them.

Recalls Dr. Sedevi, '*Dr. Sulo was the epitome of grace and an inspiration for all the women on the campus. When Dr. Abraham first faced the challenge of coming to CIHSR, she encouraged him to travel to and from Dimapur every month at a time when she already faced several physical ailments and needed a man in the house to support her. During her visits to CIHSR, she mobilized the women and the College of Nursing students and taught the exquisite art of quilling. She also taught her cooking skills to the girls on the campus, created lovely workbooks for the children's Bible clubs, taught any medical subject to students that there was a deficit in, and took on any role that would contribute to the growth of the staff and students on the campus. A warm and generously caring person.*'

24

Sulo: Dimapur Days

When Abraham decided to take up the work in Dimapur, I agreed to take up a professorship in a medical college in Amla, Trichur, (Kerala). I worked in Amla for three years till the new department I was helping set up, went through the process of being recognised by the University. Travelling back and forth to Trichur by train from Vellore and living in a single room in the guest house was not easy at my age with the disabilities of the knee and fingers that I had developed. I was greatly encouraged by Dr. Benjamin Pulimood, the former Director of CMC, Dr. Jasper Daniel, the Professor of Microbiology, Professor Dr. Charudathan, and Dr. Jose of the Community Health Department who constantly kept telling me how much I was needed in Amla. But I sorely missed the family, being part of the CMC community and our church St John's, in Vellore. I was also in a lot of pain with a bad knee.

Once the department had been set up and after three years in Trichur, I decided to join Abraham in Nagaland. Both of us missed each other, and the kind of work he was doing needed support and encouragement. Before leaving for Nagaland I had my left knee replaced. It was good to walk again without pain. I was happy to be able to join Abraham in Dimapur. At CIHSR, we were given an apartment on the ground floor as I could not climb the stairs. Beeti, the cook and general helper at the guest house came over and prepared meals for us. This little Assamese girl was so talented and so willing to take care of all our needs with such gentleness. She made sure I was comfortable in every way and nothing I asked was too hard for her. Soon she learnt to make South Indian dishes for guests who came for a week or to help out in different departments in the hospital. We had the privilege of sharing fellowship with Dr. Lionel Gnanaraj, Dr. Jacob Chacko and Mrs. Barathi Jacob and many visiting faculty from CMC, Vellore and other places. Since there was a great need for a Psychiatrist not only to see patients but also to train the Dip NB trainees and nursing students, Abraham invited Dr. Deepa Ramasamy, Sr. Psychiatrist in CMC, Vellore, to make periodic visits to CIHSR. It was a great pleasure to have Deepa staying in the guesthouse upstairs and have meals with us in the Director's house. Those days were filled with much laughter and camaraderie.

At a time when I was unable to do all the things I loved to do – caring for patients, tending to plants, embroidery – and being so far away from the family, I was feeling sorry for myself. It was God's grace that I saw a beautiful handmade greeting card one day. I was intrigued by it. The craftwork on the card was stunningly simple and unique. I had never seen anything like it before. I wondered how it was done and decided to try it. Abraham helped me slit coconut fronds to roll strips of coloured paper and manipulated them to create different shapes. I glued this together onto a card to create a decorative design. I loved making these cards and pictures. When Priya, my daughter-in-law saw them she said, 'Amma, this is quilling'. I had learnt an art without even knowing what it was. Priya supplied me with the little instrument to roll paper, and some sets of coloured paper.

As I got better at it, I made cards and pictures for family and good friends. Everyone loved it. The nursing students at CIHSR were fascinated by it, so I taught them how to 'quill'. They learnt the craft very quickly and began earning a little extra money by selling cards and pictures. This craft was a God-given gift for me at this particular time. I was far from home and family and dear friends; away too from a lifetime of work and instead of feeling sorry for myself, here I was enjoying learning something new and passing on the joy of it to others.

I was also very happy to have guests. Dr. Sushil Daniel came to CIHSR to set up the Department of Ophthalmology and had all his meals with us. Though I had not met him before, my friendship with him, his lovely wife, Starly, and his mother, grew into a warm and wonderful one. Says Dr. Sushil, *'Dr. Sulo was a master at culinary arts – be it Asian, Indian, Continental, Savoury or Sweet. Her dishes were not to be taken lightly. Each deserved to be tasted and relished with respect and time, not to be gulped hastily. And so the time spent over the meals, especially dinner, were the ones I looked forward to. Not only were they delectable but they were peppered with numerous anecdotes narrated by Dr. Sulo which would be followed by bouts of rollicking laughter by those at the table. For me, away from my own home, this was the balm I needed not to feel lonely.*

'I learnt over the period I knew her that she was an extremely talented lady. I was fortunate enough to see the beginnings and her journey to mastery over the art of quilling. Over time, she encouraged me to walk with her and I was so surprised to hear her identify the local flora, their Latin names – Callistemon,

Cassia Javanica, Lagerstroemia speciosa — these names rolled effortlessly off her tongue. I could see she loved the gardens.'

Another highlight of our time in Dimapur was the opportunity to spend time with Dr. Mammen Chandy and his lovely wife Anu. Mammen had been my personal physician for years and our families were close. Around the same time as when we were serving in Dimapur, Mammen had moved to Kolkata. Their home in Kolkata became a favorite 'rest stop' for Abraham and me as we broke the journey between Chennai and Dimapur. Their kindness and hospitality made our travel pleasant and memorable.

I didn't expect my time in Dimapur to be so blessed, but it was. Even though mobility was still difficult, it was wonderful to have Abraham to myself for a good part of the day. To spend so much time together going for short walks and visits to the homes of staff during late evenings was indeed a great pleasure and something we had not been able to do in Vellore while we had busy lives. Abraham never left my side — he was always there holding my hand lest I tripped on the cobbled stones. I think this was the nicest time of our life together.

I loved the people of Nagaland, their friendship and innate ability to welcome you with their unique culture, art and music. When it was time to leave, I left with a heart full of gratitude as I had experienced life and friendship and a culture so very different from the southern states.

25

Our Stories Of Faith

Sulo

When I first put my hands into Abraham's strong ones, I did so with the firm faith that although I didn't know exactly where we were headed, that God would lead us according to His will. I came to Dimapur with the same faith that God would lead both Abraham and me during this stage of our lives, just as he had led us when we began our careers. We were no longer young and strong and I had some difficulties and disabilities to cope with. Through the amazing quilling experience, I knew that God was with me. The foundation for my faith was laid in growing up in my Christian home. At first, for a little girl everything was a routine and a ritual. Sunday morning and evening church services were mandatory. It meant that I was dressed in crisply ironed embroidered dresses, painstakingly made by my mother and grandmother and ready on the dot of time to go to church. Singing joyful hymns and choruses, attending Sunday School, listening to the Bible stories, all gradually led to my journey of faith.

My sister, brother and I shared a bedroom. Early in the morning, I would find my way to my parent's bedroom and squeeze myself between them. The comfort that I received was tremendous — a feeling that they were there to love, cherish, and protect me. As I woke up, I would see my father kneeling by the bedside, fully engrossed in prayer before he started his routine for the day. He would change into khaki shorts and a white T shirt and proceed to the playground and participate in the physical training activities along with the resident students. Back home, he would sit at his office desk and spend a good half hour reading the Bible, grasping its contents, and then contemplating on his work at school and seeking guidance from God for the day. Observing this person whom I adored, going through this ritual day after day, certainly played a major role in my journey of faith.

My faith was tested early in my childhood. My cousin who was the same age as I, lost his mother and was in great anguish. Even without my realising it, I was able to comfort him with my childish words. Right from that early age of four, I felt very strongly that God had used me not just to comfort him, but also to help him on his journey through childhood without his mother.

I suffered from severe eczema which forced me to stay at home for a year, thereby missing school and time with my friends. In all these challenging times, I witnessed the silent, strong, unwavering faith of my mother who quietly sheltered my little world and the home, provided excellent nourishment and ensured that my education and faith in God did not suffer. Through her unspoken acts of goodness, I witnessed Christ's love in our home. My maternal grandmother who came to live with us had a role to play too. On nights, when my parents were away, I would lie down next to her, look at the starry sky and learn to appreciate the wonder of God's creation.

My journey of faith was further enhanced when I entered CMC in Vellore. The evening chapel service on Sundays, participation in SCM activities, caring for my patients, and watching my stalwart teachers in action, helped my faith grow even at times when I questioned everything. My faith and love of Christ were further inspired by Abraham and his way of life. It was so clear to me right from the beginning of our relationship that he had a firm belief that he had been called to a particular task and that he had to be faithful to that calling. He was deeply committed to the poor and the needy – and now looking back, he had a remarkable way of witnessing his faith. There have been challenges, ups and downs, happy times, troubled times, and times of rejoicing and loss. Despite all of this Abraham has been able to face it all with calmness, equanimity, and inner strength and share this with me. His strong faith has seen us through many difficult times. Through many years of marriage and bringing up our children, we grew in faith together.

I remember waking up early one morning in Bombay when I was doing my post-graduation. I had taken my father's alarm clock to help me catch up on my preparations for the MD examination, well before our children woke up. I put off the alarm and tiptoed to my parent's bedroom, and there was my seventy-five-year-old father kneeling beside his bed before the day began, praying with folded hands. Since then, Abraham, (and the children whenever available) and I would sit side by side on the bed and read the Bible, the Daily Bread book of mediations, and the various versions of William Barclay's prayer books and pray together before our day began. This ritual has been as constant as the rising sun.

My children say that my expression of faith is quiet but solid. The anchor and captain of the ship is unquestionably Christ. I try and put my faith into action by helping the less fortunate women whom I work with, whether it is a widow, a woman who has suffered from domestic abuse, helping educate the children of our home helpers, building a home for the people who work for us; supporting the healthcare of a less fortunate friend or teaching embroidery or quilling to young girls who are jobless or suffering from a terminal disease so that they too can earn a livelihood. My greatest joy is to know that I have in some way helped my children to have faith in the Almighty.

I was at the bedside of my parents, my brother and my sister, and my mother-in-law during their last moments. As my father lay in bed semi-conscious, Reverend Dr. Fritschi our friend and pastor, gave him his last communion. Rev. Dr. Fritschi placed a cross in his hands and my father whispered the entire Nicene Creed. My heart just overflowed with joy and gratitude – to think that even at this stage when we are dying, when our memory has faded when every cell in our body is slowly ceasing to exist, our faith learnt from childhood still remains. This strengthened me so powerfully. Some days later when he took his last breath and was gone, Appa had a lovely smile on his face as if to comfort us that he was with his heavenly father.

My brother Chakko had a terminal illness and was deteriorating. The day before he was transferred to the ICU, he called me on the phone and between severe bouts of coughing said to me, ' Sulo I am going to the hospital to have a peg put in and as soon as I am well again, I will come to India to care for your poor patients.' But on June 12th, 2004, my brother-in-law Ranji called to tell me that Achachan was admitted into the ICU. I left Vellore immediately to be with him. Ranji took me directly to the hospital and to the ICU where I spent the next three weeks at Achachan's bedside. Slowly his BP and heart rate kept dropping. I could not take my eyes off him. I pleaded with God. ' Please heal my brother. Please give us a little more time together.' I prayed with all my heart for just one miracle. Time just dragged by. When the nurse came in, I asked for a stethoscope. I bent over him and listened to his slow heartbeat. After a few minutes, I heard that very last beat. His heart had stopped and was still and at peace. But mine was shattered.

For almost twenty years now I have faced the pain and the loss of my beloved brother. I am comforted by good memories of us being together at his home where Susie, his wife, welcomed us warmly. The time that I valued most was the stay in Denver after my brother's stem cell transplant and when Achachan, Susie, Manu and I went for long walks in Vail, amidst rows of Aspen trees with golden yellow leaves shimmering in the sunlight. Achachan told me about the sterile surroundings of the ICU and the devotion with which Susie had looked after him. She too was heartbroken and together we mourned. Susie remembers this period well. In a note to me she wrote, *'You have given me your share of love and strength and faith. Thank you for coming and spending a month with us when Chakko, your brother, was dying. It meant a lot to the family.'* The Bible assures us that God is especially close to those who weep and are broken-hearted. It is so true. Every time I prayed for peace or comfort or hope, God blessed me with it.

Some years later, my sister Rebekah was in liver failure and deteriorating rapidly. The last few words that she spoke before she became delirious were to recognise her own faith journey, recorded by Dr. Vadivu, a Gastroenterologist who was caring for her. 'I am privileged to see Christ at work here at CMC. I am so glad and thankful to see young people working in a coordinated way, like a dance.'

My journey of faith grew with each of these losses. It was hard seeing our parents grow old and infirm and to see our siblings pass away with illnesses. Through each loss, I learnt that our questions of, 'Why' will not be answered on this side of heaven. We just know that God is in control of our lives and we fit perfectly into his tapestry of love. Each of us has a place and a time. With each loss, I learnt that we are on this earth for a short time. Therefore how we live and what we believe in, makes all the difference.

It would be incomplete if I did not mention my children and grandchildren. I am richly blessed as each of them has contributed in their own way to the larger picture of my 'Journey of Faith.'

Abraham

I was born during the Second World War in my mother's home in Vadaserikara, Kerala, a small village along the river Pamba. My mother often reminisced that her grandfather, who was a hundred years old and blind at the time of my birth, took me in his arms and committed me to God's service. This story was repeated so often during my childhood. At that time I didn't think much about it. But now when I look back at the various phases of my life, I realize that the faith and hope of my great-grandfather, and the faith of my parents, especially that of my mother influenced me greatly even without my being aware of it.

The rhythm of our daily lives was set by morning prayers and evening calls to prayer and relaxation. However, it was my mother's quiet life of service that had the most significant impact on me. Her simple faith and gracious manner made for a delightful childhood. Although I had many household chores to do, perhaps more than most children my age, they did not seem a dreadful chore. Because of my unusual childhood, I learnt to love all of God's Creation from an early age.

Even before my career began, I experienced Christ's hand in my life. Despite my plans and efforts to study engineering, God closed every door to this career for me. Instead, I was granted admission to the prestigious Christian Medical College, Vellore, as an open candidate with no obligations to serve in a Mission Hospital after my course. The peaceful Christian atmosphere of chapel services, sacred choir music and the inspiring conversations with former students who were serving the country in areas of great need, along with the wisdom and guidance of my mentors, Dr. V. Benjamin and Dr. Fritschi, led me to dedicate my life to serving the poor and motivated me to specialize in community medicine, one of the least popular subjects at that time.

My father strongly believed in the traditional idea that parents should choose their children's life partners. However, I had a different perspective. I had found a life partner I was getting to be fond of, and as I got to know her, I truly believed that we shared the same values and ideals and that she would best help fulfill my dreams of helping the less fortunate in our community. After thoughtful consideration and prayer, I decided to marry Sulo. This was a significant decision. It meant going against my father's wishes. Yet deep within me, I knew that God was leading me and that I had to trust him. It was a very difficult time – should I obey my father? Or listen to the voice that was calling me? I decided to trust the voice and have never regretted it. I have since learnt to listen to that little voice inside my heart and trust the One who very quietly whispers into it.

Sulo has been the pillar of our family much like how my mother was to my siblings and many others in need, regardless of their caste or social status. She has been instrumental in keeping my faith alive and has worked tirelessly alongside me, if not more than me at every stage in keeping the flame of faith burning.

During several challenging difficult times at work, we just knelt and prayed, and trusted that God would lead us on the path that He had chosen for us. Seeing how our faith was shaped during several crises and family losses, our children and grandchildren's faith too grew with daily prayer and Bible readings and the rituals of going to church and being actively involved in the church community.

Singing in the choir, preparing sermons for Sunday services, being active in various church committees were all ways in which both of us demonstrated our faith outside the work sphere. Of course, it was time-consuming, but as committed Christians, we felt that this too was our Christian duty.

My faith was tested during the period when my parents got older and frailer. They were in Maramon and I in Vellore. They were difficult days. I was their youngest son, a doctor, and far from them. I felt a little helpless. I knew I just had to trust God to be with them when I was not there. During the last few years of his life, Appa would sit in a corner of the front verandah of our home in Kerala, staring at the stretch of land leading to the river. He had once watched his house being built brick by brick. This house was built for his family before they relocated to Kerala from Ceylon. Now he would sit silently in his corner and wait for the grandchildren to come and play a game of caroms with him. It saddened me deeply to see such a major change in him. Three weeks before he passed on, my brother Moniachayan came down from Saudi hearing that Appa was not too well. I too went immediately and paid a brief visit as I had several programmes and important meetings scheduled for the next few weeks. As I bid goodbye to him, he looked away silently; he probably knew that it was perhaps our last meeting. At his funeral, I could only thank God for his life of sacrifice and the many ways by which he had strived to make us who we are.

Ammachy moved to Vellore after we had a house with a bedroom on the ground floor of the college campus. At the age of 93 when she finally came to live with us, she came walking in by herself, but in three months, she could only move about in a wheelchair. Yet, she was always cheerful. Ammachy's faith like her life was simple and encompassed everything good and noble. It was hard not to be touched by her faith, love and life's example I was her youngest and much loved child, and I loved her dearly. When she passed on, Sulo, my sister-in-law Rajamma, and I were beside her, holding her hands.

Sulo also looked after several members of our family – her parents, my mother and our siblings on both sides during their last days, sharing love and care. To both of us, caring for our parents as they grew frail and journeyed slowly towards their end was another way of sharing our faith with our children and grandchildren – showing them the hard Christian way of taking up our crosses and caring for and loving those who had once been the mainstay of our lives.

As a couple we have built the foundation of our marriage and family life on Christ and Christian values. The joy of being able to worship with our community and the freedom to praise and worship and share our faith through our work are blessings that continue to hold us in good stead.

26

Sulo: Deep Loss

The story of my life would not be complete if I didn't tell of two people whom I have loved so much and whose loss I feel deeply every day.

I had known Ranji, Dr. Mani Modale Mani, from my childhood, but it was only when my sister Appukochamma started working in CMC as a Dietitian that I got to know him better. I would seize any opportunity to come to Vellore to spend a few days with my sister who stayed in Small Bungalow in the hospital campus. I can remember more than a few occasions when Ranji would meet me at the bus stop, and take me for a masala dosai before dropping me off at my sister's place. I took it for granted that Appukochamma was at work or that my brother, a medical student at CMC could not get away from his classes. Much later on, I remember Ranji telling me that my affection for him was pure 'dosa love' or 'porter love'.

After my sister and Ranji got married, I attempted calling him 'Ranji Achachan', but he would not hear of it. Ever since he became a part of our family, he was truly the big brother to me in times of sorrow and joy.

After Appukochamma and Ranji left for the United States, I missed them sorely. They would come to India once in 2 or 3 years, and, as years passed by much more frequently to see my aging parents.

When I did my post-graduation in New York, Appukochamma and Ranji opened their home to our children Priya and Vinod, and this selfless action ensured that they were not left behind in India without their parents.

Every time I went to Kansas, Ranji and Appukochamma would be there at the airport and he would greet me with a big hug. I loved the visits to their beautiful warm house, so tastefully decorated by my sister. We would visit their daughter Rachel's bakery of which they were so proud. They would also take me to the homes of their friends and their church and introduce me as ' the little sister from India.'

Ranji was a plastic surgeon par excellence. At a time when cosmetic surgery was becoming popular and plastic surgeons were in great demand, Ranji chose the less glamorous role of specializing in the treatment of burn victims and caring for these helpless patients. He was the Medical Director of the Gene and Barbara Burnett Burn Center in Kansas until his retirement and a very popular doctor. He and Appukochamma were actively involved in their church and he often taught and preached the Bible.

As Ranji and AppuKochamma grew older, the cold, icy Kansas winters became unbearable for them. So they chose to come to India where our winters are mild and warm. They would come and stay with us in Vellore for a few months. I loved the time that they spent with us. We would chat, reminisce, discuss, disagree and eat wonderful meals together. We would visit our good friends and do many sisterly things together. While Appukochamma walked around the garden, enjoying the plants and flowers and the warm sunshine, I would get the special South Indian Narasu's coffee for Ranji. He was so easy to please. At the end of the stay as they left for the U.S. I would tearfully bid them farewell, although I knew that they would visit the next year. On their last visit in 2020, they had planned on a much shorter visit. But Covid extended their stay.

Although Appukochamma was happy going around the garden, listening to the birds and rejoicing over the varieties of mangoes, her little bag was always packed, ready to leave at the drop of a hat. One morning, she woke up looking sleepy and tired and lay curled up in bed which was most unlike her. Vinod came over and after a quick check wanted to take a blood sample. The results looked gloomy and frightening. From then on, all I can remember clearly is that she sat beside me in the living room holding my hands. As she got into the car to go to the hospital, she turned back and waved to me. Perhaps somewhere at the back of her mind, she knew that she was leaving the home and family she loved, and moving towards her last journey.

After Appukochamma passed on, Raghu, their son came to accompany his father back to the U.S. 'I find it hard to carry on without the love of my life', Ranji said sadly. He, always the planner and the strong one, seemed tired and helpless now. As he left our home, he assured me that he would be back in winter. This was not to be. Nevertheless, he kept his promise of calling me every day at the same time for a little chat, 'just like what Appukka did'. During that little time he had left, he compiled a beautiful little book in memory of my sister. A few weeks before he passed on, the phone calls became less frequent and he passed away on 6th of August, 2022, at his daughter's home amidst family and friends. According to his will, his ashes were brought to Vellore to be buried next to his beloved wife.

A note that I received after his death said, 'I am blessed with a loving family and many loving friends. My wealth is counted in friends, in thousands, in all walks of life.'

There are no words to express my sorrow or how much I miss them both.

27

A Different Pace

Now that we are finally 'retired', our routines and way of life are much slower. We still begin the day with prayer, thanking God for keeping us, our families, helpers, and those close to us safe during the night and surrendering the activities of the day to Him. Our breakfast, lunch, and dinner are prepared by Amutha, who takes care of all our needs. Amutha, a young widow with three grown-up children and a mother-in-law to look after, was desperate for additional work. She needed a job where she could return home to her family every evening. She came to us as our helper in the garden. She kept our garden and the surroundings clean and devoid of weeds and as both Abraham and I loved the garden, we got on well with her.

Then came Covid and the lockdown and we were finding it difficult without our kitchen and home helpers who were unable to come to work because of the lockdown. Amutha , who lived close by, offered to work for us full time doing the gardening, cooking and cleaning. At the time, my sister Appukochamma and Ranji were also with us and I needed help. Amutha was a fast and keen learner and quickly learnt to make beef fry, aapam and stew and almost all our favourite dishes. A cheerful and willing helper, she is always there to look after our needs and we in turn support and encourage her.

Most of our neighbours are older than us and we are happy to visit them and keep them company and care for them when the need arises. Retired life in our neighborhood involves a fine balance of giving and receiving. Several of our neighbors whose company we enjoy are 80, 90, or the rare 100-year-old. Caring and helping them brings us much joy. In as much as we love to give of our time, we have also been blessed to receive help and love. On September 23rd, 2023, I suffered an embolic stroke. Abraham reached out to our dear friend and neighbour, Dr. Lionel Gnanraj. Within moments, his wife, Dr. Jessie, their daughter Karen, and son-in-law Jebu Jacob, also both doctors, responded immediately to Abraham's plea for help. It was their kind and prompt action in our time of need that permitted me to survive without a neurological deficit.

The sisterhood of elderly friends, like Alamma Kochamma, Nalini Padmanabhan, Leela Ramaswamy, and Amy Jesudasan have provided me with hours of fun and laughter. Trips to visit Dr. and Mrs. Abraham Verghese have taught us ways of aging gracefully and with a sense of purpose still.

Abraham spends a lot of time in the garden which my father and he planted many years ago. The 'cat's claw creeper', a climbing vine covers our entire front wall. After a heavy rain, it breaks out into an abundance of yellow flowers. The colourful bougainvillea lines the footpath in front of our house. Various varieties of adenium, with white and various shades of pink, red, and pale orange flowers add to the beauty of the garden. I have always loved the colourful flowers and trees of my childhood at

Napier Gardens and it gives me enormous pleasure now to tend to these in my own garden.

The fruit trees – mango, banana, coconuts, and lime, need pruning at the right time and careful looking after to keep them pest free so that they can yield fruit. The baskets full of organic fruits are shared with family, friends and neighbours. While I am still able to, I enjoy making pickles, chutneys and juice, and Abraham makes his own manga – thera. These too are shared with family and friends.

There is so much in and around the house which needs Abraham's attention. Something is always breaking down and needs fixing. Abraham's love for engineering has taken shape in a new avatar and he loves pottering about and tinkering with things, trying to fix them.

Quilling is something I enjoy and Abraham helps me mount the artwork onto colourful backgrounds and we make them into calendars which we give away as gifts. Decreased vision has prevented me from reading as much as I used to, or doing the fine needlework, that I once loved.

We love visiting the campus at CMC. We think back to how this oasis of trees, gardens and sprawling stone buildings set among velvety green lawns has evolved over the years. While the campus certainly holds precious memories of our own college days, the sweetest gift offered is the secure playground it provided for our children and grandchildren.

The hours the children spent biking, walking, running, and climbing mango trees all with wild abandon and without a fear in the world, built confidence and a deep love for Nature in them. The immaculate gardens of the Big Bungalow bring back vivid memories of grand potluck dinners where staff shared their finest dishes with students and other faculty members on holidays, staff farewells, and other important community events.

The best part of being retired is spending time with each other. We began our lives with a commitment to a cause and in taking every step towards it, developed a closer relationship with God and each other as husband and wife. Abraham /Manu has been my right hand and support in all that I have done in my working days. My decision to work with him amongst the poor in the villages was a fulfillment of my promise to him before our marriage. Looking back, it was the best decision I have made in my life. My strength and happiness multiplied severalfold as I worked with him. Manu's vision, his calm endurance in dealing with challenges, helped me handle them with a similar equanimity when faced with difficulties. I wish I could have imbibed from him how not to respond before thinking twice when faced with problems.

When my parents moved to Vellore, he cared for them with much love and dedication. When we had to face the loss of my parents, the tenderness and patience with which he handled every situation was something that I admired. After retirement, I had difficulty with my vision and my mobility, Manu has always been by my side holding my hand and walking me through every difficult and unknown path. He has been a tremendous blessing indeed.

At my farewell when I retired from CMC, I made a statement that if I have another life, I cannot think of anybody other than Manu (Abraham) taking that place. I feel the same today nineteen years later.

Nurturing our marriage and caring for our family has always been a priority for us in spite of our busy work schedule. Baking something special, making each one's special dish and seeing their happy faces brings me great joy. We always gathered around our large dining table not only at mealtimes, but also for good conversations, lively debates and expressing challenging differences. Now friends and former students visit us and sit around the same table and we chat about our memorable bygone days.

The foster family system of 'adopting' a student into a family, to mentor and nurture them during their student days that CMC encouraged for its community was a great blessing to us. Our family got larger with the addition of these wonderful boys and girls who were so talented in many ways, and we and our children learnt so much from them. There were evenings of laughter and spontaneous cooking and baking sessions which gladdened our hearts. Some very special ones we can never forget are Antony Joseph, Satish Kuruvila, our foster sons, and Shalini Govil and Geeta Chacko, our foster daughters. Their company made us feel like a large family.

Our lives have been happy and blessed indeed. I thought back to what my father Kuruvila Jacob said during the celebration of his and my mother's golden wedding anniversary. He said, 'It is a gift if you have been blessed with work that gives meaning. It is a gift if you are able to give yourself for a cause other than your own benefit. It is a gift if you have good children and good friends. It is also a gift if you don't have to make decisions based on money or other pressures. ' It was so true of our lives as well. How blessed were we!

Often we just sit and reminisce about all the places we have been to and the amazing things we have done in our lives. Evenings in Vellore, as the sun sets and the sounds of the birds fade into the night, often find us alone, reminiscing about the most cherished times we've had with our family. The times when we could get both Vinod's and Priya's families together are the loveliest of our memories.

I remember the early morning misty jeep ride together in the Kabini Forest Reserve, searching for the elusive mother tiger and her cubs. We played Pictionary in the evenings at Mahabalipuram while listening to the lull of the Indian Ocean waves as they brought in weary fishermen. When the children were little, the standard request was, 'Can you chase and catch me Ammamma?' All of a sudden, Tara would turn around and chase me. It was fun.

There were also pontoon boat rides in the Wisconsin Dells, and the Christmas snowfall in Rochester as we desperately tried to get Sasha, Priya's dog to pose with us for family pictures.

We remember with awe, trips with Vinod and Priya's family to the Andaman Islands, where Abraham and I learnt to snorkel for the first time. What an adventure that was! In Malaysia our taste buds exploded when we feasted on fragrant dim sum, tender satay, and gigantic prawns.

The long car rides with Alex and Priya's family to Maine was an adventure too. We caught frogs in slushy ponds, played cricket with church members and kayaked on serene lakes. What incredible experiences and memories our children have given us and we are thankful for every one of them.

My childhood desire of seeing the Niagra Falls was fulfilled when Abraham and I went to Toronto with Alex, Priya and the children to attend the CMC Alumni (GOTC) get together one year. The day after the formal meeting, the six of us made a trip to the Niagara Falls and took a boat ride which brought us very close to the Falls. It was simply unforgettable, seeing the gorgeous view of sparkling white water come crashing and swirling down the Niagara Falls in all its splendour. A dream come true.

Besides our own family, we have another one that God has blessed us with – the one created by the CMC Alumni in North America. It was such a joy to meet them at Alex and Priya's home in Rochester. The warm hugs from Sam Asirvatham, Sanjay and Manju Kalra, Priya and Vincent Rajkumar, Prathibha Varkey, Ranjith John, and Dr. and Mrs. Carman—all reminding us constantly of the bonds that cannot be broken when seasoned with love, prayer, and God's grace.

During Priya's recent visit home, while we were in a reminiscing mood, she was very insistent that our lives be documented for future generations in their families. ' We have the story of Appachan Kuruvila Jacob. We need to have your story documented as well for those who wish to know your history. Vinod too was in agreement with this idea. Priya asked our good friend Usha Jesudasan, a renowned local writer to document our story and hence this book.

Abraham and Sulo enjoying the beach together.

Abraham Joseph Family at Elsa and Enoch's wedding, 7th January, 2023.

Alex and Priya

Vinod and Priya Aley

Priya's Family

Vinod's Family

The Blessings Of Children

Memories Of Our Daughter, Priya Mariam Alexander

Priya, our daughter could sing well from the time she was a little girl. Mary and Susie, our friends, encouraged both Priya and Vinod to sing in church. While Priya took to singing, Vinod learnt to play the guitar and the piano and the two of them formed a good pair. Often when visitors came home, they would ask Priya to sing for them and quietly, Vinod would stand beside her and play the guitar or the piano at her request. Naturally, Priya would get all the praises. Noting this, I made it a point thereafter to ask Vinod to come forward to accompany her. Priya, one day came to me with genuine doubts. 'Amma, whenever anyone asks me to sing, you promptly call Vinod. Do you love him more than you love me?' I sat her on my lap and explained to her. 'Priya, anyone who comes to the house, asks you to sing. Vinod is always there to accompany you without any hesitation. Both of you are equally loved and both of you have different talents. Wouldn't any mother want both her children to be treated the same?' Priya's response as usual would be a tight hug and an 'I love you Amma.'

Priya had a good friend who lived just outside the campus. One Saturday afternoon she came back home swinging her arms around. One look and I realized that she had gone to Shalini's house with an armful of bangles which were now missing. On asking her, the prompt reply was, ' Amma, she did not have any bangles and she loved mine. So I gave them to her.'

Priya was the outspoken one. Both of them would be up to some mischief and when found guilty, Priya's immediate response, realizing that they would be punished would be, 'Amma, who is going to beat us? ' Anticipating the answer from the child, my response invariably would be, ' Well, who do you want to punish you?' The very quick answer would be, 'Appa please, Amma.' After chasing them around for a while with a ruler, Priya would come out with the truth. 'Appa's hand goes up but will never come down, while Amma's hand will immediately come down heavily on us.'

Abraham recognised the interest that Priya and Vinod had in athletics and would take them both for workouts to the college playground in the mornings on holidays. Both she and Vinod represented their school at athletic meets.

The year in Kansas had a positive effect in instilling self-confidence in both of them. On their return to Vellore, both in Vidyalayam and Scudder School, they excelled in sports. While Priya became a Prefect, Vinod was selected as School Captain. Throughout her school days at Ida Scudder, and her college days at CMC, Priya was always ready to share her knowledge and help other campus kids and juniors whenever they needed help with their studies, especially during examination time.

———••———

Priya's Memories

Memories of my early childhood are blurred. My brother and I were born less than a year apart. I've heard my mother say that we were happy children, supporting each other and often getting into trouble. Our home was happy and full of cheer. My father's rule was that children should not be punished until the age of two. My father (Appa) never raised his voice or punished us. The only time his facial expression changed to disappointment, was when we did not practice enough before a sports competition. My mother (Amma), on the other hand, was the disciplinarian. Acts of disobedience were met with disapproval, but immediately afterward, Amma would follow up the punishment with a kiss or a hug and give us the reasons why she had to resort to the punishment. My early childhood memories include spending a lot of time with our maternal Uncle (Ranji) Aunt Appuammachy, and our cousins Raviachi, Raghuachi, and Rachakka. My parents lived with my aunt and cousins on the CMC Hospital campus until Vinod was born. We moved to the college campus after one year. Even after we moved, we still spent our weekends enjoying the love and affection of my cousins, uncle, and aunt.

Appa and Amma were disciplined and hardworking. They would leave the house for work by 7.15 a.m. on most days. My father always dressed in crisply pressed starched white kadhar shirts and crisp white pants. My mother was always so beautiful in her simple starched cotton saris that spoke of class and elegance. Her hair was tied in a figure-of-eight bun and held secure with a wooden clasp. For the rest of the day, we were under the care of our 'Akkas' Kanaga and Muniamma. They were wonderful. Both had been well-trained by my aunt and mother and we could find no fault with them whatsoever. Kanaga's crisp masala dosas, aloo parathas, and chutneys made from any plant that grew on the planet are vivid memories to this day. Muniamma made legendary spicy beef and ball curry. Our snacks at tea time were heart-healthy, but at that time, who knew? All I remember was the joy of sitting at the table eating salted boiled peanuts, tender boiled beans, and of course, my mother's incredible marble cake, peanut butter cookies, or chocolate cake. Amma's baked goods were made every Saturday in a small box oven whose front glass was cracked, but held together by a broad adhesive.

The dining table was (and till today is) the epicenter of the Abraham home. It was here that we were taught the value of not wasting food and the importance of learning and speaking our mother tongue, 'Malayalam'. The ultimate consequence of failing to do so was losing our rights to desserts like chocolate, mangoes, and other favorite items. My brother and I always had a trick up our sleeve to earn the treats. At meal time, we would not speak a word of Malayalam, but just when a bowl of luscious mangoes appeared at the table, we would look beseechingly at our parents, and with doleful eyes and outstretched hands, we would politely say, 'manga tharamo' (mangoes please). It never failed, but we never learnt good Malayalam. The dining table was also where we would play board games (monopoly, scrabble), decorate eggs for Christmas and Easter, and of course where we would execute the military operation of birthday cake decorations.

Church and family prayers were a fundamental part of our lives, and even today, the 6 a.m. family prayers are a ritual that is never missed. Church was where we first displayed new clothes. Christmas and our birthdays marked the occasions for brand-new clothes. I do not recall wearing store-bought clothes until late in our teens. My grandmother, my aunt, and my mother were unmatched seamstresses. They could create anything. Using cutouts of brown paper, yards of beautiful material were snipped and sewn together to make dresses of the latest fashion. When my brother and I were little, we were often dressed as twins in clothes that you could not find in any exotic showroom today. Beautifully embroidered ducks, cats, swans, and fairies, magically came to life on our clothes. For years, I owned gorgeous smocked outfits. My mother also made beautiful, handmade smocked dresses for each of her granddaughters. Amma ensured that I learnt every kind of stitch known to women, but in comparison to her meticulous immaculately tidy needlework, mine paled. Amma was also industrious. Earning and living off a small salary meant that we could not afford a brand-new uniform every school year. But none of my friends would have ever imagined that our uniforms were occasionally recycled. I still remember my mother ripping apart my sun-faded grey uniform, turning it inside out, and sewing it together overnight so that I had an 'as good as new' uniform for the brand new school year. Her ingenuity in managing within our means remains truly impressive.

My parents believed that spending time with our family and knowing our roots was vital for our upbringing. So every summer, we would either visit Kerala or Bombay. Kerala was particularly special because many of our cousins, along with their parents, would gather in Maramon, our father's ancestral home. The time we spent there was priceless, filled with fun games, entertainment, and delicious food prepared by our Ammachy and the aunts.

I remember that preparations for going to Kerala included taking gifts. Our gifts were always amazing Indian sweets made by Mr. Krishnamurthy. These delicious treats were made in our backyard, and the elaborate cooking session took place over a few days. Mysorepak, Mixture, Jillebi, and Laddu would be divided into large metal tins that would be packed as gifts for Maramon. Our parents taught us that it is not expensive gifts that mattered, but rather the thoughtfulness, simplicity, and care that went into them.

Mornings and nights in Maramon were punctuated by the call to worship, which began with my Ammachy's melodious singing. The whole family would gather together for prayers in the living room.

Looking back, I now realize the significance of a home that invested so much in family prayers; this is what kept us all united and grounded in an unspoken faith in God.

Back home in Vellore, we cherished the days when families would visit us. Appa's cousin, the Right Reverend Alexander Thirumeni, the Metropolitan of the Mar Thoma Church, would stay with us during his visits to Vellore. While Amma was nervous about his visit, we soon learnt that he was a lovely and simple person with no airs about him. One Sunday, he was asked to preach in St. John's Church. Shortly after we were dressed and ready to leave for church and seated in the car, Amma was summoned to attend to a complicated childbirth in the hospital. She asked us to proceed to church, knowing she would be delayed. I wondered whether Amma was doing the right thing. 'Shouldn't she be going to church, especially because Thirumeni Appachen was preaching?' I thought. Very timidly, I asked him, 'Thirumeni Appacha, is it alright if Amma does not go to church when you are preaching?' With a gentle smile, he patted me on my back and said, 'Molae, your Amma is doing God's work. I am only preaching.' I could hardly believe what he said. Every night we would have prayers. With Vinod on the guitar, we would sing along to some favorite hymns with Thirumeni Appacha. I adored him and waited eagerly for his visits.

While consistent academic performance was encouraged, Appa was far more enthusiastic about excellence in sports. A week or two before sports day, Appa would wake us up at 5.30 a.m. and take us to the sports field to train us for running. He was an exceptional short-distance runner, and he spent hours teaching us a good running style. His advice to us was to participate and do our best. I recall when I was in Scudder School, my father timed his return from the U.K. so that he could watch me walk up to the dais to receive the Championship Shield. Sadly, that was not to be. Although I had done well in all my events, I tripped and fell ten meters before the finish line in the last event. As my friends ran past me, I could have burst into tears and walked away, but I could hear my father's voice saying, 'Get up and finish the race.' The message was always about sportsmanship, competing, finishing the task, and never giving up. Winning was not everything, but doing your best was. I am grateful for all these memories.

My parents selflessly cared for their own parents. It was extremely important to them that their parents were respected and taken care of until the very end. I witnessed three of my grandparents pass away in our own home. Looking back, I realize that I have benefited greatly from the kindness and compassion they showed to their parents. Taking care of elderly parents is a significant responsibility, but my parents embraced it with grace and love.

I grew up in a family where material wealth and social status were not the most important things. What mattered most was how you treated and respected others, regardless of their social standing. I am grateful for the values that my parents instilled in me. Their selflessness was always evident as they put others before themselves, whether it was my brother or me, our grandparents, or the community. They demonstrated a way of life that I can only aspire to follow. I am incredibly thankful for the gift of my exceptional parents and for the love and life they have given me.

Leaving our home country for the United States of America was a difficult decision, but my parents never dissuaded us, despite how much it must have pained them. They did everything in their power to make our lives easier. My father was willing to be alone and make do with whatever he had, while my mother took the long journey every summer to be with us. She didn't know how to drive, so she took the kids by bus or train to Vacation Bible School, hospital check-ups, carnivals, or the park. She did everything with love, making sure that our children never felt they had less than anyone else. My mother filled our little house in Boston with the love of Christ and the beauty of God's creation, and to this day, my children love my parents more than anything else. It is a testament to my parents' wonderful character that they managed to raise me with such strong values. I am forever grateful to God for the lessons they taught me, and the love and values they instilled in my children.

I am painfully aware that my parents are ageing before my eyes. Their most valuable gift to me is their faith in Jesus, and their commitment to living a life that reflected that faith. Every morning, they sit together, holding hands, reading the Bible, and praying for us, for our families, for the sick, the elderly, and those in need. Their lives are so beautiful. At the start of each year, my mother gives my brother, me, and our children a copy of the Daily Bread. On every page, she writes down important dates to remember, such as birthdays, wedding anniversaries, and death anniversaries, and they both pray for everyone on those days.

I pray that God will continue to bless my parents, and that my brother and I will live according to the values they have taught us.

Memories Of Our Son, Vinod

While Priya and Vinod were just 5 and 4 years old, we stayed in the Rural Hospital premises next to Shanthi Illam- the Nurses' Hostel. Since there were no other children around, they would make friends with the nurses in the evening and enjoy their company sitting or swinging on the low branches of the mango tree. On one such occasion, the 'Nongu' (Palm fruit) seller lady came along and Vinod dashed off into the house to get the 10 paise that he had saved from his pocket money. At 2 paisa each Nongu, he got 5 'Nongus'. Vinod had planned to get one each for each of us – his Appa, Amma, Priya, and himself, and one for Mary, his friend who was with him on the tree. When he got back home with only three fruits, we asked him, ' Where is the fruit for you?' He replied, ' I gave mine to Susie, who had come to visit us and who didn't have any.' This was Vinod – kind and generous always.

On our yearly visits to Kerala, he made sure that he carried a duster cloth with him to make sure that the bedroom where we stayed was absolutely dust-free, as I was a bad asthmatic.

In all the three houses that we stayed on the college campus, he took a lot of interest in gardening. He would work with his father planting tapioca and later on, preparing the beds for flowering plants – marigolds and 'four-o – clocks' were his favourites. While he was in the process of trimming plants, I got a frantic call, that a bit of his fingertip had been clipped off and that he was searching for it. In schools, both in Vidyalayam and Ida Scudder School, he was selected to be the Head Boy and was also a President Scout. I am told that he always stood up for justice and readily helped the juniors who came to him for help. He also represented the school in the Interschool athletics meet.

As he grew up, he showed a lot of interest in cooking and he would make chocolate fudge pudding or marie biscuit pudding to share with his friends while on confirmation trips. He would carefully cut out the pieces he needed for his friends and leave the rest for the family. At the meet, he would happily give up his share assuming that he would have some at home. Unfortunately, his share at home would also be eaten, but he had no complaints. While in the medical college, despite being tied up with the examinations himself, I have seen him helping his friends and classmates who needed help prior to the exam.

He was very fond of my Uncle Chandypappa and Aunt Mariamma kochamma. He would visit their home in Madras at least once a year and spend the weekend with them keeping them company or helping them with various chores. After my uncle passed away, he made his visits more frequent. His attitude of caring for the elderly was evident in the way he would take care of my father, mother and Abraham's mother, more so in their last days.

Over the years, he was always there to help anyone in need. Whether it was Ankamma, the ayah who looked after Tara when she was little or an attender who needed help, it was all the same for him. The small deeds of kindness, sharing and honesty in him is truly admirable.

Vinod's Memories

Our parents were (and are) very different, but these differences complemented each other. Our mother was very systematic, meticulous and very particular about details; she would be the one to look into our studies; she was very much into cooking and embroidery; while our father was keen on and particular about involvement in extracurricular activities and physical activity. Carpentry was one of his hobbies; while gardening was something they both enjoyed.

The same characteristics came out at work. Our mother focused on meticulous documentation, careful systematic organization, drawing up protocols and initiating audits; she was always more cautious.

Our father often focused on community engagement and development, medical education and so on. He was prepared to venture into the unknown and to take risks. Wherever he went, our father would always be on the lookout for ideas to bring back to the department.

The work and building up of the hospital and department were very important to both of them. On most days they returned late, tired, but would still be on call. That meant that if they were needed, they would drop whatever they were doing and leave immediately.

Often, both of them would go together for some emergency. Priya and I were both quite small at the time and would just sit and wait for the front door to open to know that everything was okay.

Both Priya and I were always dressed simply but neatly, often in identical clothes. The salary for both my parents was very low, so there was no unnecessary spending. However, we did not lack anything and at the same time, we were taught careful spending.

Family prayers every morning were important and would not be missed unless both our parents were tied down in the hospital at the time.

Family was very important to them. We spent a couple of years with my mother's parents in Bombay while she did her post-graduate studies, and with them again when they later moved to Vellore. We saw them at varying frequencies through the week but always had Sunday lunch together. On holidays we spent time with them. Our father's parents lived in Kerala. While we didn't live there for a long time, we visited them every year for at least a week during the summer holidays. We continue to be close to our cousins and these family reunions definitely helped us bond together.

Our parents had close friends among faculty and that helped us as we were all in the same situation with just about enough to make ends meet. But within those means, we would go out for picnics in and around Vellore. The focus for all of us was on having a good time and those close relationships still continue.

Our home was always open to younger staff and their colleagues. We got to know a lot of them and have so many stories of pranks which we were all a part of together.

Birthdays were always special. Nothing was bought from anywhere. After we went to sleep the previous night, our parents baked a cake and together they would come up with new ideas for the shapes and icing. The cakes were simply spectacular. The parties were great fun with lots of homemade food, games and so much fun with our friends.

When we got married, our spouses and later our children too were an important part of their lives.

Our parents would do anything for their grandchildren. Our daughters always had beautiful embroidered dresses made by our mother. All school programs were attended by the grandparents and they cheered and clapped enthusiastically. By this time, my wife Priya's mother had also moved to Vellore and having two sets of grandparents so close was a real blessing for both us and them. There was always a wide variety of food, planning and executing birthday parties, attendance at all their programs, and being available whenever we needed additional help and someone to step in.

Memories Of Our Son-In-Law, Alex Alexander.

I remember Alex as a perfect gentleman from the first time I saw him in St John's Church. Alex had come to the church with his friends Suresh and Rekha. No sooner had he alighted from the car than he proceeded to hold the car door open for the others in the car. This caught my eye at once. A few years later when we went to meet Alex and his parents in Ernakulam, (as Alex's parents, Ach and Kochamma could not travel to Vellore, as he had just recovered from a major heart attack) what impressed Abraham and me was that he was soft-spoken and extremely polite. We also learnt that when his father was critically ill, Alex resigned his job in the U.S. and came back to Kakkanad in Kerala to take care of his parents.

Alex who had done his MBA in Kerala, had plans of seeking admission in the Kennedy School of Government while in the US. His parents and their health was much more important to him.

There are many things I remember, from the time that Alex stepped into our home. After meeting Priya and agreeing to the marriage, he was very sure that he would only get married after he had a secure job. For Alex, his family always came first, which is evident from the many sacrifices that he has made over the years to see that Priya, Yohan and Lisa are cared for and secure.

Soon after their marriage, Alex was working in Bombay. I was coming from Malaysia and the suitcase which was lifted onto the stand for security screening, fell onto my leg. Alex sat up all night, giving me warm fomentation and keeping me comfortable.

Alex is a stickler for neatness and cleanliness and you can notice it the minute you enter their home.

When the family moved to Boston, I travelled with them. At every point I saw how gentle he was with the children. Later in Boston, I remember him waiting patiently in the Kid's store, before Lisa could finally decide on her Barbie. From the time we got to know him, I have been aware of two of Alex's admirable qualities. Early in the morning he would be up and about emptying the dish washer, putting back the dishes and cutlery in their place and getting his coffee. The second thing was that he would be seated on his favourite chair reading the Bible and organising his day by going through the daily readings and seeking God's help in everything that he planned to do.

He was kind and considerate to the helpers at home and to this day, Kannan, who worked for them for several years till they left for the US, holds his 'Chettayi' next to God.

Alex loves Indian food and the day I arrive in Rochester, he would have two containers of dosai mix. I loved making crisp dosai for him. He was quick to learn what our likes and dislikes were and went the extra mile to ensure that these food items or other favourites were available whenever we visited them. When I retired from CMC in 2005, although it was hardly a year after they went to the U.S. all four of them returned to Vellore and made me feel very special by being there for me at my retirement functions. Had it not been for the help of Alex, Vinod and the two Priyas and eight-year-old Elsa, it would not have been easy to shift our residence to Kamalakshipuram, after living for 40 or more years on the CMC campus.

Alex's father Rev. K.T. Alexander and his mother Dr. Aley Alexander were lovely, God-fearing people. They came to Vellore for Priya's deliveries as Priya wanted their blessings before she was wheeled into the theatre. Later Achan baptised both his grandchildren in Vellore. His mother, an obstetrician had helped resurrect many Mar Thoma Mission Hospitals which were on the brink of closing down. Both of them together, worked in the Mar Thoma Ashramam Hospitals and had been of great help to both the rich and the poorest of the poor.

I was privileged to be considered by Kochamma as her younger sister. They were there too, as very much a part of the family, at my retirement.

———•∘•———

Alex's Memories

Appappa and Ammamma are wonderful, kind and caring. They received me into their home and treated me like their own. Each had different ways of sharing and showering their love and affection.

Ammamma is the pillar of the family. She makes it clear to everyone, and in no uncertain terms, that her family comes first. It is an incredible quality, and I often gently suggest to Priya that it would be a desirable trait to emulate. Her fierce loyalty was equally demonstrated to every member of the small family unit – to her husband, children, in-laws, and each grandchild. She worked hard to demonstrate her love and affection every moment, and all the time. No matter how trivial the act may seem, it was done with a full heart, from mastering each person's favorite dish, paying attention to simple quirky details. She is one of the most dependable people I know. When she commits to a task you know it will be completed, and with sincerity. She is a woman of deep faith. Her annual gift of Daily Bread with reminders of birthdays, and anniversaries is a testament to her earnest desire to ensure her children walk the path of Christ. She is always ready for fun and adventure. We enjoyed her love for bacon, Mike's Hard Lemonade, baby back ribs, and fish sandwiches from McDonald's. She built with small bricks, a big home, and to her credit is a financier unparalleled.

Appappa is quiet, reserved, and thoughtful. His manner of showing love and affection is subtle. He is wise and brings to the relationship a deep faith, an unshakable trust in God, and a hope that goodness will rule. His relationship with me was a reflection of his infinite love for his daughter. He was there for us in tough times, standing up for our needs, and always trying to work for the larger good. I have seen his dedication to his work, and his mission to stand up for the less fortunate through his day-to-day actions.

Like Amma, he had a sense of pride and joy in the family. Playing board games, being creative in constructing play tools for Yohan and Lisa, tending to the garden, and priding himself on the fruits in the orchard, are some of the ways he showed his love. His manga thera was a treat. His enjoyment of Malibu, Tequila, cheese, chocolate and nuts are endearing.

The different ways in which Ammamma and Appappa made efforts to support us in every way possible as we took on the daunting task of settling down in the U.S. is admirable. It is hard to think of how we would have made it without their help. They are a blessing in our lives.

―――・●・―――

Memories Of Our Daughter-in-Law, Priya Aley

Priya Aley George came into our lives in the year 1989. It was during the Community Orientation Posting that we first saw her- a dainty, pretty, timid girl. I had some doubts whether Vinod had set his eyes on her, but at the time there was no reason to come to such a conclusion. At the end of the posting, while preparing for the presentation, she approached me for help. That is when I realised that she was very shy. A loud question directed to her would make her shiver. After few months, Vinod told us that he was interested in her. We had no objection to their relationship, but told him that her parents should be told as well.

Many of Vinod's and his sister Priya's class mates would come home for meals and we looked forward to having them over. My parents, who would join us for meals on weekends also liked the company of the young students. On the sports field, Priya excelled in athletics. We saw more of her as the years went by and she was very much one of our own. When my father passed on in 1991, she sat with me through the night comforting me and doing whatever was necessary, as a daughter would. In their final year, Priya Aley informed us that her parents would like to meet us to officially formalize the wedding.

I was the one who was nervous and trembling after all that I had heard about Priya's mother Susheela's expertise in cooking. I was anxious to prepare the best meal ever for my ' would be daughter-in-law's parents. We had a happy first meeting which went off well, and the ' Pennu kanal' (seeing the girl) was fixed for the summer holidays.

Although we had known Priya for 3 years and approved of her as a suitable wife for Vinod, we followed this formal Kerala tradition. Six of us from our family set off for Kottarakara – Priya's paternal grandparent's home to officially 'see' the girl. Priyas's mother, well known for her culinary skills, had an elaborate spread – Karimeen, tender cashew thoran, and several other Kerala specialities. The table was decorated with beautiful vegetable carvings. It was a feast for the eyes and the palate. The engagement was fixed for the following year after their final examinations, and the wedding in December 1994. Manu who was excited about this family event got his words a little mixed up and made us laugh when he said, ' We had three children by the end of December, of which one was by marriage!'

Priya and Vinod spent a year in a leprosy hospital in Wayanad, and a visit to their home was the time we got to know her parents, Dr. George Mathew (Ranji) and Susheela well. Ranji was an ophthalmologist in Kasargod and Susheela managed a school, did a lot of catering and also assisted Ranji in his practice. He passed away in 1995, and following that Susheela came to Vellore. At our request, she agreed to manage the CHTC canteen. Having her manage the canteen was indeed a blessing. Although Susheela has several disabilities following an accident, there is very little that stands in her way and she is a good role model for me.

As for Aley Priya, I am blessed to have her as my second daughter. She has stood by me as a pillar of strength on various occasions – through my several surgeries, through a stroke and even at home whenever the need arose. Priya gives me a complex many a time; be it her cooking skills or her thoughtfulness. At a time after my shoulder surgery when I had difficulty in managing nighties without help, Priya brought me pyjamas, and shirts with buttons stitched right to the end. Actually, Priya thinks of these things even before I do.

When my sister was ill during COVID days, Priya was always there for me, ready to stay with her, seeing to her every need. On the last day of my sister's life, Priya and Vinod stood by her side holding her hand and singing hymns to comfort her and gently helping her as she passed on from this world to the next.

Priya Aley Joseph's Memories

When Vinod first took me home to his parents, I was a little nervous, but also excited. Until then, Uncle and Aunty had been my teachers, but now, I hoped that they would like me and that the relationship would grow deeper. They were very welcoming and did not judge me in any way for which I am very grateful. I would go for lunch every Sunday and stay over and study. Vinod would then walk me home in the evening, so I became a part of the family even before I got married to Vinod. Amma is a woman of amazing thoughtfulness. I didn't come from a very well-to-do family, so birthday cakes were not part of my life. Amma found out that it was my birthday and even though she was out of town, arranged for a beautiful cake to be delivered to me. It moved me to tears. She is a woman of great determination and a talented artist. Her creative and observant eye catches everything of beauty and she is able to replicate it in some form. Her love of gardening, which I admire, is something she has passed on to me – especially the artistic way she arranges colourful flowers and pots in the garden from season to season.

She is a woman who holds her family tight with strong cords of love. She is the glue that holds the large extended family together – she needs this connection and she has also taught us how important this is for our family life. She has also taught me how to bake and has willingly and generously shared her recipes with me for which I'm so grateful. Something I've been very grateful for is her financial wisdom – her advice to save for a rainy day, like for example, my daughter's wedding, has held me in good stead when the time arose.

Amma and Appa will do anything for us, and have often gone out of their way to be there for us. Appa too like Amma, enjoys close family relationships and has built a unique bond with me. I appreciate their strong faith, unwavering integrity and honesty, and their wisdom. Their simplicity is something I admire too. One of the things I love about them is that they are always ready for fun. They have been parents to me, nurturing me, loving me, and looking out for me from my student days. I have been blessed to be in their family and have received way more than I have given, been loved more than I have loved, and cannot count the number of times they have been there for me when I needed them. They have loved and guided us and our children wisely, and have been examples to us of the kind of people we should be.

Adorable Ammamma with grandchildren

Proud parents and grandparents at Lisa's graduation

Happy grandparents at Yohan's graduation

Elsa at her graduation with Tara

Proud parents at Tara's graduation

Our Grandchildren

Our Granddaughter, Elsa Anna

Elsa is Vinod and Priya Aley's daughter and our first grandchild. For the first few years, Elsa was in our house during the day. Priya, would drop her at home where 'Ammanja' her paternal great – grandmother would be dressed and ready to receive her. She spent a lot of time with my mother, singing to her, reading little books to her, and 'taking care of her.' My mother had a large wound on her leg and Dr. Ravi Korula would visit her on alternate days to dress her wound. We kept a dressing tray ready and little Elsa took charge of it. As soon as Dr. Ravi's car turned the corner she would be waiting, ready with a 'Moda' and the dressing tray, by my mother's bedside. The little three-year-old stood behind the curtain watching the procedure. At the slightest wince on my mother's face while the doctor cleaned and dressed the wound, Elsa would say, 'Ravi doctor don't hurt my Ammanja'. This was my compassionate little granddaughter.

When Abraham's mother came to stay with us a few months before she passed on, Elsa would climb onto the sideboard of Ammachy's wheel chair, give Ammachy a hug and a kiss and say,

'Vellia Ammachy' and in return Ammachy would bend her head down and affectionately call her 'Kochumolae.'

After my mother passed on, one day while I sat beside Elsa coaxing her to have her food, she was distracted looking at my mother's photograph. She then came out with her little story of the 'thereafter'. 'You know when Ammanja died, my Amma picked me up from bed and brought me to this house. It was very dark when we left the house in Kamalakshipuram, but when we came here to see Ammanja, it was bright. Now I know that my Ammanja has gone to a brighter place and she does not have to worry about the darkness'. The relationship which she nurtured with her great-grandmother was just beautiful.

A year went by after Elsa's Ammanja passed away. I came home from work earlier in the evening to take Elsa to the sports field. The Vidyalayam school sports was going on and this was one of her outings. Apart from the field events, one of the other attractions was the vendors on the roadside selling ice cream, potato chips, soft drinks and other small eats. Elsa was not interested in any of these. She had her eyes on the parents and children filing past a man advertising heart-shaped, halogen red balloons fastened to his hand with a thread and as he moved his hand up and down, the balloons were bobbing up and down. It cost 5 rupees each. The doting grandmother that I was, got her one and the little one was prancing up and down happily when all of a sudden, she let go of the string, and her red balloon went up, and up, higher and higher until it was but a red speck. Seeing her forlorn look, I got her another one but this time, I fastened the string onto her little bangle. Elsa was of course delighted to get a replacement and with her new balloon fastened securely to her bangle, walked back to the stadium, swinging her alms. To her utter dismay, a man walked across and in a fraction of a second, the balloon was beyond her reach as the bangle slid off her hand. For a brief while she could not control her tears and between her sobs watched the balloon and her bangle going higher and higher. As the little red dot was disappearing behind the clouds, the crying stopped and she turned to me with a pleased look saying, 'Ammamma, I am not sad anymore, my Ammanja will get my balloon and the bangle and she will be happy that I have sent it to her.' There was no more talk about her balloon or her Ammanja for the time being. One could see that Elsa was happy and went back to the sports field to enjoy the rest of the evening. To this day, Elsa continues to be a child who is happy to share and give. God bless her.

———••———

Elsa's Memories.

Some of my earliest memories are with Ammamma, sitting on the wooden steps in the old house while she taught me alphabets and numbers with painstakingly drawn pictures and activities in an old diary, going to feed the gold fish in the pond at CHAD and running on the beach, because age will not stop Ammamma from being able to enjoy time with her family. We have also spent many hours in their backyard with Appacha, picking mangoes and eating fresh tender coconut. Summer holidays in our school years were spent at our grandparents' houses, learning to cook, paint, sew and garden.

Over the years, I have watched them go through trials, illness, grief and have often wondered to myself, 'Aren't they tired?' And yet, in every circumstance they have relied on God's grace and goodness, not doubting for a moment that their Saviour has them in the palm of His hand. In situations that warranted frustration and anger, I have seen God teach them to be wise, gentle, loving and gracious. In Ammamma, I have seen selflessness and generosity in all her relationships, dedication in her work, creativity and resourcefulness in her art and most importantly, her faithfulness in supporting Appacha, walking alongside him and encouraging him in his work and ministry through the many decades of their service. In Appacha, I have seen a kind and gentle heart, rarely angry, frustrated or resentful, facing challenges and setbacks without wavering in his faith. I have seen his care and service to his family in small and big ways, and most of all, in his love for Ammamma. Their marriage has also been an example for us, in standing alongside one another, supporting each other, caring for one another and at the heart of their marriage, glorifying God in everything.

We have a very big family, scattered all over the globe. It takes effort, time, care and patience to stay connected. Appacha and Ammamma have been the glue holding our family together, making sure we call each other, remembering everyone's birthdays and anniversaries, arranging family get-togethers and making sure we are all involved in each other's lives no matter how far away we are. When I first told them about my (now) husband, they opened their hearts to him immediately, welcoming him into the family, telling him that they were not 'uncle and aunty' to him but 'Appacha and Ammamma' from then on.

We have been so blessed to have them walking in front of us, teaching us by example, how to walk in faith, to love well, to be steadfast and kind and to use our time, talents and gifts in the service of God and others.

———•———

Our Grand Son-In-Law, Enoch Joy Das.

Enoch made his way into our hearts in 2022, when he and Elsa made a promise to each other. Elsa was pretty sure that she would choose her own partner for life. When she declared to us that she had come upon the man of her choice, we were not surprised at all. It was the church where they worshipped that brought them together. Enoch, a 6 footer towered over Elsa and it reminded me of my father, a good 6'2 ½" and my mother a mere 4'11". In the year that we have known Enoch, he has walked into our lives with ease. He has a gentle sense of humour and his faith is very much like Elsa's – strong and steadfast. Nahum and Rofina, Enoch's parents, with their missionary outlook in life have been able to reach out to many downtrodden and needy people in the North, despite many challenges. Enoch and Elsa together manage their home, their cooking, complementing each other in every way. Seeing them together, we were assured that they have made the right choice prayerfully and wisely.

———••———

Enoch's Memories

Being a new addition to the family through marriage with Elsa, I guess it is understandable that I still am only in the early phase of making memories with Ammamma and Appacha. But even in this short span of time (around 2 years), the life experienced with them has helped me get a glimpse of their values, faith and love.

My fondest memory of Ammamma and Appacha will always be how they welcomed me and my family into theirs. The smile of trusting me with their precious granddaughter, the hug of assurance of acceptance in the family, and the words of entrusting their beloved granddaughter, I can never forget. The first time, Ammamma hugged me, she gently whispered, 'Elsa is very precious to us, please take care of her', and when I heard this, I was overwhelmed (in a good way) with the experience of care and love that they had for their family, but I never expected that the same care and love was awaiting me, when I was finally married to Elsa.

I come from a family where love is expressed more through actions than words, but now I am experiencing both love in words and action from my new family because I guess Ammamma and Appacha understood the need for both and cultivated that value into the family. At times it seems like they have unlimited bandwidth for loving the people because they go far and beyond to care for the people they love. I know that this love stems from their faith in our Lord Jesus Christ, and values that are deeply rooted in the Bible, and always, their actions are driven by the desire to glorify God.

I have hardly experienced life with my grandparents, so I always thank God for Ammamma and Appacha that I am able to experience their love and care.

———•◦•———

Our Granddaughter, Tara Rachel Joseph

Tara, our fourth grandchild is always full of smiles and laughter and keeps us all laughing with her cute little sayings. When she was about four, she came bouncing into the room where my brother-in-law, my husband and Tara's father were seated around having a serious conversation. She looked seriously at my brother-in-law and asked, 'Kakkuappacha, are you married?' 'Yes Tara,' 'to whom?' To 'Appuammachy,' ' Oh No!'

She then went on to her grandfather and asked the same question. Finaly she went to her father. After each answer, she responded with 'Oh No!' After asking all of them, she said with utter disappointment, 'Then who will I marry?'

We had gone to Kerala, for my nephew's wedding reception. It was a new place as far as the children were concerned, but she made sure that she was 'at home' no matter where she was. The new bride had a headache and it was a matter of concern for everybody as the reception was just an hour to go. Tara couldn't be spotted anywhere. As we were desperately trying to locate her, the bride's mother reassured us that Tara was with Monisha the bride, trying to relieve her of her headache and fever. Tara had placed a wet towel on Monisha's forehead, squeezing out the water every now and then and replacing it with a moist one. Tara has maintained her sensitivity to other's needs.

She was particularly good in athletics and her crowning event was when she won second place in hurdles in the All India Inter school ISC sports meet. The parents, both good athletes bought a couple of hurdles and trained Tara every evening after a hard day's work. After a full day of studies and practices at school, Tara would do her best as advised by her parents. Her acting talents were demonstrated when she was in Shrishti School, when she acted as 'Fiona'. Her acting was superb. While Elsa would turn out exotic dishes, Tara made delicious cakes and cookies and deserts.

Tara's Memories

My grandparents have always played an important role in our lives. For all my exams, the more stressful part of it was the intense questioning by my grandfather the day before. To him, as long as I knew that Na and Cl together made salt, and if I knew what 2+2 was, I would pass my 10th grade board exams!

Unlike many of my friends, I was blessed with a born storyteller in our family. My grandmother is more famous in our family for being the best storyteller than for being a gynaecologist. Ammamma is the reason I know how to make crepes, hot chocolate and 'pigs in blankets'. Appacha insisted that the best arm workout would be to pluck as many mangoes as our arms could manage.

Appacha taught me that the only acceptable number of dosas I should be eating for a Saturday morning's breakfast is 6 and I learnt this the hard way: by having dosa-eating competitions with him so often that it became a routine. He taught me how to play sudoku and how to run after crabs on the seashore for long enough to get my Ammamma to start chasing me instead. Ammamma's endless stories to get me, Chechi, Yohan and Lisa to go to sleep is an irreplaceable memory. Appacha and Ammamma's almost automatic response to any of us complimenting something in the house is always, ' Would you like to have it? Take it, it's yours. What will we do with it?'

Their selflessness and dedication to their family's upbringing and the development of CHAD is a testament to their character and their sense of love and responsibility, an area where they have never fallen short.

Our Grandson, Alex Yohan Alexander

Yohan was born in CMC on the 28th, December, 1999. It was a joy to have Priya and Yohan with us for three months and Alex coming every weekend to see their little son. Elsa, the big sister would run up the steps calling out to her aunt, ' Ammai, I am here, now you can give him a bath.' She would smother him with kisses. Ammai was of course cautious, but nothing would keep Elsa away from the baby. She was always the big sister. Yohan took his first steps with Elsa standing a distance away, encouraging him to walk. Once Priya and Yohan left for Bangalore where they lived, we bought a larger vehicle, so that we could go to Bangalore more often to visit them. Alex, Priya and Yohan made frequent visits to our home in the campus and we would go to Bangalore whenever possible. Yohan at that stage would run from one end of the room to the other with his little hands outstretched, to convince us how much he loved us. Once we reached Bangalore, there was no question of going back to Vellore, while Yohan was still awake. We then revised our plans and decided to leave early in the morning. By the time we reached the outskirts of Tamil Nadu, Alex would call us and hand the phone over to Yohan. Between heavy sobbing, his question was, 'Why did you leave me without telling me?' This continued even after they left for Boston and in Rochester too. They would get around Alex for permission to skip classes to be around to say their tearful goodbye, when we left for India. We found it equally difficult to leave the U.S. without the children.

During our last visit to the U.S. we were a little frail and needed help. Yohan was in high school then. During lunch break, he would make a quick visit home to see whether we had enough for lunch or any other needs.

It was wonderful to see the change in Yohan's attitude to studies. At a very young age when most children have not even decided their profession he had set his mind to do neurosurgery. This interest was sparked by the interaction he had with Dr. Ari Chacko, the Head of Neurosurgery at CMC. Yohan continues to keep in touch with us by calling us 2 or 3 times per week to check on us and to let us know about his well- being and his activities.

———•·———

Yohan's Memories

My Ammamma and Appappa have been an important part of my life, and my sister and I have been fortunate to be able to spend almost every summer with them, either in Vellore or in Boston. Consequently, there are several stories that come to mind when I think of the impact that they have had on me.

During our summers in Vellore, my sister and I would share the same bedroom upstairs in our grandparents' house on Godown Street. At approximately 6:30 in the morning, Ammamma would come upstairs to wake us up. Of course, this was not what two young children on their summer break wanted to do. Some mornings, we were woken up by their dog, Chippy, who would jump onto the bed and lick our faces till we were up. As soon as we got out of bed, Ammamma would get us to make the bed in the same way her mother had taught her. She responded, as she always would when we wanted to procrastinate, 'Time and tide waits for no man.' After the`bed was made, we would have prayers in their bedroom. My sister and I would each read the devotional that was ascribed to us, Ammamma would read the Bible verse, and Appappa would pray for all members of the family and whoever in their extended community was in need. After prayers, we would go up to their terrace and watch the sunrise and look for all the birds and animals that visit the garden they created. Or we would walk through their garden as Ammamma would tell me about stories about each plant, their significance to her, and if there were any imperfections in their care, she would fix it right at that moment – not wasting any time. Sometimes we were able to see the contraptions that Appappa had designed for the garden. During our daily morning routine, my grandparents showed me why I should be awake to enjoy the beauty that surrounds us, and to ground myself in faith to enthusiastically meet the challenges and excitement of the day ahead.

As the day progressed, visitors would often come to the house. Often, these would be old students, patients, or friends. For each visitor, my Ammamma would tell me their life stories, their connection to them, and further go on to tell me stories about their children and families. To this day, the names, and stories of all the people are etched in her mind, as well as their struggles and stories that they have shared with her. I learnt how important it was to keep an open door to the community you live in, how as a physician your patients become a part of your family, and to do what you can to help people around you and allow them to help you.

When it was time for lunch, my sister and I were always served our favourite foods including kovakka, cutlets, and fried fish. One day, Ammamma had a treat for us and had bought veal to make beef fry – also one of my favorite foods. When I bit into it, however, though it was delicious, I said, 'Maybe it is too soft.' When my Ammamma heard this, she responded saying, 'You should not cast pearls before swine.' I had to laugh. Ammamma always knew how to deliver her lessons with a hint of humour.

In the afternoon, Ammamma and Appappa would take us to see our cousins, Elsa and Tara. We would arrive at their house before they came home from school so that Lisa and I could practice piano and guitar. This was very difficult for Ammamma as it was an impossible task to get me to focus on something as boring as practicing an instrument. While Ammamma was not successful at getting me to practice an instrument, a few years later when I needed to study pre-algebra during the summer so that I could advance to a higher level in mathematics, Ammamma, again, needed to try and convince me to do something I did not want to do. It was difficult to convince me that this was a good use of my time, as it entailed studying during the summer for the purpose of taking a harder class. Because of Ammama, I was able to pass the exam and I moved ahead in the math class the following year. Now, looking back, I am happy I did this. When I struggle to play basic guitar chords, I wish I had practiced the guitar more. In those afternoons, I certainly learnt about persevering and the importance of doing things that weren't always interesting. More importantly, I learnt to always listen to Ammamma!

In the late afternoons, I would spend time with Appappa. We would either drive to their farm, collect fruits in the garden, go into Vellore town, or, when I was younger, build birdhouses out of wood. A very special memory of my Appappa is when he fashioned a baseball stand out of a car's tailpipe and commissioned a welder to build a basketball hoop, so that I could practice basketball and baseball. During these afternoons, we did not speak much, but I learnt how he thought and how his actions were slow but intentional. From my Appappa, I learnt how actions were far more important than words, and to think before you act or speak.

At night, Ammamma would put Lisa and me to bed. Here we would hear more stories about Appappa and Ammamma's parents and grandparents, siblings, and teachers. Though I would never call my Ammamma a 'storyteller,' she is excellent at keeping us engaged with the various details of her experiences, and I will always want more stories from her.

Now, we do not have 3 months every year to spend with Appappa and Ammamma, but I still try to speak with them as much as possible. My conversations with Ammamma consist of her telling me details of their day or old stories that are appropriate for whatever problem I seem to be facing at the time. My conversations with Appappa are still as brief and to the point as always. My day does not feel complete until I talk to them, and I continue to learn lessons from them as they face their daily challenges. They are my best friends, and I will carry their lessons with me always.

————·•·————

Our Granddaughter, Lisa Aley Alexander

Lisa is our little princess. Right from her early childhood, she was very independent. When she was about seven, she hurt her brother by being rude. She waited for a few moments and then came down the stairs singing, ' I came back to say I'm soddy, I made you kwy, kwy, kwy like a fool I went and hurt you----- ' It ended with a big hug for Yohan and all was well again. She would adjust easily and never bore a grudge against anyone. I remember a time when Yohan had to have a minor surgery and as he was recovering, both Alex and Priya were with him. Lisa just about six, and I waited in a small waiting room outside. I was ready with snacks and juices and books to satisfy Lisa for an hour or two. She was uneasy after a time, obviously tired and bored of waiting. She looked at me saying, ' Ammamma I want to go to the toilet.' There was no toilet in the vicinity and I said, 'Really Lisa?' ' No, Ammamma,' she said shaking her head. Then, realising that she had told a fib, she looked me in the eye and asked anxiously, 'Ammamma, is my nose growing ?' I did not know whether to laugh or cry! That was Lisa through and through. She learnt to adapt quickly and saw the better side of everything and everyone. Lisa adores her brother and holds him in high esteem. On her first day in the Montessori school, she went up to Yohan's teacher and said, 'Please take good care of him!'

Lisa was a little charmer and that worked with her father especially. She had a lovely voice, but when asked to sing, would take off 'Amazing grace' in a falsetto voice, that we had to ask her to stop! As she grew up, she was chosen to sing in the Honours Choir and that she did beautifully. She is an avid reader as well. In the bitter cold of Minnesota, she had no hesitation in participating in social protests in support of the wronged and underprivileged.

She was a 'lawyer' at home, with her friends and in the place of work as well. She has grown into a loving, thoughtful young woman, always conscious about the helpers at home and their children. The fact that they have so much less than us is a deep concern of hers. Lisa is extremely sensitive to people's feelings and that has gained her many friends, who stand by her when in need.

———•●•———

Lisa's Memories

Every memory I have from a young age has a glimmer of my Ammamma and Appappa in it. I can't begin to think about the person I would be, without them. When we first moved to America, I remember being excited, as my mother had been away from us for a couple of months. While for any other children, this might have been terrifying, I remember my Ammamma being there with me and making the journey an adventure, rather than something to be scared of. My first memory from our home in Boston is filled with laughter because of my Ammamma opening the back door into the backyard with complete confidence that it was a bathroom. To be around my Ammamma was to fill memories and time with joy, love, and faith. Not only did my Ammamma create a childhood full of joy, but she was also influential in teaching me values, generosity, and kindness. A great example is when Ammamma was packing her bag for India. She had packed her bag with a couple of copies of 'Our Daily Bread' to take home to family. For some reason, this was too much for me to handle, and I became distraught that Ammamma was 'taking all of our books'. While I threw a tantrum that I can now laugh at, Ammamma handled the situation with utmost grace. She returned all the books and waited patiently to be able to have a conversation with me about why her taking the books upset me so much. Once I had settled down and shared my perspective, Ammamma taught me about the importance of generosity and sharing when possible.

That was Ammamma, always teaching me lessons with gentleness and clarity. When I would sleep in and miss breakfast with the family, Ammamma gently reminded me 'that time and tide waits for no man'. When Yohan and I would hurl accusations at who was responsible for some mischievous accident, Ammamma would emphasize that we shouldn't find sticks in others' eyes when we have logs in our own.

One of the most important lessons my Ammamma taught me, is how a woman can do and be so much. Not only was my Ammamma an incredible OBGYN who strived to serve Christ and so many people in the community, but she was also a talented artist. She was a whizz at embroidery and, later in life, found her passion for quilling. She also efficiently managed the house, planning meals, cleaning, and organization. While I owe much of who I am and what I know to my grandmother, we also had our good share of uninhibited fun. I think of grace and blessings when I think of Ammamma. I also remember her accompanying my brother and me to Canobie Lake Park during church trips. She even assisted me in my mischief occasionally as she would quickly eat all the food I couldn't finish at Appuammachy's (her sister's) dinner table. Or even recently, when Ammamma and Appappa would completely decimate me in Scrabble or Othello, and I could never help but laugh as we read out our final scores.

As for my Appappa, he was always present in my childhood, in a different way than my Ammamma. He was always a sense of security in our visits to India. When we were coming to India for the summer, my Appappa would never stop looking for new activities for me and Yohan to do and to learn from. One activity was taking us to see the different farmlands they care for and teaching us about the land; another would be cutting up coconuts with Yohan or taking us to the basketball court to play with other kids. One of my favourites was when he called the coconut tree climber who would cut down the coconuts in my grandparent's backyard. I loved watching how skilfully the man would use rubber straps between his hands and feet to help propel himself up the tree. This memory symbolizes one of the greatest lessons that my Appappa taught me, which was to admire the skills, talents, and beauty that people in our lives have. My talent that my grandfather always encouraged me to share and admired is my love for singing. When I was young, I remember singing Amazing Grace so poorly on purpose to make everyone laugh. I would belt the song with many voice cracks and flat notes and never let on that it wasn't my actual singing voice. Even though I sounded pretty awful and any sensible person would beg me to get another hobby, my Appappa only encouraged me to keep trying and get better. I stopped doing the lousy singing voice bit and even joined competitive choirs in high school. My Appappa heard that I was in choirs and never failed to ask me to sing him a song. Though I am not shy in many ways, singing solo is where my bashfulness finds me. And though I usually find a way to weasel out of singing a solo for my Appappa, he never fails to ask with a big smile on his face. I love seeing the joy on his face when he asks me for such a simple favour, as he is so excited to see his grandchild's talent. Appappa also shared his talents with me. My first memory of a strategy game is absolutely tied with Appappa. I remember looking over his shoulder as he played solitaire quietly on his laptop or filled out a sudoku puzzle. Though I was pretty young, Appappa still took the time to show me how to play the game, and I would log onto the computer and try to replicate his winning strategies. Now I wake up, open every New York Times game (wordle, connections, the crossword), and send my achievements to my friends. I learnt to love games that mentally challenged me through watching my grandfather's passion for it. Appappa also taught us lessons in a different way to Ammamma.

While Ammamma made sure to teach us as we went through life, Appappa taught us amazing lessons through action. He showed me the importance of keeping yourself busy with hobbies and talents, which I highly appreciate now that I'm older. When my Amma and Appa moved to the United States with us, my Ammamma came with my Appa to help settle us, the children, in Boston. When we moved to Minnesota, Ammamma and Appappa were some of the first to stay with us and make our new house, a home. I cannot imagine being the person I am now without them. I cannot thank God enough for all the blessings in my life, especially the two people I call Appappa and Ammamma.

———————•●•———————

Our Nieces And Nephews

Abraham

Every time I became an uncle and held the newest little one in my arms, it felt like the first time I held a niece or nephew – a delightful experience of looking into those sleepy eyes and coaxing a tiny smile. Having the little ones snuggle into my arms made me feel very protective of them. Then at a later stage, experienced the joy of having them run and jump into my arms as soon as they saw me. Although it was the busiest time of my life, I enjoyed every opportunity to be with them and play with them and generally be there for them as they grew up. Each one of them brought something wonderful into my life. I love being their Manu Mama and am so grateful for their love and as I get older, for their friendship, which I cherish.

————•●•————

Elizabeth (Liz)

Manu Mama is my mother's youngest brother. He and Sulo Ammai and their children were my family during the 5 years of schooling and working as an Occupational Therapist (OT) at CMC.

Coming from Canada, I must admit being quite confused when everyone else also referred to him as 'Uncle', until I heard the oft told story of how they met. One of my recollections is doing rounds with Manu Mama during the newly formed community health OT placement. Having heard of his strict reputation during rounds, I cowered in the back hoping he wouldn't call on me.

There are many memories that have stayed with me over the years: Manu Mama's affable nature and wry sense of humour; Sulo Ammai's marvellous eggplant curry and artistic needlework; and of course, growing up with Priya's bubbly and infectious charm, and young Vinod's sweet nature and fine-tuned ear. And the towering presence of Sulo Ammai's father and the quiet grace of her mother added to my family away from home.

What has influenced my career is Manu Mama's and Sulo Ammai's compassion for the vulnerable and their mutual passion for community health. My daily lunch with them for over 5 years offered glimpses into developing the physical, social and financial health of the population. For example, hearing how Manu Mama convinced the bank to finance sewing machines for the village women to improve their welfare and the prospect of their families' well-being. This is what I now know as addressing the social determinants of health.

———••———

Vinita Chacko

Manu Mama, Dr. Abraham Joseph, the universal 'Uncle' of CMC is my mother's youngest brother; my real uncle or Mama —

Manu Mama as we fondly called him. From childhood we looked forward to the visits of Manu Mama and Sulo Ammai. They were the youngest and the most fun-loving couple and my favourite amongst all my aunts and uncles. Sulo Ammai was, and still is, the greatest storyteller. All of us cousins sat around her in splits of laughter, listening to her tales, most of them were about the hilarious things my Manu Mama did.

Even though they were both busily involved with their work at CMC Vellore, they valued and appreciated family time. Manu Mama travelled widely as an international consultant, and he made it a point to seek out relatives in every place and visit them, even if for a short while. Humility, love and always considering others before themselves were their core characteristics.

For me, they were a role model in so many ways. As a couple they demonstrated Godly love for one another, and you can see that even today. Their marriage has been an example for us and many others. When I studied at WCC, they were my local guardians. Observing the way they handled their children, the housework and hospital work, I learnt so much on parenting, and how to have a healthy life-work balance. Their two amazing children Priya and Vinod are a testimony to this. Strong Biblical values that they practiced was the foundation for everything they did.

It is amazing to see how they used their lives to bless and build up so many lives.

———•♦•———

Sunil Daniel Thomas

Manu Uncle as he is affectionately known has always been much loved in our family. As a child I was in boarding school and some holidays were spent with them. I remember joining the family for Christmas carols and the joy of getting a present at church along with the other kids, although we weren't there with our parents. I also have fond memories of visits from them when we were in boarding school – which were a wonderful treat.

Later in life, I lived with them for a few months while preparing for exams and got to meet my cousins' classmates, when they visited. It was inspiring to meet the medical students and though I never made it through the entrance exams, their hospitality to me and others was a learning experience.

Manu uncle although busy, always had a kind word and encouragement for me which I will always appreciate. More recently after my father passed away, I cherish the time he took in sharing his recollections of my father with me. His humour and love for my father have been a blessing.

His example of service to the community is one I have never had the courage to follow, but maybe in time I may. He has been an anchor for me as an example of a life well lived and I feel privileged to be a part of his family.

None of this would have been possible without Sulo Aunty. We have this vision of aunty rushing around between home and hospital, running with her inhaler tucked into her crisp cotton sari. We always knew she was the engine, driving the family behind the scenes, unsung but always with a smile and infectious energy. She regales us with stories and anecdotes of us as little children bringing a smile of embarrassment from me when she recounts some of my more mischievous moments.

Her home was most welcoming and I have been the recipient of so much of her hospitality. In a happy twist of fate, I am married to the daughter of one of her close college friends, who was delivered by aunty at CHAD all those years ago.

---·•·---

Vijay Verghese

Uncle and Sulo Aunty have been a big part of my life for as long as I can remember. They gave me a children's version of 'Pilgrim's Progress' soon after I learnt to read and it had a deep and abiding effect on my spiritual journey.

Once we made a trip to Vellore and visited CODES. I remember seeing lines and lines of baskets and my parents evaluating and buying baskets.

Manu Uncle didn't teach me directly in college, but he would check on me, encourage me and challenge me throughout my MBBS and post graduation. I recall a time four years before I joined MBBS. I was still at school. Three of my classmates and I were visiting Vellore to get some exposure to medicine. Our school had arranged for us to be given a tour of the hospital by someone. But after we arrived in Vellore that person wasn't available. As soon as Manu Uncle found out that we had time on our hands, he arranged for us to be exposed to Community Health instead of CMC Hospital. We sat down in a CHTC classroom and a social worker, I think his name was Ranjit, opened our minds to the social determinants of health. It struck me then that health was determined largely by things that happened outside of hospitals and so needed to be addressed through multiple fields of work among and with local communities. We then joined a mobile clinic team and saw community health in practice. When I started medical school, I think I was already sold on the idea of community health. As fascinating as some of my other subjects were, and I came close to choosing some of them for my career, the bigger picture was more important to me. There were and have been other influences that drew me to Community Medicine, but Manu Uncle's intervention planted a seed. When it was time to decide what to apply for, nothing seemed as worthwhile to me as Community Medicine.

His success was to a large extent his ability to motivate and lead people. At CHAD his core team was a diverse and extremely competent group of people who are all titans in their own right. I wonder how he brought about a common vision that held the team together. The work culture he established at CHAD is unique and gave birth to the processes and systems that made CHAD what it is today. I've worked in or with Community Medicine departments in 3 other institutions and I believe the reason for the difference between the CHAD story and the discouraging state of most other departments is the culture that was established and has been passed on.

As a medical educator, he established a community based medical education program which was a radical educational innovation that was far ahead of its time at its inception. It has been a transformative experience for students over successive decades.

Sulo Aunty was the Head of Community Medicine during my undergraduate studies. During socio-economic case presentations in the department and later in private, she perceived needs and was motivated to act on those needs.

As undergraduates, we were tasked with preparing for College Day and Graduation events. There were faculty who volunteered to help with specific preparations. A friend of mine was working on the jasmine chain, and he was shocked to find Dr. Sulochana sitting on the ground working on the chain with her hands, right there alongside students and support staff. He came and told me later that he couldn't get over the fact that a Professor and the Head of Department was doing that. It flew in the face of many of the values that are embedded in academia and society in general.

————•₀•————

Marianne Thomas (Anupama)

They say it takes a village to raise a child, and I was fortunate to be loved by what seems like a village full of aunts and uncles who saw me through my childhood and teenage years. My mother Sara's, younger brother, Manu Mama and his wife Sulo Ammai were always an important part of my life. Being just three years apart in age, Amma and Manu Mama shared a close bond and their affection for each other reached out to us their children too.

As an obstetrician and gynecologist, Sulo Ammai was present in my life right from the very day I was born. Their commitment to their work was unwavering, yet one of them would always be there to show their love and support for our family. Sulo Ammai was there to bless me on my arrival to this world, and Manu Mama came to visit when my brother was born.

Until I was ten, we met almost every summer at the Pamba river-side residence of my grandparents in Maramon, for the annual family gathering. A closer mentoring association began with Manu Mama when my brother Rohan and I came to Chennai. For the next ten years, our school holidays were divided between five places- Calicut, Maramon, Vellore, Nilambur and Bangalore. At Vellore, it was Mama's 'doctor's bungalow' – the first one we can still see as we leave CHAD – a cool building surrounded by shady tamarind trees beside the canal. Whether it be matters of faith or values or life lessons, I learnt those from Mama and Ammai not so much by words, but through observing their example and adopting it.

People in our school or work circles walk with us for a while, but family is lifelong. I watched and learnt from Manu Mama and Ammai through confirmation ceremonies, weddings, and funerals of various family members. I have learnt from watching Manu Mama about being a caring sibling, spouse, son-in-law, father-in-law, and grandparent. I saw him stand by Sulo Ammai through her parents' and siblings' passings; and be beside his daughter-in-law Priya through the accident of her mother and later the sudden loss of her father. I have seen him zipping to Bangalore in his famous red Qualis after retirement, to help out his granddaughter in distress. I saw him serve missions in the far Northeast of India, post-retirement when most people want to slow down. We weren't done yet. Mama and Ammai became our primary support for almost a decade from the detection of my Amma's cancer to helping her resettle in Vellore till she passed on in 2015. Today as I write this, my family has lost all but two of Mama's siblings; Manu Mama and his older sister, my aunt Leela . Manu Mama stands as a testament to how God's radiant glory can shine through us in every season of life. I am so grateful that I am his niece and for the opportunity to have been touched by his very special light.

———••———

Sulo – My Memories of Ravi.

I can never forget my nephew Ravi's birthday – the 3rd of September, 1962. It was the same year that I appeared for the CMC entrance examination. I had German Measles at that time and so missed seeing my sister who was expecting Ravi. Sadly I could not be around to see my little nephew when he was born. When I did get to see him, he was a plump little baby, who would go into fits of laughter at the drop of a hat. He would leap into my outstretched arms, grab my plait or ear and start sucking his thumb.

Back in Vellore, after I joined CMC as a medical student, I would seize every opportunity to visit my sister to play with my little nephew.

Ravi was one for coining names. Sulokochamma became 'Shokko.' To this day, all my nephews, and niece and their children and the children of colleagues call me Shokko. I just love this endearing term.

I was fortunate to spend much of my free time, and 3 years after my MBBS working in CMC, staying at my sister's house. Priya was born on August 10, 1970, and the siblings Ravi, Raghu and Rachel were overjoyed to have little 'Kochupappa' with them.

Ravi was a very thoughtful child and as he grew up became even more so. Knowing how much we liked the National Geographic Magazine, he would send me a parcel of these year after year.

When I visited my daughter in Rochester, Ravi made it a point to bring Mia his daughter and son Eli 'to get to know Shokko and

Manchi better.' He hasn't changed much over the years, he is still the same with his loud laughter, love and thoughtfulness.

————•••————

Ravi Mani's Memories

I have known Sulochana (my aunt whom I nicknamed Shokko) my entire life. Shokko was my mother's youngest sibling and still at Women's Christian College, Madras when I was born. The only thing I can say about Shokko is that she is Love Unqualified. Regardless of who you are – whether a friend, colleague, nephew, niece, cousin, there is just love. No complaints, no qualifiers, no questions, just pure love. If you have a question or concern, there is an open channel and then she will let you know her opinions. It is still your life and you make the decisions. And regardless of the decision – unabashed, unqualified love. We should all strive to emulate this quality of my aunt Shokko.

When you see Uncle Manchi, look out for that twinkle in his eyes. That brain – always thinking, always looking for solutions for problems not yet defined, always pushing you to be the best you can be.

I have always known that if any questions, concerns or issues arise, both Manchi and Shokko can be counted on to go the extra mile for us. This is not a family obligation or friendship issue – you just ask and they will do what they can.

They are a matched pair, Shokko is the pragmatic, implementer of the solution while Manchi is the innovator, thinker and tinkerer. I love them both dearly.

————•••————

My Memories of Raghu

Raghu was born on July 24th, 1964, second in line in the Mani M. Mani family and the first grandchild to be named after his maternal grandfather Kuruvila Jacob. From the word go, one look at his bright eyes and wide grin, you could see that he was full of mischief and also that he had a mind of his own. When he was a little over 2, his maternal grandmother would fondly make little bloomers and matching shirts and painstakingly embroider animals or birds from all those nursery rhymes that he had learnt. Raghu would refuse to wear anything of the kind, unlike Ravi who made no fuss at all.

My sister left for America for 6 months for the last part of Ranji's study leave, so my mother came over to help us out. Everything was organized so well. My only duty was to pack and send food for the two boys and supervise their homework. On many occasions Raghu drove me up the wall with his pranks. One evening Muniamma, the helper called out to me as Raghu was walking a goose with the end of a rope tied to it's leg. I wasn't sure whether it was retaliation in support of his brother, who had been bullied by the owner of the goose.

Soon we were allotted a new house in Harley Street, not too far from Shanti Illam. Vinod our son was born in the midst of all the shifting and chaos. Although Ravi, Raghu and Rachel were not happy about us moving into another house, Raghu who was fed up with all of Shokko's rules announced, 'My Dekku and Amma will be coming back soon. I will not come to your house after that'. A few days later, after their parents got back, Muniamma knocked at our door to hand over a basket of eggs. I could see Raghu peering from behind Muniamma. He called out to me very timidly, 'Shokko, can I stay with you from now on?'

Raghu has not lost his mischievous twinkle and hearty chuckle but most importantly has evolved into a fine human being. His capacity for compassion, love and caring has been an anchor on which we as a family has often leaned on. He stood by me several times and specially after my brother's demise . His family relations further fostered by his lovely wife Julie 's determination to build family ties has manifested in innumerable ways. Raghu, Julie and their two lovely daughters Anjali and Asha have visited us regularly every three to four years. Manchi and I look forward to these visits.

————••————

Raghu's Memories

I have always felt fortunate that I grew up in a household where my aunts and uncles were important parts of our lives. The bond that my mother had with her sister was very special. That closeness extended to us to the point that my brother, sister and I felt that we had not one, but two mothers. Growing up in Vellore and then visiting Vellore in the summers after we moved to the US, my relationship with my aunt and uncle continued to evolve, but the closeness I feel to them has never changed. They have always been Shokko and Manchi.

My memories of my early childhood days with them come primarily from Shokko's stories about us growing up on the CMC campus. Especially during 1970-71- when my parents were in the US, leaving the care of the three of us to our grandmother and our aunt. I have no memories of those days, but Shokko has endless stories about the three of us and all the trouble we caused.

My primary memories in Vellore come from our extended visits in the summer. We would arrive from Madras by train and they would be waiting for us at the train station and we would go to their little house on the Bagayam campus. On a much later visit, I walked by that old house, and it was tiny. I have no idea how they squeezed all of us in there for our summer visits. As children, we had no idea how busy they must have been back then. Working at CHAD, having two young children of their own, and having all of us visit. What I remember is that they made time for us despite the responsibilities of their jobs. We would have raucous games of Monopoly where the rules were only guidelines. We learnt very quickly that Manchi was extremely competitive when it came to games of all kinds and we loved that he would make time to play with us.

The other memory that stands out was when we would leave Vellore by train, and Shokko would stand in the station waving and sobbing as we left. Shokko told me later that our being halfway around the world was really hard on her as she felt that part of her heart was being ripped apart every time we left, as she never knew when she would see us again.

One year that stands out was the year both of them spent studying in the U.S. Their children, Priya and Vinod stayed with us and became part of our family in Kansas City. My brother and I moved out of our bedroom and it was given over to Priya and Vinod. To us, it was the same as when our parents went to the U.S. to study and we enjoyed being in a full house with all five of us together. To this date, Vinod and Priya are as close to me as my siblings.

When I finished college, I came for an extended visit to Vellore. This was when I learnt that they were actually working professionals. I got to see them working in their jobs and was exposed to some of the innovations they were doing at CHAD. This continued to be the theme for my next visit, when Julie and I came after we were married. Manchi took us around to visit the villages as well to see some of their other endeavors including the CODES project. As a young professional in the business world, it was amazing to see the level of complexity that they were implementing in Vellore. I remember thinking back then that it was the type of work that should be made into a Harvard Business Case study on how to change a community organically. As I learnt more about the mission of CMC, it is clear that they exemplify the CMC Motto in all that they do: *Not to be ministered unto but to minister.*

I have thoroughly enjoyed the next stages of our lives, getting to know them from a completely different perspective. Watching Manchi delve into agriculture at the same time that I was becoming a farmer in the U.S. has been a lot of fun. We do things completely differently in the U.S. but tasting a ripe mango or ripe peach off the tree is just as delicious no matter the country. Shokko still talks about the time I sent a box of peaches to her when she was visiting Priya in Boston. I can match that story on a visit to Vellore in late August to find that my uncle had stored some mangoes in straw just so they would keep for my visit.

As I find myself reminiscing about growing up with my aunt and uncle, there are so many things about them that are special. From the deep relationship they have with each other; to the incredibly close family connections with their children, grandchildren, siblings, cousins, nieces, and nephews; to the incredible legacy they built at CHAD. But what I will remember most is the incredibly close relationship they had with my parents throughout their lives and especially during the pandemic when they were quarantined together in their house. My parents are gone now, but I know that I have another set of parents that are waiting for our next visit to Vellore.

My Memories of Rachel

Rachel, my only niece was born on 14th October, 1966. My sister was in labour but continued to work till it was time for her to deliver. I was in the 3rd year of my medical studies and as soon as I got the message of Rachel's arrival, I packed a small bag and arrived at the Mani's household to take care of – No! to keep company with the two boys till my sister arrived with baby Rachel.

Ranji left for the U.S. for his study leave for 3 years and I started my internship in June, 1969. My sister suggested that I stay with her and the 3 children. I was delighted with this idea as I didn't have to stay in the Lady Doctors quarters. I had all the meals with the family and enjoyed both the company and the wonderful home-cooked food. All three of them, Ravi, Raghu and Rachel would climb into the bed with me after dinner. The boys would finish their homework and join the storytelling sessions. After they had enough, the boys would retire to my sister's room for the night, whereas Rachel on a routine basis would pretend to be fast asleep. Then when she finally fell asleep, my sister would carry her back to her bedroom.

All of a sudden, almost at the end of my Obstetric posting of internship, my marriage to Manu was fixed for 15th September, 1969. One other person would be joining the family. Rachel though excited about attending Shokko -Manchi wedding was a little vary too. All she knew about weddings was the sound of blaring music and drums which we could hear regularly from across the wall where local wedding festivities were usually held. Rachel was excited practicing her part for the wedding, 'dum dakka, dum dakka Shokkokku Kalyanam.'

In June, 1970, I finished my internship and planned to join the Clinical Pathology Department as a Demonstrator for two years. We were expecting our first child. On the day I joined work, I had premature labour pains and had to take leave for a month and be on strict bed rest. My constant companions were the 3 'Rs' and particularly Rachel who rushed home from the nursery school to look after Shokko'. This was the time when Rachel and I became bosom pals. Priya was born in the early hours of the morning. The day after Priya and I arrived from the hospital, Rachel arrived from her school with Suji and Sashi and 2 or 3 other friends.

Once more we had to shift – this time to Harley Street, very close to Shanti illam. Ravi, Raghu and Rachel helped us shift and were excited about the new baby who was to arrive soon. Vinod was born on the 16th July, 1971, just over three weeks before Priya's first birthday.

The 3 R's visited us almost every day. In the next few years, we moved to the Thoracic quarters and then to the house in the Rural Health Centre campus. The role played by the Mani family has indeed contributed to the relationship which has lasted for over half a century.

———•●•———

Rachel's Memories

Shokko, my beloved aunt believed that the meaning of life was to share love and make it easily accessible for everyone to experience. Her nurturing nature and genuine interest in people created a warm and welcoming environment. Her house was an open place where we grew, learnt, thrived, and learnt to love each other.

Her kind demeanor, warm smile, and gentle but firm ways, demonstrated the humanity we all should experience. She treated people of all ages with kindness and respect. Teasing each other for fun was tolerated and encouraged.

Shokko was a mother figure to me and my brothers. She played a significant role throughout my life, especially my early life, helping my parents raise us when they went to the U.S. Over the years, I have modelled how I parent my children and grandchildren, nieces, and nephew with the same approach I learnt from them. I enjoy her playfulness on our WhatsApp chats which keeps her active in our lives.

Shokko allowed me to be a curious child, encouraging exploration and creativity while establishing a balance between play and following rules. She has many stories about our antics and smiles with approval as she shares them with others.

She and her husband, Manchi, exemplified a beautiful partnership in marriage. They supported each other's visions, cared for one another, and contributed positively to their family and community. Both share a love of food and sharing the bounty of their harvests especially with the 'manga thera'. I enjoy their playful banter and concern for everyone in their life. I have seen that faith is the strength that holds them together.

Shokko cherishes her relationships with family members, particularly her close bond with my mother and her 'sibling' connection with my father. She shared stories and maintained strong connections, emphasizing the importance of family ties. Shokko took such good care of her parents and my parents. We all feel the love halfway around the world.

Shokko taught me that preparing and sharing food with love, grace, and laughter was essential. The table was a place for conversation and enjoyment and food was a means of nourishing both the body and soul.

I learnt culinary skills and the art of layering flavors from Shokko. Her expertise in the kitchen allowed you to experiment with dishes and recipes. The lessons on how to caramelize onions before adding in the garlic and ginger, when to add the spices and how to cook rice properly gave me the foundation for cooking professionally. I remember making spring rolls and momos from scratch in the hot kitchen in Vellore, the lesson was roll faster and fill quickly. The taste still lingers.

The kitchen became a space of bonding for both of us. She encouraged me to share my American recipes with her and we would discuss how to make apple pie or her favourite chicken pot pie in Vellore.

Shokko's talents extended to various art forms, from embroidery to quilling. Her attention to detail and passion for creativity inspired me and others. She made beautiful sarees and dresses that my mother and I still cherish.

Shokko's openness to learning new things, including quilling after her eyesight began to deteriorate taught me the importance of embracing new skills and experiences. Her willingness to share what she learnt and not fear the unknown served as a valuable lesson. She encouraged discussions on a wide range of topics, fostering a culture of curiosity and continuous learning. Watching her, I learnt not only how to talk to people, but to listen to them as well, as if what they were saying was the most important thing. I am so grateful to have Shokko who has influenced my values and actions, shaping my approach to family, relationships, creativity, and personal growth. She continues to live on through the lessons she imparted and the memories I cherish.

Sulo's Memories of Bikku

Bikku, my brother Chakko's (Achachan) and Susie's first son was born in Trivandrum. Bikku was named Kuruvila after my father. He changed his name to Bikku, a shortened version of Baby Kuruvila.

Achachan, Susie and Bikku along with Ashwin who was just a baby, moved to Bombay where Achachan worked as a Nephrologist in Jaslok Hospital. Prior to one of their visits to Vellore, Bikku and Vinod had a conversation about cars. Bikku told Vinod that his father had a Mercedes Benz car. We did not have a car at that time and Vinod was at a loss. He could only think of his own father being in charge of the Rural Health Centre in Bagayam, Vellore. So he promptly told Bikku that his father (Abraham) was the Governor of Bagayam. On the day of their arrival at Katpadi station, Vinod pleaded with his father to rent the red Volkswagon that belonged to CHAD to meet Achachan and family at the station. Bikku was suitably impressed that his cousin Vinod's father, the Governor of Bagayam had a red Volkswagon. Bikku, Vinod and Ashwin included Priya in their play time when they found it convenient to have her around. Otherwise,' no, no she is a girl' was the routine chorus. Bikku, Monisha, his wife and Kabir, their son, came for Elsa's wedding. Even though it was too short a visit, we enjoyed it.

Bikku Kuruvila's Memories

I remember Shokko and Manchi for their great warmth and love and the wonderful welcome we were always given whenever we came to Vellore. This is what I associate most with them as a nephew — the love and warmth. Yet I know there is so much more to them. I remember going with Shokko on visits to the villages outside of Vellore to see their thoughtful public health work with leprosy patients in the 90s that bridged understandings in different professional disciplines long before it seemed fashionable in the Western academy. Working with a national institute in Delhi in the early 2010s, I also know the deep professional regard that CHAD, CMC under their leadership was held by policy leaders nationally. They certainly exemplify deeply the spirit of service that CMC has cultivated and is known for nationwide.

Ashwin Mathai Chakko

Ashwin is the younger son of my brother and Susie. Shortly after his birth, the family moved to Bombay and lived in the quarters provided in Jaslok Hospital. Ashwin, from the time we saw him, was a happy, friendly, chubby little baby with a twinkle in his eyes. From the time he could walk, he was mischievous. In their house, he would walk up to the refrigerator and have a go at the

'After Eights' one at a time and put the empty covers back into the box!

Bikku and Ashwin on their visits to Vellore would stay with my parents in the Kamalakshipuram house. In the evenings, they would come over to our house and my father would take them back home. Ashwin visited us several times and each time was memorable. Judy, our half cocker spaniel showed signs of delivering. Vinod, Ashwin and I waited anxiously for a while when Judy ran from one wall to the other. After three pups were born, I had to go to the hospital for a caesarean section. Ashwin promised to watch out for more pups. When I returned, Ashwin with great excitement told me that there were two more pups. We cleaned the room and we were just about ready to call it a day when there was one more. Finally, after all the cleaning was done, we went to bed. Early in the morning, Ashwin came running to tell us that there was one more!

After my retirement, we moved to the house in Kamalakshipuram where my parents had once lived. Ashwin visited us for a couple of days and kept himself busy cleaning up the yard, planting stone pillars, digging up the front yard to get it ready for a lawn etc. After dinner that night, Manu and I retired to our bedroom upstairs and Ashwin proceeded for a bath. Early in the morning next day, he came to enlighten us of what had happened. He went in for a bath and after he had soaped himself thoroughly, the water ran out. He desperately tried to wake us up and since there was no response from upstairs, he searched for stored water. In despair, he took two bottles of ice water from the refrigerator to wash off the soap and had an ice cold bath. I have never heard the end of it.

Ashwin, Maya and their two children, Sachi and Jai have visited us here in Vellore and we had loads of fun. We look forward to their visits.

———•◦•———

Memories of Ashwin Mathai Chakko

My aunt, whom I call 'Shokko,' treats me with kindness, generosity, love and humor. I know that I am deeply loved by her, and that is something that carries me every single day of my life. When I would visit her home as a child, I would sleep in bed between my cousins, Priya and Vinod. Together, we ate, played and got into trouble as well. I know that I am deeply loved in the home of Shokko and my uncle, Abraham Joseph, whom I call 'Manchi.'

The home they created was a magical place and that is because of the kind of people they are. Vellore doesn't have all the consumer offerings of a big city. Nonetheless, Shokko made me feel that when I was with her, I had everything I needed in the world. She regularly cooked us breakfasts and dinners, which came before or after long days at work. She made yogurt and ice cream from scratch. To this day, I can still remember the taste of Shokko's ice cream.

One Christmas in the 1980s, either Priya or Vinod mentioned how they wished they could have a white Christmas tree, meaning a tree that would look as if it was covered in snow. I don't know if one of my cousins asked for it or if their tone indicated a yearning. Shokko said that we could have one. In an instant she went out into the garden and found a fallen branch with a nice shape. She got a pot, put the branch into it, and filled it with mud. We all went to a store and bought cotton and tinsel. That year, we had a glorious white Christmas tree. We had everything we needed.

My children have often heard me tell that story, a tale about my favorite Christmas tree ever. Last Christmas Eve, my son, Jai, who was then 10, said he wanted a Christmas tree. He went out and scoured the yard for a branch and other items. He brought them inside, and made our own tree. He said, ' It's Shokko's idea.' That is my second favorite tree ever -- one made possible by the imagination of my aunt.

This mindset of my aunt is remarkable, in part, because at times she did not believe that she could give her children what they needed in Bagayam, Vellore. Her father – my grandfather, Kuruvila Jacob, was a Padma Shri recipient recognised for his pioneering work in influencing schools in India. Shokko worried that maybe her children were not getting an elite education in Vellore and sometimes wished that she could afford to send them to one of the better boarding schools. My grandfather told her that if she so wished, he would certainly help the children get a place in a good boarding school. He also told her, that having an education in an elite school was not as important as having the children with their parents. It is humbling to know how true that was. I know it for my own life as my time with Shokko and Manchi has been precious to me.

It is remarkable to think of the life that Shokko and Manchi created. They each embody service. Before Manchi and Shokko married, a lifelong commitment to serving the poor, was what they promised each other.

My uncle, is an incredible doctor and logistician. He saw his patients as complete people. Shokko had a personal mission to make a difference in maternal health care. This takes personal commitment. Once, a man came to her saying that his wife was in labour. There was no car to take her to the patient in the village, so she just tucked up her sari and rode side saddle on the back of the man's bicycle. Shokko built up a labour and delivery ward that was delivering 300 babies a month by the end of her tenure.

As a teen, I used to ride in trucks with CMC students as they went to villages. Uncle, as Manchi was known had started a programme where medical students in their first year would interact with villagers. My cousin Priya was in one of the batches. Long lines of villagers would queue up, waiting to be seen. I still remember several of the questions because they were so striking. 'Do you know how to boil water?' 'Are you or is someone in your family pregnant?' 'If so, do you or they know where to get pre-natal and ante-natal care?' ' Do you have any untreated wounds?' These are simple questions, but, in answering them, a large percentage of critical issues are addressed, including infant mortality, cholera, and infection. These concepts have grounded me. I talk about them regularly at work. I am certainly grateful to them for the impact they have had on my work. But I would say that the deeper impact is in my heart. They love me deeply and care for me as if I were their own. They provide me with sustenance to live a life that honors my values.

———— •●• ————

Memories Of Our Loved Ones

Sulo

We were both raised with the idea that 'family' was a large number of cousins, aunts, uncles and anyone who had a link to our parental and ancestral families.

While we lived in Madras, my uncle Chandypappa and Chikku moved in with us after my aunt had passed on, when Chikku was only four.

After a few years, Chandypappa married Mariamma Kochamma who was a Lecturer in English at the Women's Christian College, Madras. Chikku and I made frequent trips to her house where she lived with her mother and younger brother. She had a wonderful ability to keep us interested in reading and in speaking good English. She also made lovely cakes and both of us used to vie with each other to lick the bowls and spoons till Mariamma Kochamma acquired a spatula. She made delicious ice cream with evaporated milk which would just melt in our mouths. When Chandypappa married Mariamma Kochamma, she became a second mother to me. Little Chandy was born when Chikku and I were 13 years old. With the new addition, the family moved from a flat in Nathan's Colony, to another house. While I just adored Chandypappa and his gentleness, I learnt much from Mariamma Kochamma. She cultivated in me a love for growing plants and my bougainvilleas and my first adeniums were from their house.

Holidays in those days were to Aymanam, which was my father's home town. My uncle Dr. Appachan, Kunjai Elemma and their two daughters, Renu and Raffia lived in a sprawling house with a beautiful garden. Every summer, Appa, Amma, Appu Kochamma, Achachan and I would spend a week or two with them. Chikku would also join us. Chikku, Raffia my cousin who was about the same age and I were partners in crime. We had splendid holidays as Kunjai Elemma was a meticulous planner. One weekend would be to the yacht club or to Munnar or Thekkadi. Appa's family house was on the bank of Meenachil river, where we spent endless hours bathing in the river. My father's youngest brother Thomachupappa and Elikutty Elemma were such good hosts. I remember the time I spent with them in Cochin where he was a Commander of the Indian Navy. Thomachupappa would keep us engaged with stories and songs. Elikutty Elemma was gentle, loveable and happy all the time. Saramma Kochamma, my father's youngest sister was a beautiful soul who would take Chikku and me to the river and make all kinds of interesting toys with coconut leaves.

As a child, I would write letters to Saramma Kochamma as she was my favourite aunt. Her house in Bangalore had an abundance of avocados and she would send a basket of avocados during the season to my father. Whenever we visited Bangalore, Manu, the children and I would often spend a day with her. Vinod would follow her around like a little lamb and one day he followed her to the kitchen when she was making curds. Very innocently he told her, 'Curds should only be made in a green bowl,' because he had only seen curds in a green bowl at home. Her last gift to Vinod was a green bowl for his house.

———••———

Thambichayan (Dr. George Cherian) and Leela Ammamma (Mrs. Leela Cherian)

Leela Ammamma, has been my heroine since I was 12 years old and to this day, she remains so. She first stole my heart with her talent in acting particularly in her role as Socrates in 'Barefoot in Athens.' I can distinctly remember the last prayer of Socrates requesting Xanthippe, his wife to repeat after him, 'Beloved Pan and all ye other Gods who haunt this city, give me beauty in the inward soul for outward beauty I am not likely to have.....' and the girl who acted as Xanthippe, while repeating the prayer broke down and continued the prayer, literally sobbing. As the curtain in the WCC auditorium closed, and the lights came on, almost all the audience, both young and old were dabbing their eyes.

Later, I saw Leela Ammamma after her marriage to Thambichayan, when she moved to Vellore. I saw her talents as a wife, a mother, and hostess. She modelled love, values of family stability; maximizing all God's richly provided gifts to be creative and fruitful, treating the helpers at home with love and respect and so many more important virtues. She brought cheer and joy into every interaction.

Thambichayan was my 'go to person', when I needed sound advice. I vividly remember one such instance when I was working in CHAD, and one of my senior colleagues reproached me for practically anything concerning my work. Thambichayan looked me straight in the eyes and said, 'Sulo you should stand on your own two feet and ignore all this. I have been through many such instances too,' to which I retorted, 'but Thambichayan you are a man.' His spontaneous response was, 'There is no difference between a man and a woman where work is concerned.'

Thambichayan was always kind and loving and had a twinkle in his eye that always put you at ease. His subtle humour would have us laughing.

Together Thambichayan and Leela Ammamma provided the finest example of a perfect marriage. Their love for each other and the joyful home wherein they raised three marvellous daughters – Minu, Neena and Rekha, served as a fine example for Manu and myself.

Over the years, Priya and Vinod, their spouses, and our grandchildren shared the same close relationship with the entire family especially with Rekha, Suresh, and the children.

———•●•———

Snippets And Memories

Dr. Palitha Abeykoon,
Director, Health Systems, WHO – SEARO

Professor Abraham Joseph, of CMC Vellore, is a very dear childhood friend. We 'lost' each other for 30 long years, and found each other again, very serendipitously. In the late 1950s, the two of us were classmates in a famous school – Trinity College, Kandy, situated in the hills of Ceylon. Among other common interests I recall we were members of the school relay team and I had to pass the baton to Abraham who did the last lap. Therefore, he got all the applause whereas we did all the hard running to get him there.

Abraham left Trinity and went back to India with his dad in the late 1950s and I lost touch with him completely. That was until 30 years later when I was working with the WHO in Delhi and attended a Medical Education Conference at AIIMS. I heard the Master of Ceremonies inviting Professor Abraham Joseph to make the presentation. It immediately rang a bell. I may not have recognised the bearded professor who came on stage, if not for the name and the characteristic walk. He had not grown much taller. I introduced myself and he immediately remembered me. It was such a happy moment full of emotion and nostalgia. We compared our notes for the three 'lost' decades – our careers and families and everything else. Since then, we have spent a lot of time together and our families have grown closer to one another. I have visited Vellore on numerous occasions for work and Abraham has been a regular examiner at our post-graduate Public Health examinations.

We have attended many conferences in Medical Education and Public Health all over the world and Abraham has contributed immensely to our work in the WHO. I find his company very stimulating, and it is heartening for the two of us to realize that we continue to steadfastly honour the values that we imbibed at Trinity College, seven decades ago. This is a snippet of our memories of our close friendship with the 30-year hiatus.

Dr. Cyril Mathai, Manu – My Childhood Friend

Abraham Joseph was always Manu to me. I recall meeting him when I was around 4 or 5, he was bigger and taller than me, and I always looked up to him, and still do. We were in Ceylon, later to become Sri Lanka. Manu lived in Asgiriya, a suburb of Kandy. My father and his father hailed from the same part of Kerala. Maramon. The two families would visit, they would come down to Matale or we would travel to Kandy. To me, Asgiriya was a fun place, Manu was always entertaining to me and my brother Cecil. We would keep him company on his routine chores. Taking out the cows and fastening to a tree or peg where there was ample grass to graze. Checking the well to make certain the pump was functional. There was also a big fish or two in the well, to keep the water clean. If the pump failed, Manu would have to carry buckets full of water up the many steps to the kitchen. Cecil and I would help, but it was quite a tough and tiring task.

On some days, Manu would have to go for cricket practice as he played for the Trinity College team. We would follow him to the practice field which was not far from his home. He was a fabulous batsman and fielder, we little folk would watch in awe, aspiring to be like him when we grew up. He was also a terrific athlete excelling at Track and Field. It was always a pleasure and privilege to watch him, when he ran and played for Scudder House in Vellore, many years later. About sports in Vellore, he was called Uncle then, and Uncle was into everything, even acting on stage. One of his favorite events for Sports Day was the 400 meters, and he was good at it. When I entered Vellore four years after him, it was my favorite event too. But I just couldn't compete against him, it didn't somehow seem right. I had several other events to choose from and one was allowed only five events for Sports Day. I had to wait until he stopped participating for Sports Day to run the 400 meters.

———••———

Dr. Lee Hoo Teong

'Uncle' Abraham Joseph was my roommate along with Graham Nathaniel Morrit in Room 123 at the Men's Hostel. They served the Christian Mission according to the dictum of our noble founder Aunt Ida Scudder whose motto was *'To minister and not to be ministered unto.'*

During the first year we were not very scholastic, especially the three of us. We loved playing a prank on each other and took part in sports and all the extracurricular activities.

Uncle was very active in the SCM. This was my first introduction to Christianity. He was active in the Men's Hostel management team and the College Students Association. He readily took part in several hostel and college dramatics and musicals. After his graduation, he went on to become a very dedicated Christian Mission doctor, first in CMC Vellore , then in Karigiri and later in Nagaland .

------••------

Dr. Johnny Oommen

The year was 1987. I had worked for a year in CHAD as a non-PG Registrar for the first year of my bond and was leaving to do my second year in Bissamcuttack, Odisha. I had enjoyed my work throughout the year. It was hard work, we were short of people. I used to spend 10 – 12 hours each day in the hospital, filling gaps and fully engaged. Just before leaving, I went to say goodbye to Uncle, expecting a vote of thanks and a 'well-done-good-and-faithful-servant' kind of speech. No way!

He said, 'Ah, so you are leaving for a Mission Hospital in Odisha. Very good. There are some things I have been wanting to tell you that I have noticed about you. You tend to be quite rude. You don't respect your seniors. You can be quite arrogant. Now, don't behave like that when you go to this new place. Don't say, 'In Vellore we do it like this'. They may have a reason for doing it in their own way. Keep quiet and learn before you change anything.'

I was livid. I was insulted. I was seething inside. But I did my namaskars and left. The problem was that everything he said was 100 % true. And it hurt. But once I had gotten off my high horse and thought through what he said on the long train ride to Odisha, I realized how valuable the advice was. And it held me in good stead. Thirty – six years later, I am still in Bissamcuttack; still reasonably arrogant; but able to get on a little better with others.

I am afraid we PG students were a tough lot, in CHAD, in the early nineties. And after one such disagreement with authority, Uncle called me aside and told me something very interesting. He said, 'You know, what you are saying is actually right. But the way you say it, is the problem. You are grandstanding, making it a prestige issue, where, if I have to agree with you, I have to lose face. So I resist. Then what happens? The issue that you were raising loses out. So you need to decide whether your aim is to get the issue addressed well or is it to score points and prove what a great guy you are.'

Again, brilliant, brutally honest advice that has held me in great stead since.

————•••————

Dr. Gift Norman

In 1976, I was a fourth-year student at Christian Medical College (CMC) when I first encountered Dr. Abraham Joseph, Uncle as he was called. He was a faculty in the Community Health Department and would accompany us on field visits to a nearby village on a bus that made you feel every bump on the road. The sweltering 3 p.m. heat and the thought of tea with friends back at the hostel or hitting the hockey field, tempted us to give Uncle the slip, whenever the bus rounded the college's second gate. But Uncle soon realised his miraculously disappearing flock and positioned himself at the back of the bus. It wasn't a deterrent, though he noticed us, he chose not to say anything.

In the early 90s I left for South Africa, but always kept in touch. He soon became a friend but never stopped being a mentor. As a public health doctor, you always have doubts and I readily sought his counsel. He always kept tabs on his students and was always ready to guide both professionally and personally if asked, with his wisdom.

When I returned in 2001 to serve in Karigiri, he soon took over as Director. Having known each other for some time now, we worked together in developing some large-scale projects together. Uncle remains the authority on advising developing projects. Whenever I had an idea but wanted to give it wings, Uncle was the first person I'd consult regarding funding, project management, budgeting, etc. However, the most important lesson learnt was endurance. If you believe in something, you never let go, however long it took. He is a living testimony to this.

————•●•————

Dr. Madhulika Jonathan

Dr. Sulochana is fondly known as Dr. Sulo or Aunty. I met Dr. Sulo as my group observer in 1987. She always came across as a very dedicated teacher, compassionate and caring, and with a great sense of humor. I was in their home a lot as Priya her daughter is my batch mate from CMC and a close friend. I have fond memories of dance practice and class prayers in their home which usually ended with rummaging through the refrigerator and cleaning out the pantry.

The internship in CHAD was demanding, and after a long day or night shift, Priya and I often sought refuge in the warm hospitality of her family home. One afternoon, we stumbled into the kitchen, famished and seeking sustenance. The aroma of a delicious meal filled the air, but we were hesitant. It was the time of MD Community Medicine's final exams, and external examiners were expected for lunch. We didn't want to intrude on their meal.

Priya and I scanned the delicious spread in the kitchen, searching for something 'non-interesting,' something the examiners wouldn't likely be interested in eating. Our eyes landed on the humble pot of curd rice. It seemed simple, innocuous, and perfect for our hungry selves.

Without a second thought, we whisked the pot away, giggling as we tiptoed up to Priya's room on the first floor. We devoured the cool, refreshing curd rice, relishing each spoonful. Just as we licked the last spoonful, we heard a commotion downstairs. Dr. Sulo rushed into the kitchen, searching frantically. Realization hit us like a bolt of lightning – the curd rice was meant for the vegetarian examiner!

Filled with remorse, we rushed back downstairs, ready to confess and face the consequences. But to our surprise, Dr. Sulo simply chuckled. She explained how she had anticipated our mischief and prepared another dish for the examiner. Relieved and sheepish, we apologized profusely.

That afternoon, though initially driven by hunger and a touch of mischief, became a memorable reminder of Dr. Sulo's kindness and understanding.

Dr. Sulo ignited a passion for maternal health within me, forever shaping my life's trajectory. She saw the potential for a powerful duo when she said, 'Suranjan (my partner) in infectious diseases, you in maternal and child health – Public Health has a vast canvas!' Her words unveiled the immense impact a public health professional can have. We learnt from her- 'boots on the ground' experiences from the simple PTCHW- the Part-time Community Health Worker to her teaching Maternal Death Inquiry to International Students at Uppsala University in Sweden.

Dr. Sulo is always impeccably dressed, kind, and helpful, and a thoughtful and inspiring teacher. Her influence continues to guide my journey in maternal health, a testament to her enduring legacy.

———•———

Dr. Madhavaram Balakrishnan -Medical Officer, Global Vaccine Safety, WHO

Upon being chosen as a registrar at CHAD in 1990, I was brimming with joy. Prior to this, I had been serving as a tutor at a private medical college, confined to an academic bubble. I can distinctly recall delivering lectures, donned in a pristine white lab coat, to groups of over 100 eager students. The zenith of my pride was attained when I secured a coveted spot in the MD Community Health program at CHAD. However, this sense of achievement was swiftly deflated, akin to a popped balloon, during my initial visit to the CHAD Hospital campus, where I encountered Sam, the CHAD office secretary in the office.

I can still vividly recall the memories as I prepared for my first day at CHAD. Donning a spotless white coat, I meticulously reviewed my joining documents within my briefcase and ensured that my polished, black shoes gleamed in the morning sun. With an air of confidence, I entered Sam's office and, perhaps somewhat haughtily, announced, *'I am Dr. Madhavaram. I've come to meet Professor Abraham Joseph and commence my duties.'* Sam, engrossed in his typing, didn't even lift his gaze. Upon finishing his sentence, he nonchalantly replied, without lifting his eyes, *'Abraham isn't here. You can head to the OP.'* I was taken aback. *'What?'* I exclaimed. Sam peered over his glasses and repeated, *'I told you, Abraham is not here. Go to the OP.'* Up until that point, I had been accustomed to secretaries addressing supervisors with titles like 'Professor sir,' 'Professor,' 'Prof,' or at the very least, 'Doctor.' Sam's casual reference to 'Abraham' was an eye-opening moment, one that would linger with me for the following three years and beyond.

In a dazed and bewildered state, I wandered into the OP. Inside, I was met with an extremely overcrowded, noisy, and bustling outpatient department. The registrars, interns, and others all rose from their seats to catch a glimpse of the differently dressed newcomer, as if I had just landed from another planet. That day marked the realization that an individual's essence transcends mere appearances, and CHAD cherished the authenticity within each person. From that point onward, I exchanged my lab coat for a simple cotton shirt, a stethoscope, and MCR slippers—wardrobe essentials throughout my tenure. The 'Black Book,' a quick reference guide, also became an indispensable addition.

Affectionately known as 'Uncle,' Dr. Abraham Joseph (and his wife Dr. Sulochana Abraham) inhabited an office that radiated simplicity. His wooden chair and table mirrored his unpretentious demeanor. However, beneath this unassuming exterior lay the brilliance that revolutionized the field of community medicine. Uncle's humility was his defining trait, despite his remarkable achievements. This humility fostered an inclusive environment where every voice held importance. It also forged trust, allowing us—registrars, colleagues, nurses, field staff, and others—to confide in him as a reliable mentor. I was fortunate to witness this first hand, an experience that indelibly moulded my character and perspective.

Uncle's remarkable sense of humour served as a buffer amid the complexities of daily life, transforming them into vibrant discussions. This gift united people, shining as a beacon of light in our shared human experience. I will forever remember his intervention during my final exams when I struggled to explain 'cluster sampling.' Recognizing my predicament, he simply supplied the correct answer, concluding with, '*...now you understand.*' Such moments are imprinted in my memory and have become the bedrock of my approach as an examiner in community medicine in Tamil Nadu and Kerala. Carrying these invaluable lessons with me, I strove to maintain fairness and understanding, particularly when candidates face anxiety or forgetfulness during their examinations.

These CHAD memories are just the tip of my iceberg of memories. As I reflect on the journey I've traversed over the years—progressing through various roles, from a community health teacher to medical students, PGs, doctors, and other healthcare professionals, subsequently pioneering the establishment of the polio eradication program in Kerala within the Directorate of Health Services, collaborating with anganwadi and kudumbashree workers, and engaging with a plethora of humanity including NGOs, doctor associations, Health Administrators etc —culminating in senior positions at WHO India, first as the National Surveillance Coordinator, then at SEARO as the Medical Officer for VPD surveillance and Measles Control, and finally on a global scale as the focal person for vaccine safety at WHO Geneva—I'm profoundly grateful. These experiences have sculpted me to be the person I am today, thanks to the exceptional training, guidance, and mentorship provided by Uncle, Auntie, and my teachers and colleagues at CHAD.

Dr. K.S. Joseph

My years in CMC Vellore from 1977 to 1991 were a formative period and Professors Sulochana Abraham and Abraham Joseph were among the important influences that contributed to my professional and personal development. The Community Orientation Program in the first year of medical school, and in subsequent years, had a significant impact on me, and I chose to specialise in Community Medicine. It was during my MD training that I became more closely acquainted with Dr. Sulo and Dr. Abraham. The 6 years I spent working in CHAD Hospital and the Community Health Department were intense and filled with numerous learning opportunities and challenges. It was through these many memorable interactions that my relationship with 'Uncle and Sulo' was forged.

My MD training in Community Medicine sparked my interest in epidemiology. The exposure to obstetrics and pediatrics in CHAD Hospital, combined with an introduction to epidemiologic methods in the Community Health Department, continues to inspire my current work as a perinatal epidemiologist.

I fondly recall being involved in many clinical encounters and research projects along with Dr. Sulo and Dr. Abraham. On a personal level, they provided an open house for my family – my wife, Jyothi, our son, Nene, and I spent many delightful evenings having dinner at their house. I cannot sufficiently express my gratitude to Dr. Sulo and Dr. Abraham for the many years of friendship they provided us during our time in Bagayam.

————••————

Dr. Jyothi Jayaraman

When did Dr. Sulo become a friend of mine? It happened subtly, I think, and probably began in 1984 when K.S. started his MD Community Health and I joined CHAD as a Non-PG Registrar. By 1985, I was doing my MD in Biochemistry but our friendship continued to deepen. Dr. Sulo became a great support to us when we were expecting our baby in 1986. The last few weeks of my pregnancy were a bit turbulent and there were late night visits to CMC – all in Dr. Sulo and Dr. Abraham Joseph's car.

It was only Dr. Sulo who was with me in the labour room (they did not allow spouses in, in those days). And, so, she is the one who saw our son, Avinash (aka Nene), first! And that, I think, is the real beginning of our long and loving and close relationship. Sulo became Shokko to Nene, as she was to her nieces and nephews.

There were many evening walks with Nene which ended in Shokko's house. Sometimes we would drop in at her parents' house too; Don Don Ammachi and Appacha as Nene referred to them.

How many wonderful meals did we share in Sulo's kitchen? It became Nene's particular playground where he created great 'mish-mashes' while Shokko patiently granted his demand for many varied ingredients. Her children's books became Nene's and their copy of the movie Mary Poppins was watched so many times by Nene (and K.S.) that K.S. has memorised vast portions of it!

We left CMC in 1991 and are many miles away now, physically, but we still remain friends. Sulo (as she insists I call her, now) was such a sweet and constant presence in the first 4 years of Nene's life that he (and we) will always remember her with gratitude and love.

———•———

Dr. Margery Emmanuel (Karigiri)

I met Dr. Abraham Joseph for the first time at my interview before joining Karigiri in the year 2003. My husband and his brother Barnabas arrived in Karigiri before I did, and Dr. Abraham Joseph was there with cups of steaming tea. This was a small gesture that meant so much to my husband. I later got to know Dr. Abraham as I worked at Karigiri. One thing that has stood out to me is his genuine heart and care for the marginalized. He would do the utmost for them. Through his time in Karigiri, I saw him identify talent in such people and train them.

One more aspect is his strong work ethic. He worked hard and expected the same of others as well. I also saw him constantly looking for creative ways to bring up the hospital. When I first joined Karigiri, we used to run an evening clinic in Old Katpadi. My understanding was that he saw that locating an OPD in this area would generate income for the hospital and of course be a service to those in the vicinity. In the Golden Jubilee year for Karigiri 2004, the foundation stone for the Paul Brand Integrated Health Centre was laid. About a year later the building came up. I have seen many patients from all walks of life students and professors from VIT, migrant workers and those from the local areas, benefit from this service.

In the journal clubs at Karigiri, he encouraged everyone. I did not see anyone being put down if they did not explain a concept well. He wanted everyone to grow.

On the personal front, when my husband had a brain tumor and needed surgery, we did not know many people at CMC. He made numerous phone calls and did all that he could to help us in lightening our burden.

I also saw in him, a good administrator. He had a way by which he could diffuse a complex situation and solve it without much fuss.

Some memories about Dr. Sulochana. I have always been moved by her affection for me and each of the members of our family. When Tim was born, she brought him an embroidered diaper cover which was so nice.

Those of us who have visited their home will see that she is very creative much like the woman in Proverbs 31, and has decorated their home with art work done through quilling. She is a lady who will not sit quietly and want to be served but keeps doing what she can in all circumstances.

If you ask them to preach a message, they may not do so. BUT – I often think that through their lives they continue to be the hands and feet of Jesus which speaks so much more.

———•●•———

Mr. Christopher,
Director's PA, Karigiri.

It was May 1976, when I joined the Community Health Department at CMC, as Steno Typist. The office and field staff were relaxing after lunch when a young man in white and a French beard entered the office like a whirlwind, finished dictating and then vanished. Later I learnt that it was Dr. Abraham Joseph, Head of the Rural Hospital, better known as 'uncle' among the medical students and faculty. Five years later, in April, 1981, I was appointed as his steno typist in Karigiri.

I appreciated his work ethics and the values he initiated by his example – punctuality being one of them.

————•●•————

Dr. Sushil Daniel

'Dr. Abraham I presume,' I said, on first meeting Dr. Abraham Joseph at his Director's residence in Dimapur. 'Dr. Daniel,' he said, as we shook hands with each other.

The Director's residence was the domain of another Abraham – Dr. Sulochana Anna Abraham, a charming and extremely gifted and humorous individual. Little did I know that their residence would be my comfort zone where I warmed my legs, partook of exotic dishes and learnt many life lessons from Dr. Abraham and Dr. Sulochana which would colour my outlook in life.

I had come to CIHSR to set up the department of ophthalmology. Building a department from scratch required an infrastructure plan for developing the department, procurement of equipment for both OPD and theatre and selection of staff. This required frequent interaction with the Director. It was through these interactions that I learnt the depth of Abraham's knowledge, his strict attention to financial integrity and the ability to accommodate to the legitimate requirements.

In the four years when I worked closely with Dr. Abraham the qualities I learnt from him were integrity in work and finances, and perseverance. These were the qualities that I saw, so exemplified in Abraham which I chose to imitate in myself.

One lasting image that I have of him is Dr. Abraham with his spectacles peering with intense concentration on the daily exercise of Suduko in the newspaper. This was Abraham's solution to stem the progress of age and keep his grey cells as vibrant as possible.

Dr. Sulochana was seated at the dining table when I entered her house that afternoon of November 2012. Lunch had been laid out and by the aroma that filled the air I suspected that the food would taste just as good. Dignified, stately, accomplished, multi-faceted and extremely talented, Dr. Sulochana is a lady with a wonderful sense of humour. She was and is the perfect complement to Dr. Abraham.

If Dr. Abraham was the iron fist in the velvet glove, Dr. Sulo was the one who interacted with the staff and students, especially the ones in the nursing college, and helped draw out their potential.

It spoke volumes to me when she welcomed me to have all my meals with them during my tenure in Dimapur. That innate goodness and hospitality did not extend just to me, but also to many who crossed their paths.

My four years in CIHSR, was an experience I would not exchange for anything. I was blessed by the friendship that was formed with two wonderful people – Dr. Abraham and Dr. Sulochana. A friendship that still continues and is cherished to this day.

------·•·------

Dr. Christy Simpson
Dean of College of Nursing. CIHSR Nagaland.

Dr. Abraham was a dedicated, committed, knowledgeable teacher who had a great concern for weak students. He was a father figure to everyone in Dimapur and was always very approachable. He treated everyone alike, irrespective of their gender or social status. We felt so comfortable learning from him, and we saw for ourselves his humble attitude and ways of servanthood – always giving, not expecting anything in return.

Dr. Sulo is a very humble, kind, and an excellent teacher. There are staff in CIHSR who still remember some of her explanations while taking class and conducting workshops.

She is very kind and compassionate and has much concern for the poor. She is very good at quilling and taught it to so many here, that now they earn their livelihood by quilling at CIHSR.

Dr. Sulo is a very good cook. She demonstrated to women in the church how to prepare some South Indian dishes. One of her expressions is that we should 'Walk the Talk'. She certainly does this.

------·•·------

Dr. Sedevi Angami
Director, CIHSR

Dr. Abraham engaged keenly with the community at CIHSR, learnt and blended into the local culture. He took part in all the social activities of the institute and made friends with several staff. He was loved by the community and people related to him well. He studied the people and listened to them, thereby providing him a good pulse on the various people of the region. He developed a taste for the different types of food of the region, some of which could be quite powerful.

He brought in key people in the area of Medical and Nursing Education, Allied Health Sciences, Distance Education and Disability Education who in turn developed the institute and colleges in their field at CIHSR. CIHSR is turning out to be several institutes within one campus. He encouraged staff to take on roles in starting courses even though they felt inadequate. Staff were able to thus identify their hidden potentials in teaching and administration while supporting them by way of mentoring and networking.

He initiated the various academic programmes of the Nursing college, Allied Health Sciences and DNB in medical subjects by engaging with the staff involved in refining their curriculum, networking with experts and ensuring that all the requirements were met to start the complex work of inspections, facilities, documentation, assessments and support work required.

Nagaland is a remote state in an almost forgotten location in India. By his vast networks of friends, he was able to create a circle of friends across the country and the world who came to know about CIHSR and developed support mechanisms for the institute. At CMC, he proactively searched out and engaged with several staff, mobilizing them to visit Dimapur, thereby contributing significantly to every area of the hospital service, academics and research. A very large number of staff from CIHSR were able to acquire post graduate degrees and skills in different disciplines from CMC, St John's, Bangalore, Tata Medical Centre, Kolkata, Bangalore Baptist Hospital and EHA Hospitals.

Dealing with the Government required skill, diplomacy and patience. During the time that he was in Dimapur, engagement with the Government increased significantly. His humility and credentials played a key factor which ensured that the officials in the government felt comfortable working with CIHSR and identified the institute as a vital partner in the health of the state.

He mobilized the NGOs in Nagaland to develop a common platform to address health needs.

CIHSR owes a great deal to this great and humble man, and to Dr. Sulochana, his wife. Both of them embodied the best values of Christian Medical College, Vellore, and served cheerfully through many difficulties and proved themselves to be true servants of God.

————•●•————

Mrs. Thingngamphy Vashum, HR, CIHSR

CIHSR has had the unique privilege of Dr. Abraham's services right from the time he joined in the year 2008 in the capacity of Associate Director to start with, and eventually took over the charge as Director in 2011 till 2016. To me personally and am sure to the entire staff, he was a role model par excellence as a leader of the entire organization.

From our perspective with limited comprehension of multifarious activities in multiple disciplines (Academics, Administration, Community Medicine, Research and the list goes on), the flawless progress set into motion was indeed a testament to his incisively brilliant command over details in order for the larger picture of the institute to speak for itself in terms of robust health care deliveries.

It is always a challenge communicating with the government. Yet, Sir, was extremely effective in terms of facilitating completion of projects with the government. He had the skill of communicating with them in an extremely professional manner. This helped in building relationship between government and our hospital. We continue to cherish the impactful memories of Dr. Abraham Joseph's leadership.

———•———

Dr. Susie Samuel

Sulo and Uncle were my seniors when I joined CMC in 1964. For many years I had no idea that Uncle with his charming Sri Lankan accent was Anjilvelil Abraham Joseph. He was Sulo's Uncle and ended up being Uncle to everyone, me included. My earliest memory of him is his beautiful baritone in the St John's bus every Sunday morning when he led the singing of choruses flawlessly. Sulo was someone who worked tirelessly away from the limelight for all the Women's Hostel functions. You never saw her, you never heard her, but she was the organiser of any task that needed to be done meticulously, well and with an eye for detail. She took on the responsibility of assembling the Graduation Jasmine Chain. Though it is always remembered as part of the most important walk in the lives of the graduates, many are unaware that the jasmine chain was assembled in CHAD, under Sulo's supervision for decades till she retired. The fragile jasmine chain when braided spans miles, incorporates perishables and is required to be ready on time, year after year. Most importantly, it has to survive the heat of a warm afternoon in Vellore, look fresh and smell good when held over the shoulders of the final years as a guard of honour for the fresh graduates and faculty on Graduation Day. An extremely talented craftswoman, she excelled in needlework and smocking. When her eyesight was compromised she turned to quilling, churning out the most exquisite pieces of art that I had never ever seen before.

When we moved into a retirement community at the foothills of Kodaikanal, Sulo sent us a beautiful cross as a housewarming present. Framed in glass it occupies pride of place above the lintel of our front door, blessing everyone who passes through our home. When I put off the lights at night to go to bed, the cross reminds me of a low-maintenance, uncomplicated friendship that has lasted almost 60 years. A gentle soul who is always there for her friends. Unfazed by her own health challenges, she never whined. She is generous with her time, her smile, an encouraging word and her terms of endearment. It is no wonder that I smile when I think of her.

———•◦•———

Drs. Mary and Mohan Mathew

We have known Dr. Abraham Joseph and Dr. Sulochana Abraham, affectionately known as Manu and Sulo, for over five decades. Their unwavering love and affection have been a constant source of warmth throughout the years. However, amidst recent events, their love and friendship have shone even brighter, embodying everything that they mean to us. In 2020, during the height of the Covid-19 pandemic, when our son needed a stem cell transplant in Vellore, Manu ensured he had reliable transportation from Chennai. This was just the beginning of their countless thoughtful gestures that brought a sense of normalcy to our lives. From ensuring our son had his favourite foods, to checking in on us at the end of each day, Manu and Sulo were steadfast pillars of support, always keeping us in their prayers. During the toughest times, their consistent acts of kindness, sprinkled with humour and unwavering affection, sustained us. They've brought immense love and laughter into our lives and we'll forever be grateful for their presence. Finding the right words to express our love for them feels impossible, but our hearts overflow with gratitude.

Drs. Susan & Benjamin Joseph

Our association with Manu and Sulo goes back 57 years; long enough to appreciate their wonderful traits. Their caring nature gives them the ability to detect the needs of others even before they ask. Their ability to joke about themselves and each other endears them to all who encounter them.

Sulo loves to teach and share her talents in cooking, housekeeping and hobbies. She enjoys teaching the basic principles of embroidery, which she claims to have learnt from her grandmother. She is a perfectionist, a trait she exhibits in her embroidery and quilling.

Manu and Sulo share a passion for gardening and they tend their plants with love and care. They are a couple who were there for us at the delivery of our firstborn in the Rural Hospital. Since then, they have been a support for us through the years. We hold them in high esteem. We would love to emulate them, but fall short of their standards.

———— •• ————

Dr. Shalini Govil

Mushy Rice, Love and Laughter at Sulo and Uncle's DIY Dinner with the Fosters: When I think of Uncle and Sulo, the image that comes to my mind from 1981 is an evening at their beautiful bungalow on the CMC campus when they hosted 'The Fosters' for a DIY cook-and-eat evening. Geeta Zachariah (Chacko) and I, roommates in 1st year MBBS, were chosen to join the Abraham Joseph Foster Family. Fostering in CMC is a unique tradition where Faculty informally 'adopt' students from 1st year to provide a home away from home. The Foster Family consisted of the Faculty, their family and all the current and past Foster children. For someone like me whose parents were abroad throughout my MBBS, Uncle and Sulo's home was truly a haven, a place where I was assured of a warm welcome, delicious food, interesting conversation, a sympathetic ear and loving, balanced support and advice whenever I needed it. But more than anything, what I remember was the fun and laughter at those Foster dinners! At that DIY cook-and-eat evening, each of us cooked one dish – the Malaysian/ Singaporean students made noodles/ sweet and sour chicken; I opted for rice that I planned to boil and toss with thinly sliced and fried vegetables. My dish was coming along nicely – I cooked the rice to just the right texture – not too soft but not undercooked – and because the vessel was too big for me to carry to the sink, 'someone' (and that is you Uncle!) helped me drain the rice in the sink.

Unfortunately, I did not instruct him to rinse the drained rice with cold water as was my habit to stop it from cooking further. Net result – the large pile of hot rice sat in the sink cooking more and more, into what turned into a mush. Foster brothers never let me forget that fried rice mush. The real culprit, Uncle, quietly faded into the background and has feigned innocence ever since.

Over the years, we became incredibly close; Sulo and Uncle enthusiastically approved my choice of husband since they were already huge fans of Sanjay Govil's talents as a student, singer and actor! Given the trust and comfort we had with them that superseded all our other relationships in CMC and beyond, Uncle was the one we chose to propose the toast at our wedding reception in Madras in 1987. Amongst the many nice things he said about the two of us, I remember him saying that Sanjay's performance as Che Guevera in Evita for CMC College Day was much better than the Broadway version.

Recently, I had the joy of having Uncle, Sulo and Priya stay at my home in Bangalore. It was as always, a time of endless chatting, eating and laughing.

They will always remain my role models for how to build faith-based, peaceful, loving homes and outstanding career legacies, all the while staying true to a life of simple living and high thinking.

————•●•————

Dr. Susan Varghese

My husband and I moved to Vellore in 2004, after we retired from HPCL Refinery and Andhra University, respectively, because of health issues. We had spent the major parts of our lives in Visakhapatnam and were a little apprehensive about relocating so late in life.

When I heard that the daughter (Sulo) and a son-in-law (Manu) of the great Educationist, Mr.Kuruvila Jacob, for whom I had great admiration would be our immediate neighbours in Vellore, I was excited and looked forward to getting to know them.

Although I didn't know much about their professional life in CMC, I knew Manu to be the dynamic and most resourceful Head of CHAD who expanded the Department of Community Health in all its dimensions and Sulo, his able assistant heading the Maternal and Child Health Programme.

I came to know that Manu had retired from CMC in 2002 and had taken over as the Director of Karigiri hospital and that Sulo took over as Head of CHAD after that. Sulo retired from CMC in 2005 and that is when they moved into their house next door as our immediate neighbours.

By then, I had realised that our new neighbours, the Abraham Josephs (Manu and Sulo),were no ordinary mortals, but luminaries in their field. I was awed by their popularity in the community, and this deterred me from barging into their house as soon as they arrived.

They soon set up a beautiful home with a sprawling garden, full of flowering trees, flowering plants and a vegetable garden. They both seem to have green thumbs and gardening came to them naturally. Manu was particularly good at grafting plants and it was intriguing to watch him at it. Sulo too loved plants and was not only knowledgeable about them but also took care of them personally. In fact I have had several lessons from her on gardening. To be sure, we were the regular recipients of their garden produce of all types! Not just garden produce, even cooked food would be sent over the wall to us. In fact there would be so much of food traffic that to their grand children, I was 'over the wall Ammachy.'

By then Sulo and I had bonded well and had become good friends. She is a very talented person producing exquisite works of art. She didn't stop with fine embroidery, but was exploring new horizons to express her creativity. That is how she started quilling, even before it became an established art form in India. Another remarkable thing about Sulo was that she freely imparted her skills to others. I am one among the many who have benefitted from their magnanimity. I cherish my friendship with them.

---•●•---

Dr. Jaya Hutton

The first impression one got about Sulo Ma'am was one of vigilance. She is the kind of person who has eyes all around her head, something like our mothers in our teens. But I had the privilege of seeing the softer side of her years later, when out of the blue, I got a phone call asking me if my designer daughter could convert some of her quilling art into tablemats.

She had taken up the beautiful art of quilling after her retirement. I was awestruck by the beauty of the pictures she sent me of flowers, birds, horses and elephants. Her choice of colours, and the vibrancy of the pictures were stunning.

My daughter set out to design them into 18x12 inch table mats. But the photography was not too perfect and the pictures were getting blurred when blown up. The original artwork had all been distributed as gifts.

While we were wondering what to do, Dr. Sulo came up with the design with a smaller size picture on the side leaving a plain space with a complementary colour. The result was awesome.

Both Dr. Abraham and Dr. Sulo would tell me repeatedly, 'Jaya, you can sell these tablemats.' But then even the thought of following that order was too sacrilegious.

Dr. Sulo also encouraged my passion for baking. When she found out that I even had a food licence she asked me, 'What's stopping you from selling your products?' I haven't looked back since.

What I've learnt from her is this: always follow your passion.

———— •●• ————

Abraham and Sulo followed their call and made their commitment a passion, which they passed on to generations of young people working in Community Health. Having read their story:

' What will you do with your one precious life?' (Mary Oliver)

About the Authors

Usha Jesudasan is the author of several biographies - Shaping Young Minds, Brokenness as a Blessing, And He Embraced Him, When Fears Are Grounded, Dreams Take Wings. Her own autobiographies – I Will Lie Down In Peace and Two Journeys chronicle her life and that of her mother.

Dr Sulochana Abraham retired as Professor and Head of the Community Health Department of Christian Medical College, Vellore. An Obstetrician and Gynaecologist, she is also a specialist in Public Health. As a Consultant to WHO, World Bank, SIDA, and the Ford Foundation her focus was on the health of marginalised women. After retirement, she learnt the art of quilling and has taught this to women from all walks of life. Her life is defined by her love for her family and the changes she brought to healthcare for village women and children.